"The adventure and challenge of taking over government after decades in opposition is revealed in Denis MacShane's diaries. He vividly captures the inside details of the tensions and words uttered as Labour set about rebuilding Britain. *Labour Takes Power* is an important guide for the new Labour generation in the Commons preparing for power under even more challenging circumstances."

David Blunkett, former Home Secretary

"Denis MacShane breezed in from Europe after fifteen years' exile working with social and social democratic parties on the Continent to be elected an MP in 1994. His inside story of the first Blair government reveals deep tensions over policy and progressive politics. As Labour looks to once again form a government, this book is essential reading on what entering power meant for Labour MPs in 1997."

Polly Toynbee, *Guardian* columnist and former BBC social affairs editor

"The 1997 Labour government brought in many significant reforms – more than some of our young people realise – including the abolition of hereditary peers, a Parliament for Scotland, assemblies for Northern Ireland and Wales, an elected mayor for London, the abolition of all Tory homophobic laws, a national minimum wage, a win-win relationship with Europe, the Human Rights Act and the ending of massacres in the Balkans and the death squads of the Serb strongman Slobodan Milošević. Denis MacShane was an active backbencher and commentator during this time and his diaries reveal details, anger and passions which bring to life those early Blair years in a way which history books often fail to manage."

Baroness Helena Kennedy of the Shaws KC

"The diaries of Tony Blair's former Europe Minister Denis MacShane are a compulsively readable chronicle of the first New Labour government. There's high drama, low gossip and parliamentary mischief, but what also emerges is a serious politician who spoke up passionately for Europe at a time when many of his colleagues hoped the issue would simply go away if they ignored it."

Francis Wheen, former deputy editor of *Private Eye*

"Much has been written about New Labour, but first-hand, contemporaneous accounts of the Blair government are always invaluable. Denis MacShane's book is one such, and his insider's take will provide historians and political scientists alike with a fresh perspective on a period that Labour's potential return to government has arguably made more relevant than ever."

Tim Bale, professor of politics, Queen Mary University of London

DENIS MACSHANE

LABOUR TAKES POWER

THE DENIS MACSHANE DIARIES 1997–2001

Biteback Publishing

First published in Great Britain in 2023 by
Biteback Publishing Ltd, London
Copyright © Denis MacShane 2023

ISBN 978-1-78590-839-2

10 9 8 7 6 5 4 3 2 1

A CIP catalogue record for this book is available from the British Library.

Set in Minion Pro and Interstate

Printed and bound in Great Britain by
CPI Group (UK) Ltd, Croydon CR0 4YY

FSC
www.fsc.org
MIX
Paper | Supporting
responsible forestry
FSC® C171272

CONTENTS

PREFACE

I have been writing books, articles and speeches for myself and many others ever since I was a student journalist. I honed my writing skills as a parliamentary candidate for Labour in 1974 and then as the youngest ever president of the National Union of Journalists (NUJ) four years later. Between 1979, when I was blacklisted by all media employers and had to go to work in politics across the Channel, and my return as the MP for Rotherham in 1994, I wrote endless words under my own name and for others, working to promote social justice and to end communist rule in Europe, apartheid rule in South Africa and different forms of autocratic rule in Latin America and Asia.

As I wrote political biographies or accounts of the historical origins of the Cold War and the left, I sifted through thousands of documents, letters and memoirs. If by chance in some archive I came across the contemporaneous letters, diaries or interviews of one of the principals I was writing about, it was like a new shaft of light illuminating history briefly.

So, when I was elected as the Labour MP for Rotherham in 1994, I decided, probably somewhat pompously, that I owed a duty to future historians to note down as much as possible what I heard, observed and took part in as an MP.

I had the great fortune to be named a parliamentary private secretary at the Foreign and Commonwealth Office (FCO) when Labour won power in 1997. It meant working with Robin Cook, who had been an inspiring and constructive Labour MP from Edinburgh since 1974. He was the finest orator of his generation, a shade sharper and wittier than Gordon Brown. Parliament of course comes from the French *parler*, and the art of speaking – the rhetoric taught by the ancient Greeks which is now called oracy and is still the most important attribute of anyone in democratic politics – was an art Robin Cook mastered better than most.

I also spent fifteen years working with the democratic left in Europe – trade unions and social democratic and socialist parties. I learnt not just European languages but also the complexities, histories and hopes of the democratic left on the Continent. Tony Blair arrived in No. 10 free of the burden of anti-Europeanism articulated by Labour MPs such as Tony Benn, Michael Foot, Robin Cook and Jack Straw in the 1970s and 1980s.

Blair was joined as head of government by Lionel Jospin, the socialist PM of France, Massimo D'Alema, the left PM of Italy, and Gerhard Schröder, who defeated the seemingly permanent Chancellor of Germany Helmut Kohl in 1998. Prime Ministers from sister parties in Nordic nations, the Netherlands and Portugal added to a sense that a new progressive European democratic left might be taking shape. Across the Atlantic, the progressive reformist Bill Clinton was in power. I had made good links with Team Clinton as an international trade union official working with progressive American trade unions in the 1980s and 1990s.

So, as well as twenty years in the Labour Party, I had a background in Continental European and American progressive politics. Blair sent me to the FCO, but quickly I found myself called into Downing Street as a link-person on contacts with European sister parties in government.

I noted down as much as possible in small notebooks and then dictated nearly every evening and at weekends an A4 page, or two or three, of what I saw and heard. The full diaries which I began in 1996 and ended in 2012 run to more than 2 million words – which would be dozens of book-length volumes.

They are the raw material of history and of course must be sifted and checked against other written or oral records. I will make the full diaries available in due course via a university archive.

Today in the United Kingdom, we face, as we did in the mid-1990s, the strong chance of a change of government with Labour triumphantly taking office once again. This book records what it was like to be at the heart of a major department of state, as well as in Downing Street, from 1997 to 2001.

I hope it may be of interest to anyone who wants to know how politics works and to Labour MPs who have the honour of being asked to serve in government.

Denis MacShane
November 2023

1997

THURSDAY 1 MAY 1997

The election day weather is spectacular. A warm, balmy day such as one would have in southern Europe at this time of year. I make my first call while jogging to the polling station at Oakwood school and spend the rest of the day tramping around polling stations. Everywhere there is good cheer but not a tidal wave of people turning out, just steady, brisk polling.

At the Herringthorpe Leisure Centre, all three counts for Rotherham, Wentworth and Rother Valley are being announced. We don't hear ours until about 2 a.m., when I am back with a majority of over 21,000, though the turnout is lower at just 63 per cent. The figures are roughly comparable in the other Rotherham constituencies. But nationally it is the biggest political rout of the century. Michael Portillo and other Cabinet ministers have gone. I take particular pleasure in the defeat of that filthy little racist, Nicholas Budgen, in Wolverhampton, as well as the disappearance of Norman Lamont in Harrogate.

In every single seat in which I worked, we win handsomely, but it has nothing to do with me. On the contrary, there is a bigger swing in Brigg & Goole, which was not a key seat, than in Batley & Spen, which is where the party from Rotherham worked so hard. Everybody is grinning and gleeful; it really is a revenge and a satisfaction to those who have stayed loyal to the party in the eighteen dark years. The Herringthorpe Leisure Centre is a grim place and the council have done nothing to dress the set, so I make my speech of acceptance and off we go.

The Liberal candidate, who turns out to be anti-European, was pushed back into third place and refused to shake my hand after the count. At 3 a.m. I go to bed as more and more Tory seats tumble.

FRIDAY 2 MAY 1997

The final outcome is extraordinary; 419 seats for Labour and forty-six for the Liberals. Never have the British people voted this century so decisively to kick out a party. There are three lessons to be learnt, surely. Firstly, this is a great victory for the Blair–Mandelson–Brown project. No one can take that away from them. Secondly, it is a decisive rejection of the xenophobic and anti-European politics of the Tories. We must build on this. Thirdly, it is a plebiscite or a referendum election – a giant vote of no confidence in the Conservatives rather than the sending of individual constituency representatives to legislate and represent local interests in London. It is a vote against Parliament by sending so many people down there that parliamentary proceedings will become almost surreal. All these aspects give us great possibilities.

In the evening, I go to the Labour Club for a May Day social. I give the bar £100 and tell them to buy everybody a drink, but the place is crawling with Trots and malcontents and the musicians strum their guitars and sing dirges and negative unhappy songs. Even 'The Red Flag' was sung to a tune which nobody could recognise and so nobody could sing along. This is the worst kind of old sectarian Labour.

MONDAY 5 MAY 1997

A bank holiday, so the long weekend of celebration goes on and on. We drive down to London, stopping in at the Transport and General Workers' Union (T&G) leader Bill Morris's house at Hemel Hempstead for a victory party. My old friend John Monks, the Trades Union Congress (TUC) general secretary, is there and we talk about how the trade unions need to detach themselves from the Labour Party. He said that he had phoned key leaders early on Friday morning but none of them were biting. He is completely at ease with the concept that it is the trade unions which are damaged by the insistence on holding block votes at the party conference and insisting that they form an organic part of the party's leadership and structure.

Unions would be liberated and able to make new alliances, argue new relations with bosses and indeed be a much more useful ally of Labour if they didn't attach such importance to this completely outdated link. But when I half-hinted at this to Austin Senior at a steelworkers' union meeting in Rotherham on Saturday night, he bit my head off. 'It's payback time after eighteen years and it's us that held this party together,' he snapped. Austin is president of the Iron and Steel Trades Confederation (ISTC) and a very intelligent man, but his response reflects the prejudices of most union leaders.

In the evening, Robin Janvrin (the Queen's deputy private secretary) and his wife Isabelle, John Lloyd of the *Financial Times* and his new girlfriend Ilaria, Stryker McGuire (the *Newsweek* bureau chief in London) and, at pudding time, Colin MacCabe come round for dinner. Robin says he looked in at Buckingham Palace for the mass swearing in of the privy counsellors who are in the new Cabinet. I find the obsession with titles and Rt Hons quaint and indicative of the way in which the British state quickly gets to people, but honours matter for everyone and no doubt if any came my way I would gobble them up greedily.

John Lloyd tells us that Liz Symons has been made a junior minister at the Foreign Office for Europe. 'It's a bizarre appointment. She doesn't even know where Europe is. But she is completely dependable,' said Lloyd. I am sure the adjective 'dependable' is the key. The main Minister for Europe is Doug Henderson who is filling today's news bulletins with an early flight to Brussels. Doug comes out of the north-east stable of right-wing MPs which is a core block in the Blair constellation. The last time I saw him, other than in the Commons, was in Glasgow where he was accompanying, indeed bag-carrying for, Gordon Brown at the Amalgamated Engineering Union leader Jimmy Airlie's funeral.

Joyce Quin, who had prepared the European brief and knows Europe, has been shunted aside for a Gordon Brown placeman who is likeable but knows nothing about European politics and will be putty in the hands of officials. It is messenger-boy duty not real policy-making that is valued.

MONDAY 12 MAY 1997

In the lobby, I bumped into David Curry, the ex-Local Government Minister who kept his seat and who is now campaign manager for Ken Clarke's bid to become Tory leader. 'William Hague will get it,' he told me. 'It's a non-vote. By voting for Hague, MPs can keep their constituencies happy without taking any specific line,' Curry added. This is unnerving stuff given the fact that Clarke certainly seems to have most public support and is the only really heavy-weight minister. There is a bizarre article by Simon Heffer in the *Daily Mail* in which he blasts Hague as being, well, I suppose the only word is vague, and says that despite his European credentials, Clarke is a real tough free-market minister with proven successes at the Home Office and at Education. The Tories are totally out of the opposition scene at the moment as they convulse themselves over their leadership problems. This is giving Blair and his ministers an absolutely clear run, but sooner or later, and it may be sooner, real politics will kick in.

TUESDAY 13 MAY 1997

A day spent working at home which isn't very productive as the phone never stops ringing and, of course, I keep phoning out. I had a good talk with Sarah Helm, the Brussels correspondent of the *In-dependent*. She announced that she had a new boyfriend, Jonathan Powell, Tony Blair's chief of staff. Powell's marriage to his American wife is dead, not helped by his working over here while she kept living in Washington with their children. I like Jonathan very much and am extremely fond of Sarah, so it is a nice match if it works out. She said that Labour had made a good impression in Europe but asked why they had chosen Doug Henderson as Minister for Europe 'since he obviously was completely lost and just sat there saying rather naive things'. I explained the need for neutral messengers and Blair's desire to appoint a non-controversial and rather grey team of ministers. Sarah's pillow talk is clearly going to have much more influence now than in the past. She is a fine journalist whose writing is matched by a political determination on issues she believes in, like rights for Palestinians and European partnership and purpose.

MONDAY 14 JULY 1997

I go with Doug Henderson, the newly appointed Europe Minister, to the 14 July Bastille Day reception at the French Residence in Kensington Palace Gardens. I am now named as a parliamentary private secretary at the Foreign Office. I have a pass that lets me walk into the FCO when I want. It's a bit odd as I know far more about European politics and the EU than any of the ministers, including the Foreign Secretary, Robin Cook. I speak better French than most FCO wallahs, or rather I speak contemporary political French and read *Libération* and *Le Nouvel Observateur* which plugs me into the French socialist government which has arrived at the same time as us. Most of the FCO panjandrums both in the FCO and those running Blair's European and foreign policy desks in Downing Street will read *Figaro* and other French conservative weeklies if they read any newspaper in French at all. It's rather grand being driven in a minister's car, but when we arrive at the French Residence the champagne has run out, either new austerity measures by Lionel Jospin's socialist government or the Quai d'Orsay is sending out signals about what it thinks of its new socialist masters. After nagging the ambassador for ten minutes, two saucer-type glasses – these must have been in stock since Charles de Gaulle was here during the war – of indifferent champagne were produced and that was our ration for the evening.

Doug Henderson said that my appointment had been decided upon by Tony Blair from the very beginning and that Robin Cook had refused to sign off on it until it was made clear it had to happen.

Doug is completely in cahoots with Nick Brown and Gordon Brown. Doug and his girlfriend are having dinner with Gordon and Sarah Macaulay next Saturday and he is firmly hitching himself to the Gordon bandwagon. 'There's no point in trying to strike out on your own. This place works on who you know and who likes you and 95 per cent of all jobs go to people who simply keep their head down,' he told me, no doubt prophetically. He also wondered how Tony would reshuffle the pack since clearly a number of ministers aren't up to it but they do not expose themselves to justify dismissal. Oh dear, I shall be stuck as a PPS if I remain one, for some time to come.

WEDNESDAY 16 JULY 1997

At 6.30 p.m. I chaired a Tribune Group meeting at which Robin Cook spoke. There was a good, if heterogeneous, turnout and Cookie was in brio form. He is very pleased with his new ethical foreign policy and human rights line. He said that he had got on a lot better with Madeleine Albright, the American Secretary of State, than any of his European counterparts and clearly likes finding himself lining up with the Americans in preference to the

Europeans. So much for his long anti-American political past. He told a hilarious story of a draft of a reply to a letter from an MP asking about arms sales to Indonesia:

> I am still reading through my replies before signing them and I got to the last paragraph where I found a sentence that said 'what the position of the government is on this is complete bollocks…'! I circled it and sent it back saying, 'Surely some mistake?' But it shows that getting the message through all the levels of the Foreign Office is taking a bit of time.

THURSDAY 17 JULY 1997

Up early to catch a plane to Paris for a British Council seminar on media and politics. I sat beside Andy Marr and we had a good chat. He said:

> I had a talk with Robin the other day and he asked me what I thought of Gordon's Budget. I told him I thought it was absolutely first-rate and he looked at me and said, 'Well, that's a point of view, I suppose.' I wonder how long he will stay at the Foreign Office. I still think he will go back to Scotland and seek to be top man in Scotland.

This is one of Marr's favourite themes, since a part of him is very much connected to the Scottish project and having a dramatic and radical leader like Cook up there would be the dream ticket for the radical Scottish intellectual journalists like Marr or others like Neal

Ascherson and John Lloyd. I am not sure that Robin is prepared to give up the historic status of being Foreign Secretary.

TUESDAY 22 JULY 1997

I bike over to the Royal Festival Hall for lunch with David Rennie, the very smart and very Europhile *Daily Telegraph* diarist. He is full of high-quality gossip.

'The Foreign Office all hate the new Foreign Secretary, Robin Cook, but they like the Ministers of State,' he announces grandly with the knowledge of having a father who was one of the great mandarins of British foreign intrigues as head of MI6.

David said he had written an unkind paragraph about Chris Smith and to his amazement got a call from Chris himself: 'The phone rang and a flunky said, "I have the Secretary of State for Culture, Media and Sport on the line for you, Mr Rennie," and there blow me down he was in person. He told me that what I had written was motivated by malice and was unworthy.'

I don't know to what extent Rennie is playing Peter Mandelson's game, but the knives do appear to be out for poor Chris Smith who has no real base in the post-1997 Parliamentary Labour Party. As the first ever gay Labour MP, there would be ructions if he was sacked, but he can be moved sideways and replaced by someone like Peter Mandelson.

THURSDAY 31 JULY 1997

To a team meeting at the Foreign Office, presided over by Robin Cook, who, I must say, is one of the worst chairmen I have ever sat under. He allows an endless dribbling discussion mainly based on his own experiences and we do not reach half the items on an agenda which only has six headings.

He is just back from Bosnia and Croatia where he said that meeting the Croatian President Tuđman was an encounter with the last fascist in Europe. 'He is completely barking, and as I left, the Croatian Foreign Minister apologised for his President's behaviour, which is an unusual job for a Foreign Minister to have.'

As he summed up his various forays or foreign office developments, he kept turning to the Permanent Under-Secretary, to ask him, 'Is that a fair summary, Permanent Under-Secretary?' as if he needed the approval of the machine at every stage.

I don't get the sense of a man completely at ease with the smell of manure that surrounds all foreign policy decisions.

MONDAY 4 AUGUST 1997

The big story is that Robin Cook has left his wife Margaret to shack up with Gaynor Regan, his Commons secretary. I had lunch with them once in Bellamy's and didn't realise, at the time, I was interfering in a little love lunch.

The whole story seems dodgy. Robin lives just around the corner from us in Sutherland Street in Pimlico. According to the papers, a freelance photographer just happened to be there outside his flat... And just happened to see him feeding the metre for Gaynor's car.

I think the tale stinks and it has all the hallmarks of a set-up. I expect that people in the security services listen to the right wingers in the Foreign Office who don't like Cook, and have picked up his affairs and fed it to the press.

What a filthy business. Though, to a certain extent, if he wants to make a break with his wife, then it is necessary to get it out into the open. And this may be the least painless way, though it must be devastating for Margaret, Robin's wife, who has been working as a consultant in an Edinburgh hospital while he has been cavorting about in Westminster.

SUNDAY 31 AUGUST 1997

We are in Glasgow so Granny can see her four grandchildren and I can show them something of their father's birthplace nation. But then the news arrives in the morning radio bulletins that Princess Diana has been killed and everything seems to come to a stop. Benjamin, just three years old, kept saying, 'Diana dead, Diana dead' as if it was the most important thing that could happen in his little life so far.

I am as cynical, perhaps more so, as the next person, but the tears were in my eyes at the shock of her life ending in this manner. As the hours go by, the awfulness of the event sinks in. Suddenly, all the glitz and extravagance of her life fade away and all that stands out is her holding little babies in her arms in the third world or hugging an Aids victim on a deathbed in a London hospital.

WEDNESDAY 3 SEPTEMBER 1997

The anniversary of the start of the Second World War, but no one notices. Diana is everywhere, with flags at half-mast and railings up in Whitehall to prepare for her funeral. I get a call from the *Daily Mail* asking me for a quote about the fact there is no flag at half-mast over Buckingham Palace, but I declined to get involved in their rent-a-quote stupidities.

Instead, I phoned Robin Janvrin, the Queen's deputy private secretary. I told him that if the royals were not down in London by tomorrow there would be a republic by the weekend. An exaggeration but not by much. The nation is horrified at the callous indifference of the Queen and above all Prince Charles, who made Diana a breeding horse for the future monarchy while he went off living his own life, sleeping with an old girlfriend, as if marriage and the family were a boring irritation for himself.

I told Robin to get the royals down fast to inspect the mountains of flowers, looking serious and sorrowful and trying to understand the nation's grief.

Everyone I talk to has been scornful of the royals. Tony Blair, on the other hand, pops up in a black tie and talks of the People's Princess with a look of intense anguish and grief in his eyes.

Matthew d'Ancona calls up to say the Tories are tearing their hair out because Blair is claiming or taking all the credit for defining the week as days of memorial for the People's Princess. 'There is complete panic in the Tory high command,' said Matthew. 'They think this could be Blair's Falklands – the moment when he nails himself into the consciousness of the people for a long, long time.'

I think this is an exaggeration. But there is no doubt Tony has judged the mood beautifully, whereas the palace has just got it desperately wrong. From Balmoral, Robin Janvrin tells me he is very much aware of this. 'I agree with you completely. I am trying to get the message over, but it's very, very difficult here.' It was nice of him to phone back and he was as courteous as ever. I expect he's had this conversation with many others today, but he sounded concerned about what I had to say.

TUESDAY 9 SEPTEMBER 1997

Down to Brighton for the TUC and Tony Blair's speech. Tom Baldwin of the *Sunday Telegraph* told me that the line from No. 10 on Clare Short was: 'It's not a question of her being in the tent pissing out or of her being outside the tent pissing in but simply being in the tent pissed.' It was a clever-dick phrase but absolutely daggerlike.

The Archbishop of Canterbury George Carey was the star of the show just before lunch with the most left-wing speech of the week. In fact, it was the most concerted and unapologetic exposition of socialism I've heard at a major conference like this in Britain for some time. He was a member of two unions before starting his National Service and then going into the priesthood, and he was quite explicit on the obligation of employers 'to recognise unions and not to victimise union activists' and on the need 'for new economic policies to create full employment'.

Tony Blair, by contrast, in the afternoon, gave no concessions and told unions to shape up or ship out as far as he was concerned. The core message remained business, business, business. Inasmuch as unions can help business, then they would be allowed through the doors of No. 10 to present the case but, there was no automatic presumption that simply because of the historic connection, trade unions would have any influence over policy.

THURSDAY 16 OCTOBER 1997

I get a call from Daniel Johnson of *The Times* to ask would I do an op-ed piece on state funding of parties. I write a quick article arguing state funding is a good idea but should be limited and directed more towards party work on policy, education and training and not simply a big cheque in exchange for the number of votes parties poll at their various elections. Instead, I argue that money given to parties for organisational work should be in proportion to their own fundraising and to the members they have.

TUESDAY 28 OCTOBER 1997

To the Foreign Office for a team meeting. It lasts longer than usual and there are no officials present. Robin Cook remains depressed after the rotten press he got over his visit to New Delhi, where he tried to raise Kashmir and got a massive Indian Hindu cowpat dumped on him that the UK press gleefully relayed. He exuded unhappiness. He continually referred to whether a proposal or a policy will work in terms of getting the green light from No. 10. It is curious to see a man who has reached one of the top offices of state so obviously feeling not exactly powerless but not in complete control of his destiny or able to fulfil political ambitions by constantly looking over his shoulders at a boss who controls all. Not even a boss in the sense of an individual, the Prime Minister, who has nominal authority over him but a formless entity, 'No. 10', which has the power to block any initiative, take over any glory or channel and water down new ideas.

After a lot of misery about Kashmir, I intervened and said that I thought his stewardship at the Foreign Office so far had been a big success. On Kashmir, I told him that people would have been astounded had it not been raised and certainly on the ground it was not perceived as being a big failure. Derek Fatchett, one of the Ministers of State and a shrewd Labour MP who was sitting beside me, turned and said, 'Thanks for the therapy.' Robin remains the cat that walks alone. He obviously is beginning to feel over dominated by his diary and running the department. 'Frankly, I don't know what goes on outside this office or who the thousands of people working for me really are or what they do,' he said. 'The diary just runs me around and I'm never in the country or even in the building.'

TUESDAY 4 NOVEMBER 1997

To the House to hear Robin Cook give evidence at the Foreign Affairs Select Committee. He was marvellously in control, articulate, not a comma or subordinate clause out of its place, with barely a look at his notes. Only once or twice did he refer to officials and when Simon Gass, the FCO's head of Europe section, intervened by himself, Robin looked a touch annoyed as if to say, 'I don't need any help from anybody, thank you very much.' His take on the Amsterdam Treaty was interesting, praising it for the headline achievements that were noted at the time such as border controls, the employment chapter and other little vetoes that Britain obtained. But he said it had failed to achieve institutional reforms in the size of the commission, the organisation, the council and so forth in order to prepare for enlargement.

This actually is the French, German, even federalist critique of Amsterdam, and it is interesting that Robin is spontaneously offering that. The Foreign Affairs Select Committee is the weakest of the senior departmental committees. The only senior Tory is Virginia Bottomley, who sits there playing with a lovely half-smile on her face, but her questions were anodyne. The room was crowded with journalists, diplomats, others who wanted to see the great Cook in action, and sensing the attentive audience behind him, he was completely and utterly on the job.

A vote and then Calum MacDonald offered to take me to dinner, but I said I was going home and invited him to come with me. Calum said that Tony Blair had called in all the Cabinet-level PPSs for a pep talk in the Cabinet Room, which seemed an extremely good idea. According to Calum, Tony's message was pretty simple. We will have two years on no spending and then gradually ease the restraints on cash so as to spend our way to an election victory. This is certainly a change from the behaviour of Harold Wilson in the 1960s and Jim Callaghan in the 1970s when an incoming Labour government was generous and then had to go desperately into reverse, cutting spending and stoking up resentment. In fact, the policy of Budget restraint is an absolute classic Tory policy and is what we used to condemn as 'stop, go', plus it can so easily be blown off course by events.

The current issue of *The Spectator* has run a foul Europhobe attack on Nick Soames, my pair, except that pairing is pointless now with our huge majority. The assassin is a charming but stiletto-vicious high Tory, Peter Oborne of the *Sunday Express*. I dug up some facts on the speeches that Bunter has made from the House of Commons Library and sent a letter back defending him. It will stir things up a bit as Soames is popular with the public and with a number of Tories, but it shows the complete eclipse of the Old Etonians who, in the shape of Soames or George Young, are quite sensible on Europe but are loathed by the Tory Europhobe Trotsky-ists who now surround William Hague.

THURSDAY 6 NOVEMBER 1997

The papers are full of a ghastly U-turn on tobacco advertising and Formula One motor car racing. Yesterday I listened to Tessa Jowell making a complete fool of herself on the *Today* programme trying to justify the exemption of Formula One cars from the govern-ment's programme to try to reduce tobacco advertising, which is completely in touch with what the public wants.

Over to the Foreign Office to see Doug Henderson. He was chor-tling at Tessa Jowell's discomfiture. 'She's a little goody-two-shoes and, of course, a big FOB [Friend of Blair], so she can't be touched.' Of course Doug and his gang of Brownies hate all the N1, NW3 or, in Tessa's case, NW5 gang. He told me that he had received a note asking his authorisation for the ambassador in Moscow to go and open a new British American Tobacco (BAT) cigarette factory in Uzbekistan:

I said no, because BAT and Philip Morris and all the other to-bacco companies are simply moving out of western Europe and opening the new markets for children and others in the ex-Soviet Union, but Robin countermanded my order and said the ambas-sador could go. So much for his ethical foreign policy.

Doug is a real fitness guy and has young children and I only wonder whether it was No. 10 rather than Robin that signed off on the ambassador promoting the cancer industry as long as it was far away from the British media.

FRIDAY 7 NOVEMBER 1997

Up at 6 a.m. after a bad night's sleep and an early drive out to London airport to catch a plane to Portugal for a seminar on the European social model and globalisation.

On the plane, I was quietly reading a very pro-European interview with Tony Blair in *Le Monde*, and who should tap me on the shoulder but Stuart Holland in the seat behind me. We rearranged things so that we were side by side and had a marvellous talk and gossip all the way back to Heathrow. Stuart is wonderfully egotistical and outrageous. He is an adviser to António Guterres, the socialist Prime Minister in Portugal who insists on being called Tony and who spoke at the Labour Party conference.

Stuart was full of a scheme to issue eurobonds or use the European Investment Fund and European Investment Bank to get infrastructure projects going. He said he had had a talk with Robin about this, who was very interested.

I know all of these guys. They're all of my age and generation. When I was in Rome the other week, I called up [Romano] Prodi and he immediately said come round and have a talk. I see [Jacques] Delors now and then and have tried to get him to get through to [Helmut] Kohl so that they understand that debt can be used. But, of course, the German word for debt is 'Schuld', which means 'guilt', and it's the same in Dutch so the Germans are absolutely terrified of indebtedness.

I think there is a little more to Kohl's financial prudence than the fact that the German word for debt and guilt is the same, but Stuart may have a point.

He was scathing about Tony Crosland, Denis Healey and, above all, Tony Benn.

'I told Benn he was just being a complete fool over the common market in 1975, and he didn't talk to me for seven years. He is a very dangerous man.'

Stuart claimed that Jim Callaghan had come up to him in the Commons in 1982 and said:

'Stuart, if I had won the election in 1979, I would have introduced planning agreements.' He had no reason to say this to me, so I think it was what he really thought. The trouble is that Prime Ministers are so heavily briefed they only get a chance to see the value of ideas once it's too late for them to put them into practice.

I can't believe Jim was being anything other than a flatterer and, like all non-intellectuals, wanted intellectuals to think well of him. As we spoke, Stuart consumed gin and tonics, red wine, whiskies and then bought half a bottle of Chivas Regal which he drank and drank. He was looking blotchy with thinning hair, bad skin and poor teeth as well as a fat stomach. But his capacity for storytelling and argument was undiminished and his lovely voice, which he told me had been the voice of a great singer when at university, was still a joy to listen to. We had a nostalgic hour or so going over all sorts of old ground and old struggles.

TUESDAY 11 NOVEMBER 1997

In the lobby, Alan Clark came up and in that frightful, smothered drawl of his congratulated me on my letter supporting Nick Soames in *The Spectator*. 'Peter Oborne [the *Sunday Express* writer who had attacked Soames] is an absolute tart.' Quentin Davies and Alastair Goodlad also had congratulated me on the letter with Quentin saying in his very nice way, 'It is quite preposterous that an MP can't organise his own time and it is none of the business of the whips or the journalists what MPs do providing they come along and vote as required.'

WEDNESDAY 19 NOVEMBER 1997

To an office meeting at the Foreign Office where I arrived early, having pedalled in at a furious rate for what I thought was a 9 a.m. meeting only to find it wasn't due to start till 9.30. The private office, which consists of three secretaries each at their desk in a different corner of a huge room adjacent to the Foreign Secretary's office, continues unperturbed in its work.

As usual, the meeting wanders and flows all over the place without a proper agenda. Robin's main obsession is spending more time with MPs. 'You have to stay in touch with the House. It is why we are here. Political avalanches can develop with terrifying speed. One minute the ground seems safe and then it is breaking under you and you can be swept away unless you have got an early warning system.' He proposes a day at Chevening, his country house, but the day chosen is 5 January when we will be away skiing. Tough. He then names another day in December, but Doug Henderson says he is launching a European presidency that day in Newcastle. Robin mutters and grunts about whether he can change it, but Doug stands his ground. The only substantive item was a paper by Tony Lloyd about controlling arms sales which is very critical of the French. Tony speaks very softly at the far end of the table and none of us can hear what he is saying. Robin shows no interest and later Doug tells me that Tony has been at some arms control seminars in Sweden, where they have filled his head with the usual Nordic moralism which never seems to stop them selling as many arms as possible all over the place while preaching homilies about disarmament.

I walk down the corridor to her office with Liz Symons. I tell her very sharply that she is causing a lot of trouble with MPs by refusing to sign letters and always upholding the position of her officials even when the cases are manifestly unfair. 'But Denis,' she says in that butter-wouldn't-melt-in-her-backside voice, 'I have to send out 1,500 letters a week. I can't sign them all, no one can.' I tell her that other ministers do and that she should make a distinction between routine letters and those that are important to MPs and that her predecessor, Liam Fox, certainly did. 'It's so difficult. I am working all the time. I have all these other policy matters which I have to concentrate on,' she complains. I tell her bluntly that there is an impression around that she has never done a constituency surgery and doesn't remotely understand the pressure that MPs are under. I console her by saying that everybody recognises that as FCO minister in charge of entry clearance for relatives of constituents who want to emigrate from Pakistan, India and Bangladesh, she has one of the worst jobs in government, but there is a great deal of discontent building up and this is the kind of parliamentary avalanche territory that Robin was talking about. She is obviously unhappy to get the telling off, but I hope I did it as a friend and the message gets home.

Across to the House for Prime Minister's Questions. I don't see any point in attending save to mark Blair's score card. How did he do? It was about even with one or two good spontaneous bursts, like when he pointed out that John Bercow, the obnoxious little twerp who has been sucking around Tory tits since he was in nappies, had worked as an adviser for Jonathan Aitken. This produced a real laugh and made Bercow look stupid, though he shook his head furiously. Afterwards, John Williams of the *Mirror* said Tony looked absolutely terrible and strained. Of course, John sits in the gallery looking down on Blair, whereas all we see is the back of his head, and I thought it was an interesting comment. The past ten days have been pretty wretched and we have been exposed as looking very weak.

To a Tribune Group meeting with Harriet Harman. It was in the upper committee corridor and as I went there about ten minutes early, the room next to it had its door open and familiar voices were to be heard. I put my nose round the corner and Diane Abbott was there. 'Ah, it's the sycophant-in-chief, come in,' she said. I looked around and saw Tony Benn and Alan Simpson, and realised I was attending the campaign group. Its star speaker was none other than Eddie George, the governor of the Bank of England. I watched in amazement as he courteously exchanged views with the hard left of the Labour Party. 'Tony, I think that's a very important point... Yes,

Alan, I do agree that EMU [the Economic and Monetary Union] is far from settled.' It was the Tony and Eddie show or the Alan and Eddie show and there was something gloriously comic in seeing the high priest of finance capitalism meeting the far left of the PLP and conversing so sweetly and it seemed to me with so many heads of agreement.

I had dinner in the Members' Dining Room. As I entered, Diane Abbott and Audrey Wise were at a little table for two and both gave me a public dressing-down for daring to support the government's line on welfare at the PLP this morning. They really are obnoxious, but I adore Diane. She spends all the summer on an American lecture tour and is a star of TV talk shows over there. It is the only way for a clever MP once she is off the career ladder to make herself known. But it is a crazy waste of talent and she, of course, becomes an object of parody and scorn very quickly.

In the lobby, I bumped into Peter Mandelson and he agreed to come and open the exhibition of cartoons I am planning of Martin Rowson's work. This is very good news and will pull lots and lots of people in.

MONDAY 24 NOVEMBER 1997

I did an interview on French television about whether London harbours Islamic terrorists. I gave as good as I got from the French interviewer, who said yes, we did, and I reminded them of the obligation of democracy to offer exile and asylum to political refugees. I really think I will stop doing these things on French television as there are no votes in it at all, nor much point.

Dinner with the *Critical Quarterly* gang at Groucho's. Christopher

Hitchens was there and Anthony Julius, but the real pleasure was to see Nigella Lawson turn up. With one or two penetrating comments, she helped to sum up a real issue. We had a good discussion on the need for a politics of family which got some half-hearted endorsement when I advanced my new round of ideas on the need for effective family politics, though Anthony Julius got very upset when he was accused of being a family lawyer, saying he had only done one divorce in his life, that of Princess Diana.

Hitchens made a good comment that now communism was dead, the only place where the slogan 'from each according to his means, to each according to his needs' was valid was the family, which made everybody stop and think for a moment.

I kept getting beeps saying that there was going to be a division and then that there was not going to be a division which caused hilarity with all the women around the table, who thrust the pager into their waistbands and waited for it to vibrate with the usual fairly scatological comments. I suppose I take these vibrating pagers so much for granted there is nothing to them, but if you haven't had one throbbing somewhere about your body then there is something new to it.

TUESDAY 25 NOVEMBER 1997

Question time went off OK. Michael Howard hardly rose to ask a question except a rather feeble one on Iraq. He showed no interest in his shadow teams trying to attack Robin. I wonder if he might just walk away from it all before long. He shows no interest or concern, and apart from an out-of-date hostility to Europe, has no passion or political purpose that makes itself evident at the despatch box.

I stayed for Gordon Brown's statement on what was being called the 'Green Budget' but is now called the 'pre-Budget Statement', which was meant to be an outline of tax thinking in order to have a more mature discussion of fiscal alternatives and policy choices before the Budget. But he is such a showman that he can't resist throwing powder into the fire and puff! Up he comes with two new classic welfare policies – extra money for pensioners for their heating bills and new childcare places. At the same time, corporation tax is cut on companies and there is to be a law enforcing fiscal stability. The latter to please the City and capital; the former to delight, as it did, the Labour backbenchers and the welfare constituency. It was a brilliant performance. Tony was sitting beside him looking much younger and relaxed and beaming with delight at his Chancellor's command in the House.

In the lobby, Peter Mandelson came up in a glum way and asked if I'd seen *The Guardian* leader that day. I hadn't and he said it was a filthy attack on him, blaming him for everything that went wrong. 'But at least they say Tony Blair has to shoulder some of the blame,' which I suppose is some bizarre consolation. Poor old Mandy.

THURSDAY 27 NOVEMBER 1997

This was fox-hunting day or, to be more correct, hunting with dogs day, since it is also proposed in the bill that we discuss today to stop all hunting with dogs. The House was absolutely full on both sides. I had a brief chat with Dennis Skinner before the debate began in the Members' Lobby. I said that I really couldn't get worked up about it. 'I agree with you. I am just here to go through the motions. If you think of all the problems that we face, this is absolute nonsense,' he muttered.

Michael Heseltine was the first speaker from the Tory side and early on in his speech attacked the bad wording of the bill. He ridiculed the reference to flushing foxes out and then killing them and asked rhetorically if anyone had ever tried to flush out a fox and then put it down.

I bellowed out: 'Ask Mrs Thatcher!' and the House broke down in laughter with the Tory benches collapsing and Heseltine having to stand rock still for a number of seconds trying to find his composure and not grin himself. He tried to remain serious and made some reference to having knowledge of what happens in the political process when parties get 'decimated', which brought even more howls of laughter as our benches pointed merrily at the decimated Tory side. He then got back into his speech, but I crept out since it was going to be my only chance to intervene and went off to the gym.

SUNDAY 30 NOVEMBER 1997

A lovely *farniente* day. Up late – 9.30 a.m. – because we were so tired and then a spectacularly good roast beef lunch followed by a trip to Lots Road Gallery where I put in bids for some Gillray cartoons of Peterloo and a fake Sisley done by a clever Spanish artist called Kanals. I didn't bother with the Sunday papers and instead read books and magazines and felt much better for a day without the press on top of us.

I talked to Carol Barnes, who said she had introduced the item on fox hunting in which I spoke on ITN. She said she and my old friend, Graham Miller, who I worked with at Radio Birmingham, both fell off their chairs as they saw me pop up. 'You looked much better than you usually do,' Carol said, I think kindly.

MONDAY 1 DECEMBER 1997

Across to the Foreign Office for some kind of Christmas party for the media. I had a brief chat with Tim Garton Ash, who is fretting and worrying about Europe and trying to work out where he'll want to be in ten to twenty years' time. I had a go at him for his hostility to EMU which he resents but he is backed up by Sir Nigel something or other, the old Etonian ex-ambassador to Germany whom I met in Manchester and who is still locked into a Conservative critique of Europe. None of these guys understand that Europe needs big decisions, not incremental little changes. Labour couldn't stomach sharing power over steel and coal in 1950. Now that the euro has been decided upon by Paris and Berlin as the essential underpinning of a true single market – imagine the US economy being based on California or Texas or Michigan each with its own currency – the British self-proclaimed pro-Europeans shrink in horror at having the same currency as the Germans and French.

TUESDAY 2 DECEMBER 1997

Over to Doug Henderson's office for work on the committee stage of the Amsterdam Bill tonight. But I escape from this early to go to the gym. In it there is a young Ganymede, a slight, tiny good-looking youth who I later find out is Douglas Alexander, the new MP for the Glasgow seat where Gordon McMaster committed suicide. What a contrast. Gordon was enormous, wobbly, with rolling chins and a complaisant look. Douglas is small and perfectly formed with sleek black hair and a winning smile in his perfect Athenian face. Another Brownie on the parliamentary payroll.

THURSDAY 4 DECEMBER 1997

Lunch with the *Mail*'s Simon Walters at the Tate Gallery. I made him buy two decent half-bottles of wine, the claret being a Château La Tour which I accompanied with a fairly disgusting bit of pheasant. He is in mega-flattery mode, describing me as Labour's Alan Clark. If this diary is one quarter as good as Alan's, it will be worth the effort, but, alas, Clark is a real writer; I am simply a note-taker. Also, Clark writes whereas I dictate and the difference is as obvious as between buildings thrown up with breeze blocks and one in which brick after brick or stone after stone is carefully laid one on the other by a craftsman to make a real statement.

Simon is full of an article in the *New Statesman* which hails Alan Simpson as the new leader of the left. I protest that intelligent and capable of organising as Alan is, he is a loner with no friends or followers and only bitter rivals. 'The trouble with the left is that it is divided on almost every issue. On Europe, on trade unions, on women, on free trade, on the environment, it is split every which way,' I tell him. Simon urges me to write an article about all this, but I don't think I want to wade in and make unnecessary enemies just yet.

Yet another European debate, though this one mercifully was shorter and we were finished by 8.30 p.m. as people are sick and tired of debating Europe. It was a general adjournment debate and Robin opened it. He arrived with his speech, as always handwritten in his red felt tip pen, and as usual it was a very good one. There was only one problem. No one was there to hear it. Robin has an oratorical trick of turning from the despatch box waving his hand in a gentle semi-circle behind him and pulling himself round to address his own backbenchers. But everybody had gone home. After a couple of minutes of this, I whispered to Ken Purchase that I would go out and rustle people up. I rushed into the lobby and grabbed Graham Allen and Janet Anderson and asked them to get onto the front bench.

I then went into the tea room and tapped anybody and everybody on the shoulder. 'The Foreign Secretary is making a major speech against Michael Howard and there is no one there to listen to him! Please come in and sit behind him, even for ten minutes or till the end of his speech,' I begged. The ten or so MPs sitting there were quite responsive and gulped their tea, put down their papers and trooped into the Chamber to form a reasonable phalanx behind him. It looked at least on television as if there was a bit of support and as he turned with more of his jokes against Howard, whom he was putting through the mincer on his U-turn on a referendum on the Amsterdam Treaty, there were at least a few people to smile and nod and cheer.

FRIDAY 5 DECEMBER 1997

Across to the Foreign Office for a long session with Robin Cook.

Liz Symons opened with a long paper on dependent territories like the British Virgin Islands, Saint Helena, the Cayman Islands and the Turks and Caicos Islands, as well as Montserrat, all of which have an odd status. Another one of these historic anomalies, of course, is Gibraltar. The question is, should such islands be forced to become independent, or should they be absorbed fully into the United Kingdom with all their people offered citizenship? What the territories want is lots of money. They also want the right for their people to come to Britain, but the comfortable ones like Bermuda certainly don't want to allow anybody from the UK to live, settle or work in their little island paradises.

The FCO paper was fairly useless, offering an enhanced associate citizenship. I said that one model might be the French DOM/TOM status and Robin asked what that meant. Liz jumped in and very slowly and clearly pronounced, '*territoires... outre... mer*' and I told him what the DOM (*départements d'outre-mer*) stood for. I then said that it would be very expensive though an interesting way of sending British influence out into the world. 'Every single one of them would immediately become eligible for all British rights, including any welfare benefits if there are any in a couple of years' time.' Everybody burst out laughing and Derek Fatchett said to Greg Pope, 'I hope the Chief Whip has noted that.'

Of course, if Britain were to take over the dependent territories used as off-shore tax havens, it would be a massive interference in the cosy little world of international currency speculation and tax avoidance fiddles. I pointed out it would cause a massive explosion in the City and be a major politically aggressive step. John Kerr, the Permanent Under-Secretary, who sat at the end of the long table opposite Robin, says he doesn't like the DOM/TOM solution. 'It is very, very costly,' he moaned. The conversation drifts off into a hand-wringing series of complaints from Liz about Montserrat. She says that the FCO is responsible for supervising and ultimately administering Montserrat and the other dependent territories but all the money to spend on them comes from the Department for International Development.

This unleashes a hate session against Clare Short. John Kerr asks, 'Is the Secretary of State for International Development part of the constitution?' Larry Whitty intervenes to say he had a drunken tirade against Robin from Clare at party conference in which she blamed him for the press criticism of her during the Montserrat business. Both Tony Lloyd and Derek Fatchett say relations between the FCO and the new department are very bad with Clare's Permanent Under-Secretary encouraging a climate of hostility.

The dependent territories item took up nearly half the agenda before we moved on to disarmament, where Tony Lloyd had produced a *New Statesman* article which David Clark, Robin's adviser, had written for him two years ago, setting out the ten-point plan for a nuclear-free world. 'Yes, it was a good article, I think I agreed to it while I was playing tennis, didn't I, David,' said Robin and everybody giggled at the way high policy is made. Tony mumbles and mutters through his presentation and makes some proposal that our nuclear submarines should announce they are not going to patrol but simply be stationed at their base in Scotland. Everybody looks a bit puzzled trying to work out what the point of that is with even Robin saying, 'But I thought the whole idea was that you didn't know where they were if they were out on patrol under the water and that was the element of security and surprise?' Some of the proposals make sense and if a little package can be got together on a register of nuclear weapons with the support of the big nuclear powers then it certainly would be useful.

The next subject area is the Middle East peace process.

Robin says, 'I hope this room is hermetically sealed but, of course, the Arabs know perfectly well who finances Tony.' It was a fairly abrupt and open statement. I said I thought Labour's swing to Israel was simply a reaction against the excessive pro-Palestinian and at times openly anti-Israel borderline anti-Jewish politics of the left, including the left in the early 1980s. Andrew Hood, who has close links with Israel, jumped in and started spluttering about events at the Labour Party conference where Gordon Brown at a Labour Friends of Israel dinner had made a gushingly friendly speech, whereas at the equivalent function for the Arab ambassadors and pro-Arab Labour MPs, only Clare Short had turned up and she was late.

As a result, the Arabs are convinced that the Labour government is in the pockets of Israel. Robin came up with the idea of celebrating the end of Ramadan by going to an end of Ramadan Eid feast in Cairo. 'I could do with going through Ramadan myself just to stop all these wretched meals I have to eat,' he grins. He then starts asking when Ramadan ends and nobody knows, with people talking about moons and cycles, but here you have in nominal terms all the people who determine Britain's foreign policy and overseas relations and not one of them knows the date of the most important celebration in the Islamic year.

I ask if it is possible to go and burst in on a Muslim feast and whether it is a good idea to go to Cairo where the Egyptians are always locking up journalists and generally showing something less than respect for human rights. John Kerr also says he's against the idea and instead proposes that we should slaughter some sheep and roast them in the courtyards of the FCO and invite all the Arab ambassadors to attend. I expect it will end up with a reception for them in the FCO to try to soothe their concerns and send out pro-Arab signals, though as I tell Andy Hood afterwards, the real problem is that there isn't a single functioning Arab democracy or a single Arab country in which political norms or human rights are fully respected.

THURSDAY 11 DECEMBER 1997

The papers are full of the forty-seven Labour MPs who voted against the government on the lone-parent benefits issue. It is not the 200 that Roger Berry was boasting about, but together with the abstentions about a hundred people have refused to support Blair. Blair today is meeting Gerry Adams. I was in Canada last week and it was interesting to note the extent to which people asked me about Ireland, as if that was the most important item on the North American agenda when people think of Britain.

Calum MacDonald has been appointed to replace Malcolm Chisholm who resigned as a junior minister in the Scottish Office. That is a popular move as Calum is a lovely guy, though I wonder how he will relate to Brian Wilson since both have one major passion in Scotland which is the Western Isles and Highlands and this can't be an area of responsibility big enough for two ministers. Don Touhig sits beside me during education and employment questions and says it is very unfair that Gordon Brown has been blamed for the lone-parents fiasco. Everybody is covering their ass. Victory has many authors; humiliation is an orphan.

I walk down Whitehall with Alan Simpson and he is very cheerful after last night. Last week in the *New Statesman*, John Lloyd had depicted him as the next leader of the left, but I still don't see Alan's programmatic ability, let alone the real charisma that is needed, though he is one of the most affable and humorous political opponents one might wish to have. Women in the Commons love him and he likes them. His hostility to Europe also is not going to make him new friends. He agrees that one advantage may be that government plans to cut disability benefits will now have to be put on ice.

FRIDAY 12 DECEMBER 1997

I drive to Doncaster to pick up Clare Short who is going to do some constituency stuff for me. At the station, I saw Caroline Flint. She is the intense raven-haired new MP for the Don Valley who is being ultra loyal on the back benches. She is getting unfair stick and is in this dreadful race with all the other competent, youngish female new MPs. How they must all eye each other, wondering who's going up, when, and pushed by what or whom.

Clare was full of her exuberant, emoting self as soon as we got into the car. She wriggled and fought with the seat to push it back. We drove back to my house and she was high in denouncing the events of the week, especially the big rebellion of payments or lone parents:

> Wednesday was a complete disaster. Harriet [Harman] just is in-capable of running that department. She is fighting permanently with Frank Field and there is no policy structure discernible at all. The party is really angry and fed up. The lone-parent cut is completely unnecessary and a dreadful price to pay to lose all that goodwill.

Clare rambled on and on, letting her hair down. 'Tony's become very arrogant with this obsession with control and presentation. There's a nicer Tony struggling to get out but the arrogance of No. 10 and all his little entourage is now causing us real trouble.' She said that the lone-parent cut was never discussed in Cabinet. 'Tony never reads anything. He just sits in an armchair and thinks in terms of pres-entation all the time. There is no attention paid to detail.'

34

All this spilled out pell-mell as we drove back to the house where I gave her a good stiff whisky and a little bit of a sit down before going to the Labour Club. There she worked the crowd brilliantly and is clearly very popular with Labour Party members as one of the superstars whose warmth and emotional engagement comes out from the TV screen and hugs you close. Her mistakes and excesses are all forgiven because she is a real warm created-in-the-flesh politician. The first group I took her to were all from the World Development Movement and she was immediately snarled at, as was I, about the lone-parent benefits cut. She dominated the little scene wonderfully, saying that we were wrong and that the party was hurt and the Cabinet had to listen to what the party was saying and therefore it was all the more reason to stay within the party to ensure that these messages got across.

This was exactly the right tone to take and calm people down, much more than my rather stronger line of defence might have been. In fact, I was surprised in the course of the evening at the upset and aggression. It simply wasn't ever evident before Wednesday night's vote and shows how an event in Parliament can significantly change the political balance of emotions and priorities. All during her stay, Clare was dumping on Harriet, saying she couldn't handle policy and had no real feel for her department. 'She's only ever been promoted because she stays totally on-message and never answers any questions,' Clare said bitterly. She feels thoroughly vindicated and was praising up people like Frank Dobson and Chris Smith as the old left in the Cabinet who were on top of their departments, unlike what she kept calling the Blairistas. All of this was private to me, and at the Labour Club she went around talking, engaging, holding hands, listening.

I made a little speech of introduction, pointing out all the positive things that the government had done and apologising for the Wednesday vote but saying that there was no point myself and Clare resigning over it. I was glad she was there as a kind of shield since attaching myself to her allowed my cred with the party to remain intact – I hope. Her speech also was one of regret at Wednesday, of healing, staying in the party to fight for what we believe in. 'It shows the good old Labour Party is there with its heart and its head and we all have to listen to what's being said.' She criticised nobody but sent out signals of absolute empathy with all the party members there and absolute opposition to the recent line which is asking us to swallow the tobacco funding nonsense, the Geoffrey Robinson offshore trust debacle and now the lone-parent cuts.

I took Clare home and we finished off half a bottle of whisky with more gossip. She is very angry, scornful and full of some pity for Robin:

He is losing it. His little chest is puffing out with all this crap about a People's Europe and being a leader around the world. The Foreign Office have got to him and swelled his head. It is a tragedy, the break-up with Margaret. He was getting back together with her when the spin doctors phoned up and forced him to decide. Now I hear that his new girlfriend is suffering from panic attacks and he is going through a terrible divorce case in Edinburgh. He's got bags of money with his Cabinet salary but he is trying to take the family house off Margaret. I will never forgive him for what he allowed the Foreign Office to do, or try to do, to me over Montserrat.

Clare is obsessed with the spin doctors and the on-message control system. She was contemptuous of Brian Wilson, who was her deputy in the shadow Ministry of Transport:

He wouldn't do any work. He was another one driven by his beeper, always wanting to get into the media. He may be a very good journalist, but in that case he should go and work as a party press officer if he's not prepared to do the hard work on policy. He was desperate to get into the Cabinet, but I think that probably is going to elude him now.

Clare was full and free and frank with me, but I am terrified if she says any of these things within earshot of a journalist or somebody malevolent. I repeatedly told her that Robin expressed support, admiration and fondness for her, at least in the team meetings I have participated in, but she dismissed all these olive branches and clearly has decided that the Foreign Office is an enemy body. Not really a happy government or Cabinet.

SATURDAY 13 DECEMBER 1997

I went out to get all the papers only to find gloom and doom on all the front pages. *The Guardian* splashing with this ridiculous letter that David Hill, the party press hack, has sent to the *Today* programme threatening to withdraw cooperation because John Humphrys gave Harriet Harman a hard time in some interview. *The Guardian* also had a front-page story saying that disability benefits were going to be cut. Thanks.

The Times' splash was more scandal over the Geoffrey Robinson off-shore trusts while *The Independent* had a front-page story saying that Gordon Brown had been excluded from the European Council of Finance Ministers at the Luxembourg summit yesterday and thus was starting off the British presidency of the European Union by, in effect, helping to inaugurate the two-tier Europe that we were supposed to avoid thanks to the change of government.

I took a cup of tea and these gloomy front pages up to Clare Short who was in Granny's bed. We then went down to Tesco where there was a photocall about fair-trade shopping. A good gang of people were there and the store managers were quite friendly and helpful in finding various fair-trade goods. Clare gamely sported a little Santa's cap in order to try to make the picture come to life. She is a lovely political trouper.

I then drove her down to Birmingham and had a repeat of all the venom against Robin and Tony from the night before. She said that Frank Dobson told her that 'Alan Milburn had been very helpful over the NHS White Paper even though', and this was Clare's remark, not Frank's, 'he's an old Trot. But then, Tony likes people who have got no political background like Derry Irvine and Liz Symons and Jonathan Powell, who is very nice and clever but has absolutely no political understanding or grasp at all.' Interestingly, Clare said she thought she would have more money for her department by year three of the parliament. 'Tony and Gordon have made so many promises at international meetings that they will have to match their words with real cash.'

Her mother was sitting hunched in a little chair waiting to go out to Mass. She had a lovely strong Brummie accent which Clare has certainly ironed out of her own voice. On the way down, she used my mobile to phone her brother to chat about her mother's trip to South Africa and presents for all the family. She is one of six children, pure Irish Catholic. I said that I thought one area Blair had been very good in was in backing the peace process in Ireland, but Clare is not really prepared to hear much praise for the Prime Minister:

> It has been Mo [Mowlam] who has done nearly everything, bringing people together, really working at the detail. There is an incredible hunger for peace in Northern Ireland. My Uncle Paddy lives in Crossmaglen and he says that the Republicans want peace and all this talk of a split in the Republican movement is nonsense. It is that hunger for peace that's driving it forward and Mo is the person who is actually putting it all together.

I don't disagree with her estimation of Mo's importance for a second, but the fact is that Blair has used all his authority as Prime Minister to open the doors of 10 Downing Street to the IRA and allow no excuse for the peace process to break down on the basis that a British government is not serious in negotiating. Clare made me a cup of tea and I then set off to hack my way through north Birmingham and back down the M42 and M40 to a crowded London.

MONDAY 15 DECEMBER 1997

Over to the House for the statement on the European Council. Tony is calm and serious. He is flanked by Gordon and Robin. The former scuttles out as soon as it is decently possible, but Robin stays beside the PM whispering and prompting him in the ear as each Tory rises. I have the feeling Tony doesn't really need the help, but Robin remains glued to his side, subordinate and supportive. I am simply taken by Tony's hair, which has now got plenty of white streaks in it as well as a distinct greying at the temples and a growing bald patch. I remember it all happening to me. Sensibly, he is cutting it shorter and he ought to really get a bit more brutal and admit the fact that over the next four or five years, those once long luxurious locks are going to be memories in photographs and nothing else.

I bike back home to see the children briefly. Even for thirty short minutes, it is a great pleasure in these crowded days. Then on to Random House, the publishers, just up from Vauxhall Bridge. Anthony Barnett has written another book (yes, yet another) about politics and constitutional reform. Many of the left intelligentsia of our generation dislike him strongly, but I have always enjoyed his company and admire his restless Continental intellectual vigour and energy. He is the begetter of Charter 88, which other than its absurd name, laying claim to affinity with the Czech movement, has been an excellent force for good in the country. Anthony comes up beaming as I am the first MP to turn up. 'Denis, I am so glad to see you here. You're one of the half-dozen MPs who actually reads books. I have sent a copy to everyone but I know you, at least, will read it.'

My heart sank since a book sent to every MP is destined for the bin or a raffle prize. And although I might dip into Anthony's book, which he signs for me with a flourish, I think I shall probably give it as a farewell gift to young Adam, my assistant, who is going to study politics at Edinburgh University next year. I have a nice little talk with Marina Warner, who I recall as being at Oxford but don't

really know. For some reason, I mentioned the fact that I spent Saturday and Sunday night reading a collected edition of Louis Mac-
Neice's poems, which I picked up in a second-hand bookshop on
the Charing Cross Road when out with Sarah, buying her clarinet
music on Saturday afternoon. Marina says that her next book will
be called *No Go the Bogeyman*, which was inspired by the famous
line from MacNeice:

> It's no go the Yogi-Man, it's no go Blavatsky,
> All we want is a bank balance and a bit of skirt in a taxi.

I was feeling rather cocky at being able to reel it off and she and
another TV producer, called John Ellis, all around fifty, giggled as
we thought that no one under the age of forty would have the faintest idea what 'a bit of skirt in a taxi' meant, all those days of going
round and round Hyde Park in a taxi without a rear-view mirror as
one of the safest possibilities for a rendezvous of safe fun. I asked
Marina what was in her book but she said, 'Oh, I don't really like
to discuss my book at somebody else's book launch. It's rather bad
form, don't you think?'

A taxi up to Finsbury for a very nice dinner with Martin Ivens
and Anne McElvoy. Martin is firmly embedded at the *Sunday
Times*, a paper which simply doesn't have much bite any more. To
be honest, recording this diary a day or two later, I can't remember
much conversation. Tim Allan, one of Blair's young press aides,
was also there with a new girlfriend. He is smart and charming,
but I have to be on my guard to avoid any remarks that might get
recirculated in No. 10. The other person there was Ed Fawcett, who
is an old *Economist* hand who knows Christopher Hitchens and

remembers I had written a biography of François Mitterrand which is suitably flattering. I wish I had that kind of memory about what other people had written.

TUESDAY 16 DECEMBER 1997

Over to Downing Street where all the junior PPSs were invited to meet the PM. Inside we all sat round the Cabinet table. I was in John Prescott's chair and as soon as Tony came in, he took the notes and papers that had been lying on his pad and turned them over as if to make sure I couldn't look at them. The room itself is much smaller than I expected, with pillars at either end and really a quite compact table around which the Cabinet sits. There were glassed-in bookcases at the end of the room and while waiting for him, I wandered up to have a look at them but they were full of anodyne editions of John Morley's *Life of Gladstone* or William Monypenny's *Life of Disraeli*, with the odd book by Tony Crosland or Ian Gilmour as something more up to date. But there was no particular rhyme or reason in the selection and I doubt if anybody had opened the glassed case in years.

Blair began by saying that we were in a 'post-euphoria, pre-delivery' mode. It is a snappy sound bite which was well received. He acknowledged the problems arising from the lone-parent benefits cut but bitterly denounced *The Guardian* as an enemy paper. There was a touch of media paranoia in his voice. He provided one shocking statistic, which is that we spend far more on disability benefits than we do on education. 'There is no going back. We have to separate last week's rebels into those who have a genuine concern and the out and out oppositionists.' There was more than a hint of iron in his voice and I think that if he can find some mechanism for dealing with those who publicly and continually attack him – Alan Simpson, Ken Livingstone, Diane Abbott – then he will do so.

As Ann Coffey, his PPS, who was chairing the meeting, went round the table, everybody moaned about the effect on the party of the lone-parent benefits crisis. As usual, I took a contrarian view, pointing out that if there were forty activists in each constituency who were unhappy, that amounted to 16,000 people for the 400-odd MPs, but this needed to be set against the 12 million or so who voted for us. I also said that while consideration should be given about how to handle the rebels, we shouldn't forget the 350 people who had been loyal to the government who also needed to be shown some respect. Blair was fluent, emollient but not wavering on the need to reform the welfare state. It was an authoritative seminar by a competent professor explaining political processes to his post-graduate students. There is not the charisma when he is there in person that one senses coming off the television screen or one feels the public senses about him. He uses his hands and fingers, which are very handsome, extremely expressively, splaying them out and working his hands into a little fist in front of him to make a point. He has an odd piece of vanity which is a fondness for crisp white shirts with very long cuffs which he wears with rather tacky cufflinks.

Blair confessed the failures of communication of the past few weeks:

Look, I mean, you know that we didn't get the Formula One funding issue right, but quite frankly all my time during that period was spent in meetings here thinking we might be going to war with Iraq. It's rather difficult to concentrate on the Formula One problem when you think you might be involved in a war at any moment.

He announced he was going to do a tour of party meetings in the New Year. 'I know I have to get out more. But government is different. I have to spend two days at the Luxembourg summit. Nobody gives a hoot what is agreed there or what the debates are about, but it's one of the things a Prime Minister has to do.'

There was a just a tad of a whinge and a hint of self-pity in Blair's voice. However, overall, the performance was good, convincing and he left the PPSs supportive and friendly. There were no mutterings as people struggled into their coats on what was the coldest day of the year so far with light snow flurries giving a Christmas air to Downing Street as we left. These are people who want to get on with their work and want this government to succeed. I went out to do an interview with Swiss TV and just as the reporter was about to begin the door opened and out swept Alastair Campbell who burst out laughing, 'Oh no, Denis, not you up to one of your self-promotion stunts again!' Thanks Ali.

TUESDAY 30 DECEMBER 1997

In the afternoon, I go and play golf with Papi, the children's Vietnamese grandfather, and we get round quickly. The light fades by 4 p.m., but at least there is some oxygen in our lungs.

1998

TUESDAY 13 JANUARY 1998

Every paper this morning is splashing on its front page a head-line like 'Blair grounds Cook's mistress'. The story is that No. 10 has ordered Robin Cook not to take Gaynor Regan on a series of overseas trips he is making.

It is a wonderfully English outing about sex. Of course, Robin should be accompanied by his partner if he so wishes. He is in des-pair. After a routine going-through of the questions, he asks all the officials to leave and then turns to us:

> I would like to apologise to everybody for what has happened.
> The weekend and the last few days have been the worst in my life.
> I thought the story had died down, but No. 10 has now given it
> oxygen. I have a very angry and unstable woman to worry about
> as well. Gaynor is furious with the press and the way they have
> depicted her.

I have never seen him so vulnerable and although it would be too much to say he appeared on the verge of a breakdown, he was in very great misery in front of us all. Everybody tried to cheer him up. I said we would maximise the support behind him on the back benches in the afternoon and told him: 'Robin, no one in the PLP or in the party is much worried about this. It is an internal Westminster media story. You must simply go out there and do a professional political job as a Labour Foreign Secretary.' Most of the other remarks followed in a similar vein and the only concrete outcome of this discussion was an order or an agreement to go out and rally as many backbenchers as possible behind him.

I go across to the House to corral the troops behind Robin. This actually works quite well and the benches are absolutely packed behind him. When he rises to answer the first question, there is an immense growl-cum-throaty cheer and the Tory benches, which also have a solid presence, are silenced with shame as they realise that this is one fox they will not be able to tear to bits. Robin handles all the questions with his usual skill and aplomb and such is his authority that no one dares raise the only issue that is on everybody's mind.

I went up to Rules for a dinner organised by Job Ownership on employee share ownership with Gordon Brown. Gordon took notes and sat in his usual hunk fashion, half-turned to people, I suppose to catch them with his one good eye and looking more jowly than ever. Ed Miliband sat opposite.

At the end of all the mini presentations, Gordon asked some good questions and the whole evening was a great success. It was a real coup to get Gordon to come along and discuss this issue and the presence of all the Americans committed to employee share ownership really had a good impact on him. I must remember this for the future: it's best to influence ministers not just with the presentation of arguments by Brits but to slip in a foreigner, preferably a North American, who can bring some freshness in enthusiasm and accent to the presentation of any reformist ideas.

THURSDAY 15 JANUARY 1998

Over to the House with a mound of documents for the debate on the EU Amsterdam Treaty to start. It is the usual rants by the Europhobes.

The best speech was a thirty-min drone by Bill Cash moving an amendment to delete an article in the treaty which would enable the Council of Ministers, acting unanimously, to propose measures to stop discrimination. Other Tories, like Oliver Letwin and Tim Collins, are there with their anti-European tirades and the debate, although deadly boring, is instructive in showing just how gripped the Tories are by this mad sectarianism.

Grabbing a quick salad in the tea room during a vote, David Davis, Doug Henderson's predecessor as Minister for Europe, glides up to me and says, 'You would do such a better job than your boss. Don't say anything, but I mean it.' He, I think, is being sincere though he may simply be being devious.

Someone in the tea room was handing out sheets for Labour's new hymn.

THE RED FLAG: REVISED VERSION
The People's Flag is turning blue,
Supporters don't know what to do.
Euphoria from May the First
Is fading fast; the bubble's burst.
While a tax dodgy millionaire

Is best of friends with Tony Blair,

It looks as if it's all too true.

The People's Flag is turning blue.

The People's Flag is turning white,

The government has taken fright.

For fear of Murdoch's gang's abuse,

They've turned it to a flag of truce.

They're just concerned they must not fail

The readers of the *Daily Mail*.

They've given up attempts to fight,

The People's Flag is turning white.

The People's Flag WAS deepest red,

But not all principles are dead.

So let us praise the forty-seven.

You are the salt, you are the leaven

Within the party's soggy dough.

Ignore the whips; be proud to know

Despite this most disgraceful bill,

You've kept the Red Flag flying still.

FRIDAY 16 JANUARY 1998

Up at 6.30 a.m. and a drive through London to get to Hanbury Manor, the Hertfordshire mansion where the Anglo-French *colloque* is being held.

A whole raft of friends were there, including John Lloyd, Ian Hargreaves (the *New Statesman* editor with whom I had had a long discussion the day before about why the weekly is so dull), Phil Stephens from the *FT* and a very impressive group of French businessmen and journalists including the lovely smiling Christine Ockrent and Laurent Joffrin (editor of *Libération*). The French participation was at a much higher level than ours. The most senior Brit politician was Stephen Byers, while the French had Alain Juppé who wandered around like a ghost at a feast. One of the Frenchmen said to me that no ex-Prime Minister is ever dead in France, hence Juppé's presence.

The conference opened with a remarkably arrogant presentation by Mervyn King, the deputy governor of the Bank of England, who announced that it would be the task of politicians to defend and promote the European Central Bank and ensure its decisions were accepted by the population. I thought it was a bit cheeky for him to tell all the Frenchmen what the European Central Bank was going to do given that Britain was not even in the euro, particularly as the governor of the Bank of France, Jean-Claude Trichet, was present. Trichet is the French candidate to run the European Central Bank and I wonder how he enjoyed King's admonitions.

Martin Taylor, the intellectual who is the boss of Barclays Bank and is heading a committee for Gordon Brown on how to integrate the tax and benefit system, finished his remarks with an odd line saying, 'Britain is throwing away all the levers of economic management to worship at the altar of the euro.' It came as a cold shock to realise how deeply hostile this particular representative of the banking establishment and the Conservative-thinking establishment is to the whole idea of European partnership based on common rules and mutual obligations. We have a long way to go.

Over cocktails, I talked to John Kerr, the Permanent Under-Secretary at the Foreign Office, who needed a shoulder to lean on about how disastrous the Gaynor problem is for the FCO:

Robin is in a dreadful state. We invited him up to our house for a talk, but I had to spend yesterday drafting PQs about her trips and he sent them all back saying he wasn't satisfied with my answers, but I told him they had to be published. He is also pissed off with me because I made him pay back Gaynor's fare on one of the trips she went out with him on last year. There's no problem with her going with him if she carries out some official engagements, but she didn't do the things we had arranged for her and so there was no justification at all for us picking up the tab. He was really angry, but I had to make him pay back the money.

Kerr was wearing his Garrick Club tie and puffing away at his cigarette and is a great gossipy, full-of-fun fellow. I told him that I thought the Foreign Office had been leaking bits and pieces to the diaries about Robin's behaviour and he didn't deny my allegation:

Robin wanted Gaynor to be his diary secretary and he fired the woman who was doing it. She was no good and she had to go irrespective of the fact that Robin was trying to get Gaynor the job, but now she's going around badmouthing him to the *Sunday Telegraph* and anybody else who will listen.

I am not sure it is easy to switch the blame for all the diary pieces and other anti-Robin publicity to a disgruntled Tory secretary who lost her job as the single source.

Kerr said how desperately alone Robin was. 'I asked him if he had had a talk with Clare Short since the election and he said, no, he just doesn't like her. I told him this was ridiculous and he should have regular meetings with her. After all, she is one of his political allies.' This is absolutely horrendous and makes a disarray at the top level of government in the Cabinet even worse than what we already knew to be a pretty bad set of commanders on the bridge.

I asked Kerr, who I had seen in deep conversation with his opposite number at Quai d'Orsay, if the French were going to be more helpful on Iraq. 'I wish to God we could get off this ridiculous Iraq policy. Every time Saddam burps we send an aircraft carrier. It's all No. 10's doing. They have this ridiculous desire to follow blindly wherever the Americans are going.' I try to cheer him up by saying that Robin and the Foreign Office had accomplished an impressive achievement in that it was the first time since the war that there had been a Foreign Secretary and a Foreign Office that was not the object of immense political controversy within the Labour Party and was not a divisive department of state for a Labour government. Ernest Bevin may be remembered as a great Foreign Secretary, but his policy on Israel and the Cold War provoked huge upheaval inside the Labour Party.

Harold Wilson's Vietnam and Rhodesian policies also provoked outrage, as did Labour's attitude on Europe, nuclear weapons, Cyprus and the appointment of David Owen in the 1970s. By contrast, Robin remains outstandingly popular in the party and the Foreign Office is a non-problem in internal party terms. Kerr joked that he would go and stir up some controversy if I wanted it and wandered off with a chuckle. He really is an extremely clever, nice man and it is great to have a good talk with him.

SATURDAY 17 JANUARY 1998

I drove back to London with Kirsty Hughes and David Miliband, the head of policy at No. 10 who is a very charming guy. He rattles off some stats about the welfare row and I suggested that it was a problem that had to be solved by the summer, certainly before the party conference season, or it should be shut down completely. But as we got into other areas, like foreign affairs, Europe and the international economy, it was clear that David did not have much to say, so said nothing.

It is worrying that the people at No. 10 know very little of what is happening in other countries. David agreed that the dinosaur remarks emanating from No. 10 when the French socialists were elected had been a disaster and I urged him to try to find a joint project that Blair and Jospin could attach their names to in order to give some concrete shape to the British–French relationship.

MONDAY 19 JANUARY 1998

The tedium of the Amsterdam Treaty debate goes on. Tonight it was an outing for the Tory Trotskyists. John Bercow, the funny little man who was secretary of the Monday Club Immigration and Repatriation Committee, was ranting about the iniquities of Europe. I had foolishly put on a pair of EU socks which I had bought from the Sock Shop in a rather garish blue with a little circle of yellow stars. I merely put my foot up on the bench in front of me and pretended to draw up my sock, when Bercow stopped in full flight to attack my choice of socks, with Bill Cash coming in behind him saying I had 'smelly socks'. They realised quickly how they had fallen into my little trap but ploughed on with all their anti-European nonsense.

The bill got its third reading so now goes to the House of Lords. It has been a long six weeks of debates. The key lesson I learn for the future is preparation, preparation, preparation. Doug Henderson is not an expert on European technicalities, but he seizes the main points and focuses on them and he does prepare himself very thoroughly with the officials.

WEDNESDAY 21 JANUARY 1998

The BBC yesterday had reference to Bill Cash attacking me in the Amsterdam Treaty debate even though I didn't actually speak.

FRIDAY 6 FEBRUARY 1998

At 10.30 a.m. over to the Foreign Office for a two-hour meeting with Robin, all four ministers, Robin's PPS – Ken Purchase, the Wolverhampton sheet metalworker MP – and officials.

Clare Short has gone bonkers because on Tuesday Robin announced that the dependent territories – mainly Caribbean tax havens – would have a new status, there would be a special ministry for them (I think he meant minister, with the job going to Liz Symons) and they could all have British passports. Clare has interpreted this as a grab by the Foreign Office for one of her areas of responsibility as her department funds the dependent territories and has kicked up a huge stink.

Robin said that Blair had indicated he wanted the matter to be settled between them, but Larry Whitty told the meeting that Clare had bent his ear on Wednesday night with another long diatribe against Robin. Part of the problem is the chalk-and-cheese nature of Clare Short and Liz Symons. They are both intelligent, forceful, achieving women but have such different backgrounds, style and routes up into politics that they were destined to be permanently at war once they found themselves working in the same field.

John Kerr intervenes to say that since the Department for International Development (DfID) has been removed from the Foreign Office, it has now £2 billion annually to spend. In contrast, the FCO, once its obligatory subscriptions to international organisations are taken into account, has only £50 million to spend on projects dear to its heart. DfID, complained Kerr, has a one-track approach to its job, which is to be pro-poor.

As always with Robin chairing, the meeting meandered all over the place with no proper discussion or sticking to an agenda. Half of it was taken up with a purely logistical discussion on a visit by foreign ministers or foreign affairs spokespeople from the Party of European Socialists (PES) in the context of the European presidency. Could Robin offer them dinner at his official residence, 1 Carlton Gardens? Kerr said he saw no impropriety, so the tick from the Permanent Under-Secretary was there, but I intervened to say I didn't think it was a good idea after all the sensitivities on government hospitality to use a government building and, in particular, a Cabinet minister's official residence for such an event, even if it would be the PES that would pick up the bill.

Robin got a little cross at this, saying, 'I don't see why I can't invite people to my residence if I want to,' but Doug Henderson and Derek Fatchett came in on my side. We don't need any negative publicity after the recent weeks' stories. One factor emerges that Blair is simply not interested in rolling out the red carpet for the European socialist leaders. He was willing to let them use 10 Downing Street for a meeting but not willing to give up time for a dinner the night before. This coolness to Europe that comes out in the form of these signals from No. 10 is extremely short-sighted.

TUESDAY 10 FEBRUARY 1998

At lunchtime, the usual chore of gathering up people to make sure there is a good turnout in the Chamber for FCO oral questions. I am pushing a ball downhill as Robin has created an excitement about foreign affairs issues with both his personal problems and now the Iraq story. The House is full and again he makes absolute mincemeat of poor Michael Howard and deals very effectively with every question he has to touch on. Robin thinks very fast on his feet but always retains control of his manner, speaking slowly and clearly for effect and not allowing either a speeded-up delivery or a high-pitched voice to give away what pressure he is under. Afterwards, there was a statement on Iraq.

The majority of MPs are backing the government, but I don't know how long this support will last if bombing starts and civilians get killed. The propaganda machine has sufficiently demonised Saddam, and John Major stood up from the back benches to rant about him and to demand the destruction of the Republican Guard. In fact, Major and George Bush should have a guilty con-science about not having finished off Saddam seven years ago. But the plain fact is that overthrowing a tyrant in the Middle East just opens Pandora's Box and we have no politics of democratic change or change of any sort in the region.

At 8 p.m. I had to go to St Stephen's entrance to pick up Jack Dromey, Harriet Harman's husband, and a senior T&G official who had never got a pass as a spouse for the House of Commons.

Upstairs to dinner with Nathalie, Harriet, Jack and Flavia Lam-bert. The three women talked about schooling for their girls as

Harriet is thinking of sending her daughter to Grey Coats, the Westminster comprehensive where Flavia is deputy head. She said that being an MP was the worst thing to do if you wanted a family life. 'I'll get out of this soon because the pressure is too much and it is hopeless for any kind of family life,' Harriet said. She also mentioned her sister who is a judge and earning pots of money. I think the heart of the matter is that the struggles of being an MP are as much to do with the low-earning power as they are to do with the question of children and seeing them. 'You just don't understand, my sister buys designer clothes!' said Harriet with the despair of a woman nearly fifty who has never had much money.

THURSDAY 12 FEBRUARY 1998

I had to prepare a draft for Labour Party MPs on Iraq. I bashed away at this, though to be honest my heart wasn't really in it. I don't mind bombing Saddam – except, of course, it won't be him or his elite that will suffer – but what I don't see is any strategic position or strategic analysis of what to do in the region as a whole. We live from hand to mouth. In the 1980s, Iraq was everybody's friend because it was fighting Iran. Then Iraq became the devil because it annexed Kuwait, as if anybody in Britain really cared whether Kuwait existed or not. Now we have to agree that Saddam is the most monstrous dictator and turn a blind eye to the absolutely filthy and inhuman despots that rule in Saudi Arabia and the other Gulf states.

The one line one can hang on to is to support the United Nations and to defend the upholding of its resolutions. But then the UN is a morally dubious outfit and so all that is left is the hegemonic fold of the United States with its democratic mandate from its own people and the rather pathetic support of Britain as a pimple that simply doesn't want to be squeezed from Uncle Sam's backside.

TUESDAY 17 FEBRUARY 1998

Robin opens the big debate on Iraq to a packed Chamber. He is very sombre and reads from a typewritten text, which is unlike him. Tony Blair sat beside him and from my perch directly behind the pair of them, I have to say he looked strained and tired. He is losing his hair at a ferocious rate and now has a little widow's peak sticking forward and a growing bald patch over what looks like a bad dandruff patch at the back of his head. His skin looks parched. It was made up as usual, but you can see the visible ageing. Despite the time off he takes, every moment is decision, decision, decision and the pressure must be awesome.

Michael Howard makes a competent speech but in the middle of it has a dig at Europe which goes down very badly. As others have said, it seems there is something of the night about him. Like the scorpion on the frog's back, he cannot help stinging even when it only does him harm.

Then came the first of the opposition speeches from Tony Benn. Having demanded loudly last week that Parliament should debate the Iraq crisis, he now complains that the debate is a sham and simply a means of providing cover for the government. He waffles on about having worn uniform, but as Edward Heath, who actually fought his way as an artillery officer through the last war, looks up at him, Benn has to say that he actually saw no action. I find his invocation of a non-existent warrior past curiously pathetic and he has very little hold on the House, though he is still a commanding and efficiently organised speaker. At the end, he more or less says that anybody who votes with the government is going to be directly responsible for the slaughter of innocent children, and this makes people angry, though there is simply no desire to turn the debate into a row.

After the vote, Steve Byers chuckles to me in the lobby that I shouldn't go to the theatre. This is because of a remark I made quoted in *The Independent* saying, 'Luvvies had demanded money from the state ever since Roman times.' William Rees-Mogg had devoted a whole column on Monday to attacking me, saying I would lose Labour immense support amongst artists and the world of cultural intellectuals by my stupid insult. In fact, I have written a letter quoting Juvenal in Latin contradicting the boring Father William, but nonetheless it was a slightly unfortunate slip of the tongue. Byers got into trouble on the *Today* programme the other day when he was asked what seven times eight came to and said fifty-four. I said to Stevie, 'Well, at least I can add up,' and he snapped back, 'So can I. I just have difficulties with multiplication.' It was a silly remark to make to a future Cabinet minister, but much as I on the whole like him, I can't quite work out a relationship as yet.

TUESDAY 24 FEBRUARY 1998

Up early to Hanover with David Marsh, now with the Robert Fleming bank. He speaks German fluently, having worked there a number of years for the *FT* and having a German wife.

We spent an extraordinary day with Gerhard Schröder. He is campaigning to win the Lower Saxony *Land* regional election on Sunday. If he does well, he will almost certainly emerge as the Social Democratic Party of Germany (SPD) candidate and then he is well placed to beat Kohl and become the next German Chancellor. I was there thanks to David, who has sensational German contacts and phoned up to see if he could spend the day campaigning. I came out as well and made a speech at Schröder's evening meeting.

He drives around in an armoured Mercedes which needs a huge amount of effort just to close the bulletproof doors. He talks very freely. He has a soft, easy voice and, at least to these two foreign guests, no side. He admires Britain and Blair and stresses his north German preference for links to England rather than the southern German orientation towards France. Kohl, he thinks, is finished. Schröder doesn't have much time for his old left rival, Oskar Lafontaine, who he said is caught with a terrible decision about surrendering his own claim to be the candidate but knows that Schröder is better placed.

As we drove through the countryside, the car phone rang and it was Oskar himself. He was enquiring about what the private polls were giving as Schröder's margin of victory but also started a little conversation on jobs in any Schröder Cabinet. He told us that he would make Rudolf Scharping the Foreign Minister. Scharping has come out for Schröder and thus nailed his colours to the mast.

We went to three meetings. The first was in a tiny regional newspaper office where an old building was being renovated. This was a relaxed press conference and Schröder is quite happy to indulge in long conversations with the journalists on any topic.

The second was at a small family bakers. I forget the name of the town, but in all these Lower Saxony regional towns one has a much stronger sense of infrastructure and economic activity than in their equivalents in Britain. I say a family baker but it employed 180 people and laid on an immense spread for all the local business owners. Schröder spoke in front of a gas oven, which I thought was an unfortunate image but then that is just stupid English sensibility. Here were sturdy, successful Volkswagen employees worried about their industrial future. There was plenty of beer and sandwiches as well as cakes and coffee as no German political meeting can take place without something to munch on. I did a little interview with CNN saying what a great guy I thought Schröder was while trying to make sure I said nothing that could cause any diplomatic offence.

The final meeting, a big public one, started at 6.30 p.m. in a town hall – not the *Rathaus* but the *Stadt Halle* – which was packed to overflowing with standing room only. I made a short speech in German, wishing Schröder all the best and saying the time of right-wing rule was over across the whole of Europe. I got lots of applause, though an attempt to be a bit smart with a reference to the springtime of nations and a new springtime for social democracy 150 years later fell flat. But it was appreciated and then he was off speaking for forty-five minutes without a note in a rather cool, unpopulist, almost educational manner, talking about the policies needed to face up to the challenge of globalisation. He did not attack the Christian Democratic Union of Germany (CDU) and praised Kohl, just saying that now it was time for him to go. There were no searches for applause and it was a serious affair and appreciated by this very serious, down-to-earth group of northern Germans. Schröder told us in the car several times that he now had to play the role of the statesman in order to prepare himself for the chancellorship and this restrained his natural aggressive and uncompromising manner.

We drove back towards Hanover and stopped in a small town about thirty kilometres away to have dinner. This was in a very luxurious hotel and the waiter came up saying that oxtail was a speciality

of the night. I shouldn't have but I couldn't resist, and a rather gluti-
nous blob of meat in a rich sauce eventually arrived. Schröder, who
is fifty-three and looks fit and well, said he had stopped drinking and
had never felt fitter, though he took a couple of glasses of wine with
his dinner. Again, it surprised me that he gave up so much time to us
and I wonder if he thinks I am more elevated than I really am.

We drove on into Hanover where he got out of the car outside
a modest housing block where he said he lived in a fifth-floor flat
which had no lift. It belongs to his fourth wife, a younger journalist,
and his very messy divorce seems to have caused him no problems.
I am only making a short note of this as I have written a long three-
page memo on Schröder for Blair, the government and the party
hierarchy, since I think they should make contact with Schröder
early in order to wish him well. Blair is fixated on Kohl, but we must
not make the mistakes that Major made in 1992 of overtly siding
with Bush and not noticing that Clinton was coming up the blind
side and was going to be the next President. Of course, my less-
than-perfect German means I couldn't get every nuance or work
out everything Schröder was saying to my complete satisfaction,
but I found him to be a fairly simple, very pragmatic and clear-cut
politician. We shall see if he wins on Sunday and if then he emerges
as the SPD candidate, but it was well worth the investment.

SUNDAY 1 MARCH 1998

It is a cold, blue day and London is full of the countryside march-
ers. As I went for my run in Battersea Park, I crossed a sturdy group
of men in grey and green just reeking of green fields and looking
very angry and bitter. Later in the morning, I saw more of the

upper-class countryside dwellers parking their Range Rovers, Jags and BMWs in SW1. They are clearly only interested in wandering along to Hyde Park and being seen and not actually taking part in the protest march itself. The *Sunday Express* has huge maps of how to get there, a bit like the Trotskyist *Socialist Worker* or the communist *Morning Star* twenty years ago would have told people where to join a demo against Vietnam or for trade union rights.

There are yet more people flocking in for this countryside march. Along the Embankment they look harmless holding their banners, and it is a real social movement that we have to understand and contain. Now they are focusing on the rural seats we hold with Labour MPs like Ian Cawsey and Angela Smith who are very anti-hunting being specially targeted. This is going to be a bit bigger than perhaps I had thought.

MONDAY 2 MARCH 1998

Tony is getting into a love-in with the French. He is making a speech in French to the National Assembly in three weeks' time and doing a big interview with the number one French TV news presenter, Christine Ockrent, which I helped set up. The French have stuffed us on two major foreign policy areas in the past few days. Firstly, by adamantly refusing to consider force against Saddam Hussein, they drew the sting from the threat of an Anglo-American led assault. Sending a plane to fly Kofi Annan to Baghdad also highlighted their diplomatic skills.

The other development, which is quite disgraceful, is the decision of Europe to kowtow to China and not support a human rights resolution on China at the UN Human Rights Conference in

Geneva. The French broke ranks with Europe last week and rather than facing down the French, Robin, as president of the European Council, has had to give way and now Europe is no longer putting any pressure on China on the human rights question.

We have been helped by the remarkable victory of Gerhard Schröder in the Lower Saxony elections. He made a huge break-through, getting 48 per cent of the votes and last night was imme-diately announced as the SPD candidate for the Chancellor contest in September. This means the memo I sent about him to No. 10 has proved stunningly accurate. Jonathan Powell phones up and asks me to call Schröder and give him Blair's personal congratulations. He tells me that Blair will fax a letter later on. I call Schröder's Han-over office and talk to his personal assistant. The man himself is rushing from TV studio to TV studio in Bonn, but his assistant is incredibly excited and pleased to get a call from me as a reminder of the happy day spent campaigning last week.

I go to the gym and then to a reception organised by the Oxford University Labour Club, where I glad-hand a few of these enthu-siastic children with beaming eyes. I want to tell them, 'Give up politics now. Become a banker. Become a writer. Cultivate your garden. Have a happy family. But not, not the false drug of political involvement.' But I do nothing and smile and be as friendly and agreeable as possible.

Back in the Members' Lobby, I pick up some mail from the letter board and there is a note from Blair himself, handwritten, congrat-ulating me on the Schröder report and my question at Prime Min-ister's Question Time. I bump into Doug Henderson and show it to him and he says, 'Put it away. Don't show it to anybody else. They will only be jealous.'

TUESDAY 3 MARCH 1998

Up early for yet another trip to Germany. This time to Bonn for
a seminar organised by the British Embassy with the CDU. The
team leader is Peter Mandelson, who has already set off. I travel out
with David Goodhart of *Prospect* and, like me, he is an old German
hand and very excited by the prospect of the SPD defeating Kohl.
It will shift the balance of power to the north of Europe, creating
a Hanseatic axis as outward-looking Protestant Europe has a different perspective from the ultramontane universalist Catholics.
Politics once again becomes serious and exciting.

The *Daily Mail* has published my article on the family and
pitched the headline as if I was arguing exclusively for women to
stay at home to be housewives. The strap describes me as a 'former
left-wing firebrand' and I wonder which of these words is the more
defamatory.

We land to be greeted by a pretty embassy diplomat who ushers
us off to an enormous hotel perched on the top of a hill overlooking
Bonn. It is a luxurious conference centre and hotel and extremely
well equipped with eight interpreters' booths as fixed installations
and an excellent seminar table that allows thirty or so people to
talk freely.

Wolfgang Schäuble arrives in his wheelchair. I had seen pictures
of him, but in the flesh it is tragic to see this shrunken figure almost
made miniature sitting in his wheelchair. Mandelson looms over
him chatting and David Goodhart hovers anxiously and when the
moment comes, thrusts a copy of *Prospect* into his hand burbling
about some long-forgotten interview Schäuble gave the magazine
two years ago.

I find myself talking to George Weidenfeld – yes, *the* George Weidenfeld – who is remarkably spry for what must be a ripe old age. He first published Harold Wilson in the 1940s and is one of the legendary networkers of Europe, criss-crossing and knowing people on the political, intellectual and Jewish networks in different countries. Oddly, we speak in German, which of course impresses him, and we actually get on extremely well.

I call my office and am told that Polly Toynbee is trying to get hold of me. I call her at *The Guardian* and have a chat for half an hour. She says she is going to 'put the boot in' over my article in the *Daily Mail* in support of the family. I speak to her on an 'off-the-record' basis arguing my familiar themes that we should not allow the Tories to occupy the family policy ground and that family politics can be a Trojan horse for progressive politics. I also give her the hard facts on allowances, but I can feel that since she is perhaps the chief priestess of the metropolitan elite sisterhood, I am getting nowhere. I asked her to respect the 'off-the-record' basis of the talk and not to attribute anything to me without agreement and she says, 'Don't worry, Denis. I'm just going to put the boot in as hard as I can.'

I dashed back to the lunch to find Rudolf Scharping giving a little talk. This is the only intervention by an SPD politician in the seminar. At dinner, Joschka Fischer, the leader of the Greens, is the guest speaker. He is an utterly changed man from the last time I met him three years ago. He looks about seventy with his fat, cheerful and well-dined and wined body slimmed down to almost a skeleton. I ask him what has happened because he looks as if he has had the mother and father of all heart attacks, but he says he has lost thirty kilos and wanted to stop looking like Kohl. His speech is the standard Green one about the need for a political Europe. One suggestion was to have a second chamber in the European Parliament consisting of delegations from national parliaments.

I go back to the ambassador's residence, which is a large suburban house, with Mandy, the ambassador Sir Paul Lever, Robin's European adviser David Clark and Colin Budd, who is the FCO's head of Europe. David Clark orders a brandy. I met Lever twenty years earlier in Barontoli, near Siena, at Flavia Lambert's house where he was with Flavia's sister Sophia who entered the FCO in the same year as Lever. I don't think much came of the relationship. He already had the incipient self-importance of the ambassador and the house party dubbed him 'Lord Palmerston'. We wickedly encouraged the children to push him into the pool. Now as the ambassador, he drinks a beer. I had a Williams and Mandy had what looked like a herbal tea as we chatted gently. I said that *The Guardian* would have a nasty column by Polly Toynbee attacking me tomorrow and Peter cheered me up when he replied, 'A column by Polly Toynbee attacking you, Denis? In *The Guardian*? I can think of nothing that would more highly commend you to the Prime Minister.'

I asked him if he was going to get the 7 a.m. plane with me tomorrow and he said, 'No, that's far too early. You are a workaholic, Denis, but I like to stay in my bed.' Of course, what he enjoys is being waited on hand and foot in the palatial surroundings of all these embassies. At home, he must wake up a lonely man. There he is in his mid-forties, staying an extra moment in a hotel or an ambassador's house where there is company and admiration and your shirt is washed and ironed. Perhaps this replaces the absence of family, children or a partner.

WEDNESDAY 4 MARCH 1998

My room was like a large old-fashioned hotel room with two big beds and rather chintzy furnishings. There was a bottle of whisky and gin and a bowl of fruit with sour black grapes with too many seeds in them. What there wasn't was a television, save a tiny hand-held portable. On the other hand there was an excellent shower and a mixture of British Cotswolds furnishings and German plumbing was more than adequate. We were served coffee by the chief butler at 6 a.m. and I was offered a book with history of the pictures of the residence which I declined as I had not had time to see or study any of them.

I went to the airport with Colin Budd, who is a deputy under-secretary in charge of Europe.

I asked him if we had any strategic view on how to develop an effective European policy. In effect, at the moment, we have four. One run by the PM and Jonathan Powell; one run by Peter Mandelson and Roger Liddle; one run by Gordon Brown on EMU; and one run by the Foreign Office. None of the four really dovetails one with the other. David Clark had complained bitterly last night that Charlie Whelan, who is nominally his opposite number at the Treasury, does not even return his calls.

The FES (the German Social Democratic foreign policy foundation) man in London had nobbled me on Monday evening at a reception to complain that Roger Liddle was taking money from the CDU's Konrad Adenauer Foundation to pay for trips for No. 10 staff to Germany. This is sheer madness, as if it gets out into the press that Blair's special advisers are taking money from German Conservatives, it will cause a huge stink and row.

Budd said:

Robin hasn't really shown any interest in Europe so far. He has probably the best relationship with a US Secretary of State since the war, and talks to Madeleine Albright every week, sometimes several times a week. But he isn't focused on Europe. It doesn't help that he never talks to his Minister for Europe, Doug Henderson. Doug is a lovely guy who seems very cheery and everybody likes him, but he obviously has no relationship with the Foreign Secretary. I have prepared an eleven-page memorandum on how Britain can become a leading player in Europe over the next five to seven years, but as far as I know, it has not been read or approved of by the Secretary of State.

He was full of praise for Mandelson. 'One day he will make a superb Foreign Secretary.'

Again, I said little, listening as a very experienced diplomat set his flies upon the water to see which one would produce a response. I complained that the Foreign Office had become thoroughly Thatcherised in that after about the early 1980s, it simply refused to have any bi-partisan relations with Labour and its representatives in trade unions' parties or other linked institutions. This became self-reinforcing as the Foreign Office considered that the left was just redundant or dead around the world. As a result, very few diplomats had good contacts and in the case of Germany were simply out of touch with the new forces such as those propelling Schröder to power. I told him that ambassadors should read *The Guardian* as much as *The Times* and the *Daily Telegraph* if they wanted to know what was making the left move and tick.

We landed and a car was waiting for Budd to go back to the centre of London. I asked to be dropped off in Pimlico and managed to arrive just as the children were leaving, so they gave great whoops of delight and I went to school with them and walked Benjamin on to his nursery school.

I go to Groucho's to have a drink with Christopher Hitchens who is in town to promote an updated version of his book on the Elgin Marbles. Polly Toynbee had been true to her word and has written a most unpleasant column in *The Guardian* attacking me. She completely misrepresents my position, saying I want to drive women back to the kitchen and that all fault in society lies with women. What is worse, she has broken her 'off-the-record' agreement and printed directly attributed to me lots of stuff which is a bit embarrassing, except her piece is so intemperate it doesn't matter.

Diane Abbott abused me for twenty minutes in the lobby, jabbing her finger excitedly in my chest, saying, 'If you're so keen on housework, why don't you go back and do it!' However, Diane and one or two other MPs and journalists said, 'That stuff Polly printed was off the record, wasn't it?' It was so obvious to them. Jonathan Powell's line on all of this is that everything is on the record, which I suppose is the only sure way of operating, but it makes pretty miserable conversations and no chance to explain what you're really trying to do. Hitch cheers me up by joking about both the *Daily Mail* article and Polly's response and saying, 'Like her or loathe her, there's one thing about Polly Toynbee everybody can agree on. You certainly can't read her.' That's unfair as she is a superb hardworking journalist and when you open your mouth in politics, you should expect no mercy. Christopher is in good cheer, overweight and as impish and delightful as ever.

THURSDAY 5 MARCH 1998

At 6.30 p.m. I walked over to Downing Street to attend some function for the Commonwealth. There is a reception line and we are greeted by Cherie Booth, who gives me a big 'Hello Denis,' and then a kiss which leaves her lipstick on my cheek. But she isn't interested in any more talk and I guess has a certain impatience with having to stand in for Tony. Ann Coffey comes along and rubs the lipstick off me.

Blair made a sweet, crowd-pleasing little speech. He was moving through groups of the Commonwealth guests so I didn't bother trying to talk to him and started to move out when I bumped into Sally Morgan who was full of praise about my memo on the German election last week. I mentioned that Keith Brookman had immediately paid £5,000 to the Labour Party to pay for Gordon Brown's Welfare to Work roadshow in Edinburgh and could something be done for him. 'Keith is high on our list [for a peerage] – no, he's now at the top of the list,' she smiled.

To the Travellers Club where Hitch was launching his book on the Elgin Marbles. We saw Colin MacCabe coming out and he cried, 'You have to wear a tie to get in there. I had to go to Tie Rack to buy one.' He was displaying some ghastly cheap confection. As we went in we passed Peter Hitchens, who is currently doing an odd double turn in magazines and papers with his brother. He said he had seen something I had written with which he profoundly agreed, but I didn't remind him of the *Daily Mail* article. We went on upstairs to say hello briefly to Christopher, Tony Holden and Annalena McAfee from the *Financial Times*, who had dug up a photograph of me and her on a picket line in east London in the 1970s. *Ou sont les neiges d'antan?*

SUNDAY 8 MARCH 1998

To Athens for a seminar organised by Chatham House and Kirsty Hughes with its opposite number in Greece. I said 'yes' half-heartedly and am feeling miserable as I leave the family home on a weekend day.

At the airport, I bump into Charles Grant and Roger Liddle. They are two interesting specimens. Liddle is an arch right-winger who has been opposed to the left in the Labour Party all his life, and as he tells me in the taxi from Athens airport, he goes right back to the Oxford University Labour Club in the early 1960s where he was a hammer of the left. Charles Grant is a much softer, more interesting figure. He was *The Economist*'s correspondent in Brussels, one of the bright young men from Oxford the paper always hires, but became a great fan of Jacques Delors and eventually wrote his biography. His passion is politics. Like me, he is a journalist, but that is simply a base for political engagement. He sits on the aeroplane hunched over his Toshiba hammering out pages of a speech that Blair is to make in Paris in a fortnight's time. Phil Bassett has asked everybody in the park to contribute and of course Charles is immensely flattered and works hard at it.

The flight is hideous. Four hours in a cramped Olympus Airways airbus with a filthy meal for lunch. Greece is two hours behind London, so we have to leave before midday to arrive at 6 p.m.

Roger Liddle was full of No. 10 gossip which is worth recording. The most interesting comment was that Blair was far more gung-ho than Clinton about bombing Iraq. 'He was really ready to go. I sat next to the chief of staff who said how thrilling it was to have a real leader again in Britain,' said Liddle. He also said that the targets chosen for the bombing raids were not, as I had assumed, rather safe casualty-free bits of desert but included the very centre of Baghdad. Liddle, of course, is Peter Mandelson's closest chum, so I was as noncommittal as possible. In a giveaway line, Liddle said, 'Tony, of course, can be very cruel and often shows no gratitude,' which I took to mean that the assumption that Peter was an unquestionable future star under Blair might now have to be questioned.

Liddle says he is working sixty hours a week at No. 10 and rather sadly added, 'I am no good at policy. I am 100 per cent a propaganda man. Give me a line and I will go out and sell it.' That seems rather against his image as the brains behind Peter Mandelson. Could it be the other way round, that Mandy has the brains and Liddle is the spin doctor?

WEDNESDAY 11 MARCH 1998

At 6 p.m. I got on my bike to go up to St James's Hotel, where there was a reception for the Party of European Socialists. This is a side meeting to coincide with all the European bigwigs coming in for the European Conference, which opens at Lancaster House. I had a good talk with Gerhard Schröder, who said I had been his good luck mascot to win the campaign. He said he was interested in my idea that he should write a series of open letters to people from the Pope and Blair to postal workers and miners in Germany as a way of doing a campaign autobiography.

I introduced him to Sally Morgan who bubbled with enthusiasm and he managed a short exchange in English with her. I also had a good talk with Costas Simitis, the Greek Prime Minister, who is a short, bald little chap. We talked in German, which impressed him greatly, and the fact that I had just been in Athens was extremely helpful.

Jan Kavan also came up and said 'hello'. He is in deep trouble in Prague because he was the Czech Social Democratic foreign affairs spokesman, but at a meeting recently in Prague with Javier Solana, the NATO secretary general, he asked openly if it was possible for the Czech Republic to withdraw from NATO. Not unnaturally, the heavens fell on his head as the Czechs have invested everything to get into NATO and here is someone who might be a future Foreign Minister saying how do we get out?

Václav Havel, the Czech President, attacked Kavan openly and he is being made to stand down as the Social Democratic Party's foreign affairs spokesman. I asked him why he had been so stupid and he just shrugged his shoulders. 'You have to ask honest questions now and then.' Yes, but the art of politics is to move from the moralism of European nuclear disarmament to the reality of winning and holding power. Dear Jan is a magnificent natural oppositionist, full of passion and ideas, but at times without a gram of political common sense in his head.

Blair came in followed by cameras, trumpets and noise. He entered into a conversation with Pierre Mauroy, the French socialist bigwig. Both were talking French, but it was clear that neither understood what the other was saying. Blair worked his way round the crowd and was well received, though I think there was a little irritation at the heavy presence of TV cameras. These guys are all used to this kind of attention in their own country and they don't need to be reminded that Blair is important... again.

Blair turned in desperation to Nick Sigler, the Labour Party's international officer, to ask what he should say to them. Nick burbled something in his ear and Blair was off, talking about how nice it was to see them all, about old values of 'social democracy and democratic socialism' – the S-word being used without a tremor on his lips – and other warm words that went down well. Searching for a theme, he praised Neil Kinnock who was sitting there beaming and is still networking merrily on the European socialist scene as of old. Robin Cook sat to one side, looking very 'garden gnome' and clapping politely as his master spoke. He is beginning to pick up the reins of all this euro socialist networking, but I doubt if he understands just how complex and difficult it is to bring them all together. Mercifully, the cocktail party was over quite early.

SUNDAY 15 MARCH 1998

Philip Bassett faxed over the draft of the speech for Tony Blair to be given in French to the National Assembly in Paris next week. It is absolutely dreadful. Whoever is responsible hasn't the faintest idea of how to write a speech starting from French premises, French formulations and French poetry of language. It is perfectly easy to put over Blair's ideas but to do so without using standard English clichés. There was a reference to Lord Cockfield. No one in France has the faintest idea who he is and to put him into a speech is simply out of date and plain silly.

I wrote five pages of notes with alternative phraseology and corrections and faxed them down to Phil, and it will be interesting to see the final shape of the speech.

FRIDAY 10 APRIL 1998

In La Baule for Easter and the news of Tony Blair's success in Northern Ireland dominates all the French papers. He has really pulled off something. David Trimble is the man of the moment. He has made the fateful decision to break with his past. Actually, he can't lose. The deal, if anything, will return a Northern Irish parliament which is bound to be under Unionist majority control at least to begin with. If common membership of the European Union through economic and other contacts end the barriers between north and south, so much the good. This has every chance of being the equivalent for Tony Blair what Algeria was for de Gaulle or what the Falkland Islands were for Margaret Thatcher. Once again, a British Prime Minister is a huge international star. The French papers show a photo of Blair shaking hands with Bertie Ahern. It looks like a London–Dublin deal over the heads of the factions in Northern Ireland. But Dublin is as opposed to Sinn Féin and the IRA as London, so the deal itself does not represent a victory for the ultra-Republicans. Gerry Adams may have as many difficulties as David Trimble.

SATURDAY 11 APRIL 1998

It's difficult to get the full force of the Northern Ireland agreement from the French papers. There is simply no praise high enough for Blair, Mo Mowlam and the team headed by Jonathan Powell that have achieved this, not least the Northern Irish civil servants who now are going to see themselves out of a job, though I suppose they will all transfer to being the administrative elite for the new parliament and administration. I talked to Patrice de Beer, *Le Monde*'s London correspondent, who is just back from Belfast. He is unstinting in his praise for Blair and for Blair's use of Clinton at key moments to move the process along. Given how cautious and at times downright cynical Patrice can be on the Blair government, this is high praise indeed.

FRIDAY 24 APRIL 1998

I am in Paris to attend a conference organised by the Fondation Jean-Jaurès, which was set up in 1992 as an international policy foundation linked to the French Socialist Party. To be in Paris in April is a liberating joy. The hotel is in rue du Faubourg Saint-Honoré, right opposite the British Embassy. I go there first and give my card with a little note scribbled for the ambassador, Michael Jay, to a tall upper-class Englishwoman, dressed in black but not quite as the French can manage it, who tells me with a rather disdainful voice that she is his private secretary. Her general demeanour suggested that the last thing he would be interested in and the last thing the British Embassy in Paris should have to put up with is an MP from London, and she clearly didn't have the faintest idea that I worked at the Foreign Office. How these diplomats are a caste of their own and this priestess does not want any contact with infidels who might profane her sacred temple.

To a television studio in the 15th where a new French channel, LCI, set up as the French equivalent of CNN, is staging a discussion about the first year of the Blair government. Interestingly, and to my immense pleasure, one of the people there is the French socialist Alain Bergounioux, who is an academic and historian of

the best book on *Force Ouvrière* (the democratic socialist reformist French trade union confederation) and now a national secretary for communications at the Socialist Party. He was a fat, jowly,
provincial-looking type who I assume must be on the hard right of
the French Socialist Party and thus completely in tune with today's
policies and leadership. Opposite us were Charles Hargrove, the
former correspondent of *The Times* in Paris. He is also revealed as
president of the Conservative Association in France, which helps
explain some of the reporting of *The Times* from Paris in recent
years, and now lives in retirement in Normandy. He was an old
English buffer, full of himself and profoundly out of touch and
desperately wanting to believe that Blair was a Tory. With him was
a weird woman who is now the president of the Conservative Association in France who claimed to be a political teacher at one of
the Paris university institutions, but given her French was atrocious
and her knowledge of British politics was zero, I found that hard to
believe.

The half-hour discussion was pretty useless as these two old
Tories hogged it with endless references to Frank Field, Keith Joseph
and even Samuel Smiles, with Hargrove trying to tell complicated
English political jokes in French to the bewilderment and dismay
of the very intelligent presenter who had done his homework.

Bergounioux and I, in contrast, offered a modern left line and as
far as possible supported each other. I probably talked too long but
felt fairly pleased that again I had had a good chance to promote
what Britain was doing and what Blair was doing on an influential
French media outlet. Afterwards I had a talk with Bergounioux and
we agreed on the need for much stronger party political contacts.
There are different events taking place including one in Paris on 9

June to which they are trying to get Peter Mandelson to come to address the first year of both governments and to which I will be invited as a supplementary speaker, which doesn't exactly do my ego any good. Peter, of course, now is a European-known politician, but he doesn't have much idea of how France works or what French priorities are and he doesn't speak any French.

SATURDAY 25 APRIL 1998

Michael Jay, the British ambassador, phones up to invite me for coffee. The embassy is just across the road from the hotel and after the tedious opening moments of the conference, I slip out.

He is there in a green jumper and slacks in his rather small study in the midst of this extraordinary hotel bought at the end of the Napoleonic wars and which now is the No. 1 diplomatic address in France. His wife Sylvia works in the neighbouring office and was busy manipulating a computer as I came in. We had a general talk about European and French policy and he said that things had got a lot better after the bad start following the election of the Jospin government last June. 'I try and invite them to come here. I had Anne Sinclair over for dinner because that is the best way of getting a message through to Dominique Strauss-Kahn [Sinclair's husband who is the French Finance Minister].'

I made my lament about the lack of political knowledge of the French left in London. 'It's very difficult with the cuts and the focus on commercial stuff,' said Jay. He moaned:

In the 1970s, we had somebody like George Walden here who went off and got to know the rising French socialists like Pierre

Joxe, but there isn't anybody on my staff at the moment to do that. We are completely obsessed with the World Cup, which is taking up an immense amount of embassy time.

The ambassador agreed whole-heartedly with my concept of the need for political 'aides-de-camp' who would network around Europe finding out what was on the political agenda and advancing and explaining what the government was doing but doing so with the authority of the Prime Minister or top ministers.

At the moment, each Cabinet department runs its own policy and although the Foreign Office coordinates the politics of relations with Europe and the Cabinet Office coordinates ministerial presentations, this is quite dull – very civil service, technological and administrative in its style – and misses the need for high-level political work such as is undertaken by *cabinets* in Continental administrations. Jay agreed with everything I said, though as always with these top dips, is that just prudent politeness to a member of the governing party or something he really believes in? He is rather unsmooth in his style, though far from being a hairy man. His teeth are all bucky at the front and he looked very comfortable in an American sub-fusc for his dress-down Saturday. There are problems between the French and British leaderships but just finding meeting time is difficult. Jay noted:

I tried to fix up a visit by Jospin to Sedgefield but it was impossible to get a diary time out of No. 10. I think it would be great if Tony could invite Jospin, or vice versa, spontaneously to come to London or Paris to watch a football or rugby match, but again it is difficult to fix these things up, especially from the London end.

There indeed is the rub. Prime Ministers and Cabinet ministers may want to establish good relations, but the domestic agenda has supremacy, and once they have shaken hands and left the physical presence of their opposite numbers, the need for strengthening these relations just floats out of the window and evaporates. But how good is Jay's own staff? This week *Libération* published my big full-page article on Blair and the Third Way and he hadn't even seen it. Despite having a socialist government, he doesn't read the main paper of the left himself, nor does any member of his staff think it of interest to draw attention to, even though I am a Labour MP and a PPS at the Foreign Office. It's not my own vanity quotient that I am worried about but a lack of political feeling within the embassy which hasn't reorganised itself to fit in with the new governing and political mood across the Channel in Britain.

FRIDAY 8 MAY 1998

To the Dome in Doncaster for the election count for the European Parliament by-election. Linda McAvan wins easily with 52 per cent of the vote on a 24 per cent turnout. That is not dishonourable compared to the last by-election in Merseyside, where the turnout was only 10 per cent, but there is simply no interest in European parliamentary affairs at all.

Jane Robbins is there from the BBC to do a film on changes in voting systems. I tell her that you can choose any system you like but it only delivers the goods if the policies and people are right and are popular with the public. It is a search for a philosopher's stone to think that there is a magic electoral system that will deliver automatically better government. Surely the rise of malign extremist politics under PR voting systems in Israel or Italy, to take two examples, might be a warning?

SATURDAY 9 MAY 1998

I drive down through London to Chevening, the Foreign Secretary's country residence. We are there because Giles Radice has organised a seminar for British, German and French MPs and got Robin to lend them his country home for it. It is a stunning Jacobean building and full of history as the different earls of Stanhope who owned it since 1717 have been at times great soldiers, ministers and at the very centre of the British aristocracy. There are beautiful prints, autographed letters from Disraeli and Macaulay, the library is a heaven of leather-bound books and the grounds with their imposing lake are quite delightful. Yet it feels so much like a National Trust museum if not mausoleum and although Robin says it has been a haven from the pressures of being Foreign Secretary, there is no indication that he actually lives there, not even in his bedroom with its four-poster bed and TV conveniently beside it so the Foreign Secretary and his new wife can sit there in their nightgowns late at night watching all the horrible news and current affairs programmes tearing him to bits.

The seminar is fairly routine with a lot of old sticks who are obviously professional hands at these international seminars and who tend to repeat positions that we all know in any case. The Germans all speak English but the French have never bothered to learn any other languages and in that sense are just like us. Meeting in the historic elegance of this Kent country house is very soothing for the spirit, though lunch was perfectly foul and I hope Robin gets better cooking when he stays there with Gaynor.

MONDAY 11 MAY 1998

At lunchtime, I phone Mark Seddon of *Tribune* to discuss an article about European politics, but we start moaning to each other about the problem of spin doctors briefing against each other. There have been a spate of absolutely poisonous little articles in the papers aimed at ministers before the reshuffle. The *New Statesman* said Geoff Hoon would replace Doug Henderson, then *The Sun* quoted a 'senior minister' accusing Robin of stabbing Tony Lloyd in the back and now this morning there is a story on the front page of *The Times* saying that the Permanent Under-Secretary at the Department of Trade and Industry (DTI) has written to the Cabinet Office saying he will refuse to accept Geoffrey Robinson in a transfer from the Treasury to the DTI. I say I would like to do a piece attacking this endless spin-doctoring and disloyal briefing, and Mark snaps it up.

I dash it off and go up to King's Cross where I meet him and hand it over furtively in the W. H. Smith's there like a meeting of dissidents in Prague in the 1970s. I feel slightly ashamed at having to do this anonymously, which I suppose makes me no better than the briefers, but this is a poisonous, demoralising business that needs to be checked.

THURSDAY 14 MAY 1998

In the evening to a dinner organised by Carla Powell, the woman whose salon, thanks to her marriage to Charles Powell, Margaret Thatcher's foreign policy aide and Jonathan Powell's older high Tory brother, has been the most famous in Conservative circles for years. The event is to launch a book by a man called Rodney Leach on Europe. He works at the same bank as Charles Powell. It is in a posh hotel in Knightsbridge and bit by bit a coven of Europhobes assembles. There is Paul Johnson with his watery eyes and his once flame-red hair now turning white. He is off the drink and in deep national disgrace because a former girlfriend of his revealed all in the *Daily Express* about his proclivity for spanking activities in bed.

Then there is William Rees-Mogg looking more gaunt and white-haired than ever but still passionate in his hatred of all things European. Michael Howard appears with his model wife and then Bill Cash. I spotted Norman Stone, who had come back from Ankara for the evening with his Garrick Club bow tie, looking irrepressibly vulgar. He seemed to be less bloated so a diet of Turkish delight can be doing him no harm. There was David Frost and one of the Saatchi brothers who is close to the Conservative Party.

Then the divine apparition came in. It was Margaret Thatcher, coming through a side entrance in a fluorescent light-blue dress, walking very slowly and sedately like an ageing goddess amongst her fawning *serviteurs*. The whole event was becoming more and more surreal. Roger Liddle turned up with his wife Caroline Thomson, who is now a big cheese at the BBC World Service. She giggles to me and tells everyone that I was responsible for taking her out on strike when she worked at local radio in the 1970s. I beg her to keep my militant past buried.

Roger says that Cabinet ministers were told they couldn't attend the event and the only minister there is Joyce Quin, who smiles across the room at me as if to say, 'What the hell are we doing here?'

Charles Powell is acting like a major-domo, ushering everybody into dinner. To my horror I find it is a sit-down hotel meal and I am placed, oh Lordie, Lordie!, between Polly Toynbee and Mrs Bill

Cash. On Polly's left is Paul Johnson, who stares vacant-eyed across the table, physically a pale and thinned-out version of what he once was. Bill Cash's wife, Biddy, is absolutely charming and the most perfect dinner party companion. She seems very young though she has a thirty-year-old son. 'Bill had me when I was sixteen, so we started at an early age.'

She insists that Bill is not anti-European. 'It's so unfair. He really likes Europe. He's a great admirer of Tony Blair. He is co-chair of the Jubilee 2000 Appeal [which is trying to get Third World debt lifted off the back of poor countries] which the Tories don't like at all.' I listen to her burbling on about what a nice chap her husband is and we exchange technical chit-chat about the tedium of driving up and down to constituencies. Luckily, I had given Cash a lift back to Pimlico a few weeks ago, so although I am in the opposite camp politically, I don't think there is anything personal between us.

I see David Goodhart, who is ensconced between the wife of the author and some large horsey woman, sending eye signals of despair and merriment at me and attacking the booze as seriously as he can, as indeed I do. I chat a bit to Polly, who, like me, is baffled to be there since she has common-sense views on Europe and we both subliminally agreed not to mention her column or her reactionary and silly views on family politics.

Then an introductory speech from Charles Powell and up stands the author, Rodney Leach, who is introduced as some kind of polymath because he is a great bridge player as well as being a banker and has written his book. He makes a rather tedious speech attacking Europe for its social policies, its federal inclinations and all the usual rant of the Europhobes. I mutter under my breath getting noisier all the time and I see blacker and blacker looks at me. To Biddy's right was the publisher of the book who says I am behaving disgracefully. Mrs Leach is very angry, as is the horsey woman to Goodhart's right. Paul Johnson just stares vacantly at the floral arrangements in the middle, unaware almost of anything that is happening.

I realise I have gone a bit too far and am creating a scene. Polly Toynbee says, 'I think we should walk out. This is absolutely disgraceful.' I decide not to and try to cool everything down by apologising profusely, buying a copy of his book and giving £17 to the publisher and making sure he signed it, and then after the speech is over, going round and getting other people like Norman Stone and Andrew Neil to sign it as well. Bill Cash sits down for a good chat but too much wine was taken by then and I just smiled benignly at everybody. I had good hugs and talks with Andrew Neil and Norman Stone, both of whom are effusive in their greetings and I suppose there is just a solidarity between those of us who like to be outspoken and cause a row irrespective of our politics. Mrs Thatcher is sat regally at her table with an upright back, looking neither left nor right but fixing her eyes somewhere to hold her head erect. Actually, she didn't look too bad and I wondered if she's had a bit of a neck lifting as the awful crow's skin that was certainly there two or three years ago doesn't seem to be quite so noticeable.

I left with a lot of other people and got a taxi home having drunk and eaten too much and again made a scene which no doubt will be spoken of loudly in the salons of Tory Europhobia.

FRIDAY 15 MAY 1998

I pop into the office and then go out to Flemings, the bank in the middle of the City where David Marsh has organised some kind of lunch with Josef Joffe, the editor of the *Süddeutsche Zeitung* who writes perfect English and does editorials all over the place for English journals.

There was an offensive sneering question from a tall youth in granny spectacles with a large double-breasted jacket dating from the 1950s, who I realised was Jacob Rees-Mogg, son of the Europhobe William and ex-Tory candidate. He sneered about the three federalists and talked about losing sovereignty. A bit later on I was able to say that I wasn't a federalist and that what we were doing in Europe was something quite new and the notion that any MP controlled interest rates, or indeed that any minister did, was silly. I won the argument, I think, and people were quite cheerful as I hurried up to King's Cross.

Alan Simpson, the ultra-left MP from Nottingham, had been invited to the Rotherham Labour Party General Committee (GC) tonight to speak against proportional representation. I had left a note on the board for him about coming to my house, but as I race over there to get to Hall Grove by 5.30 p.m. there was no sign of him. Instead, there were plenty of telephone messages and then, horror of horrors, a call from Joe Murphy of the *Mail on Sunday* who was writing their 'Black Dog' column and had heard about last night's little row at the Europhobe gathering. He asked me if I had heckled and walked out and I strongly denied walking out, saying on the contrary I had got the author to sign the book and had had a very pleasant lunchtime meeting with him in the City today. Thank God that had happened, which gave me a little bit of cover. I burbled away about the other things I had seen there and we shall wait for the outcome of the 'Black Dog diary', but I suspect it will be wholly negative.

Down to the GC where Alan Simpson gave his speech against proportional representation, pleading for the alternative vote system which is a nice little racket helping incumbent MPs. That is why everybody is in favour of it, as it seems to be a change that looks a bit fairer and will keep lots of Labour MPs in their seats. But when the big swing comes, as I think it will, it could cost us very dear.

The opposing speech was given by Charlie Simmons, a Sheffield Labour Party activist, who is involved with the campaign for electoral reform. He was really good, serious and coherent and easily won the argument, though a full-scale move to PR isn't really on the cards. But when a vote was taken, he got a good majority and I was pleased at the sound common sense of the party.

I took Alan as well as Irene Furnell, Anna Chester and Andy Ducker back to Hall Grove for a glass of wine. We ordered a take-away curry at 9.30 p.m. but it didn't appear until 11 p.m. and then only because Anna and Andy went down to fetch it. Alan told lots of his lovely stories about campaigning against the Tories in Nottingham, as well as problems like 'Asian infiltration'. In one of his wards, 250 Asians became Labour members in a very short time as they fought with each another to get the nomination to become a ward councillor. But generally we skirted around politics and just were as friendly as possible.

Simpson, of course, is Blair's enemy number one. He is keeping his head down until a moment of crisis appears when he will seek to emerge as the leader of a new left. But the point about leaders of the left is that they have to be brave and put their heads above the parapets when to do so is dangerously unpopular. Alan writes and speaks a bit but isn't prepared to take on the machine. In addition, I don't really think there will be a crisis in the sense that he and Ken Livingstone and the other crowd who support or who long for the moment when 'the worse the better' arrives. However, I have a fatal weakness of liking people who are actually good company and he is, so we drink two bottles of wine and eat a great oily curry which arrives in a cardboard box after 11 p.m. and people go off at midnight having had a jolly time.

MONDAY 18 MAY 1998

I look down from the Foreign Office on the G7 leaders. As the journalists assemble, I can see Martin Walker. I phone up *The Guardian* and try to find out if he has a beeper or mobile phone, but of course Martin is not a technological freak so I leave a message asking him to call me to see if we can link up.

On come all three of them – Clinton, Blair and the EU Commission president, a nonentity called Jacques Santer, from little Luxembourg of course. Clinton doesn't look as big as he sometimes appears in photos, but then all three men are quite tall. Blair rattles out his statement and then Jacques Santer makes his declaration. It rambles on and on, delivered in this ghastly Luxembourgeois English accent which we can't catch because the loudspeakers are pointed at the press conference and not up to our window. But it is clear the president of the EU is waffling on and on. Blair's body language becomes hilarious. He twitches and fiddles with his cufflinks and sneaks a sideways look at Santer as if to say, 'For God's sake, shut up, you boring Eurocrat.' Clinton, who is infinitely more used to the unspeakable ritual of tedium associated with international declaration-making, just stays his ground patiently.

At long last Santer is finished and Blair turns with a puppy look of adoration to his master and asks Clinton to speak. His face is wreathed in smiles, admiration and excitement.

Clinton is shorter and more solid than either of the previous two in his declaration, but again I can't quite hear what he is saying, so I leave after the first question or two and go back to Robin's suite of offices.

There, predictably, nothing has been prepared for backbenchers for the debate this afternoon, so I sit down and type out some questions for Howard myself.

I have a question to Ann Taylor about providing cash to allow MPs to travel to Europe, which I get out with a laugh or two, and she is fairly friendly in her reply. Later in the tea room, she says it is simply a matter for Gordon Brown. If he is prepared to make the money available we can have it, but as always in this wretched government every negotiation, even on the spending of pennies, has to go through the Treasury. An MP can go anywhere in the UK on a fiddle called 'extended travel', so I can go to any political meeting or just to the seaside if I claim there is some remote link to my constituency. But if I want to spend a penny on going to or meeting anyone in Europe – which is my main focus of political and parliamentary interest – I have to pay for it myself or scrounge a ticket and a hotel room. The jobsworths who control MPs' finances or the committees who check expenses are properly paid turn a blind eye to any money claimed for a trip inside Britain – but to show an interest in Europe is seen as political deviancy.

Later I joined Martin Walker for dinner. Martin, as usual, was in great form, talking about how Clinton had introduced Labour and environmental rights into his statement on world trade which agreed with the EU leaders this morning. I somehow don't see it making that much of a difference. The language is there but no follow-up. But Martin clings to his line that Clinton is really a leftist and that a new left-of-centre world is in the making between Blair and the US

Democrats. I wish it were true. I certainly think a rapprochement between the new European governing left and the Democratic Party is necessary, but we are simply managers of market capitalism and there is very little that is concretely left wing still in our philosophy or in what we are doing. All that is taking place is holding on to nurse, for fear of finding what we know is worse.

It was a good dinner, but I was tired and not completely on form and we had a bottle too much – but not of the most expensive wine, as Walker or rather *The Guardian* was paying.

THURSDAY 21 MAY 1998

My fiftieth birthday. I feel lost and just going on as usual. Where has that half-century gone? What have I achieved? What is left? I can't even bear to begin thinking and analysing all this because the answers are so nugatory. I will try to draw up a balance sheet a bit later. I have tried to do some good, but it really has been a life so far of physical and intellectual voluptuousness.

I write an article for *Critical Quarterly* in the morning but nothing seems to work in terms of work and I go off instead to have lunch with Simon Heffer and Colin MacCabe. Heffer is no longer drinking and has lost his puffy, tubby body and face to become more feline with his red hair. He is an extremely funny conversationalist. His imitation of William Hague and what he is trying to do with the 'Con... serv... ative Party', with each syllable hit with a rather bad imitation of a South Yorkshire accent, is very good. Colin and he are in free conversation and I join in. Nobody seems to have noticed it's my birthday and Colin and I share a bottle of passable claret while Simon sticks to the mineral water. Like all those right-wing columnists, he is still savouring the defeat of Major but doesn't know how to handle the new government.

WEDNESDAY 27 MAY 1998

I get a Swiss Air flight to Moscow. At the airport, a young Russian woman meets me and takes me straight into a VIP lounge. This is full of very shady-looking customers with a hint of despotic orientalism. We get into a horrible Russian-style transit van stinking of diesel and ride down an interminable crowded motorway turning off through birch forests to the hotel and conference centre where I am due to speak. The event is organised by the Moscow School of Political Studies. This was set up by a remarkable woman called Elena Nemirovskaya who ran a dissident's salon in the 1980s and then created this school with support from all sorts of overseas foundations to promote democratic political activity of a liberal-right nature once Russia had gone 'democratic'.

Anne Applebaum, the right-wing American commentator with whom I get on extremely well, had asked me to participate months ago and I had said yes. I didn't really notice the dates were in the Whitsun break and although that is convenient in not having to ask for parliamentary time off, it is inconvenient because it takes time away from the children. So I cut my stay down by one day and will only spend two nights here before flying home on Friday.

The conference is held in a luxurious, by old Soviet standards, hotel and conference complex in the middle of the dacha belt to the west of Moscow. It was built, I guess, in the early 1980s, with rather ghastly imitation German or Nordic architecture from about ten years previously. Everything has that slightly Third World Soviet feel to it, though my room is perfectly adequate and the most important thing is plumbing that actually works.

Anne Applebaum spoke about the British media and didn't, I think, have a lot to say. The problem was that she kept citing different English newspapers, but I wonder how many of the participants from the lower Volga or from Siberia have much of an idea of what *The Observer*, the *Sunday Telegraph* or even *The Sun* are? At any rate, it was nice to see her and we had a bit of a chat over a quick dinner served with cups of tea which at least helped to keep the alcohol quotient down.

The nice man I met there was Rodric Braithwaite, who was the ambassador there from 1988 to 1992 and then worked in No. 10 before retiring. He really was very good value, very open, very easy, very political, very John Kerrish to talk to.

The participants at the seminar themselves were mainly members of either the State Duma in Moscow or the different regional government dumas right across Russia. There were communists, liberals and right-wingers, so the whole political spectrum was covered. There were also a couple of journalists and in the session after dinner, which went on until 10 p.m., they had a great ding-dong about role-playing their way through different political positions. They were all very smart, and passionate, but the underlying thesis was a lack of order, a lack of political legitimacy and a lack of democratic control over the economy.

The real problem is I don't know enough about Russia to set all this in its proper context. Braithwaite told me that the real decision-takers were the governors of the different regions or the big-city mayors as well as Boris Yeltsin himself. 'The parliamentarians just don't get much of a look in. They are badly split. Basically, there is simply no political culture of democracy and self-rule in Russia.' There was one good joke which went: 'Every people gets the government it deserves. That's why here the government is run by Russians.'

THURSDAY 28 MAY 1998

I do my talk in the morning and it goes down very well. Braithwaite comes up to me and says, 'Now I know why Anne Applebaum wanted you to come.' Of course, the generalities one can get away with at a conference like this are quite easy to deliver. In addition, I make some flattering remarks about Russia and say that the country needs to develop a narrative, a story to tell.

As soon as I have finished, I grab one of Elena Nemirovskaya's assistants, a young graduate student called Misha, for a drive into Moscow to see the city. We take the scenic route through Dachaland. This is where Lenin, Stalin and all their successors had their dachas as well as their followers. Now the new rich in Moscow are buying property here. But the effect is bizarre. There are small plots of land with giant three-storey buildings all in bright new red-brick and hardwood imported from west Europe springing up. But they are squeezed side by side as if on a tiny estate. The lot is always sealed off with a wall and I presume is meant to give some sense of security, but what is the point of being a new millionaire and having your house built to order if they all look the same and you live cheek by jowl with your new neighbour? The effect is vulgar and self-defeating.

As I ponder this, the car comes to slow down as two police cars overtake us, crossing the single white line in the middle of the road going through the birch tree forests. Then our car stops and we wait for ten minutes, then twenty, then nearly half an hour until finally two big jeeps full of soldiers or armed police emerge and behind them a giant forty-foot long Mercedes with the Russian flag at its front. It is President Yeltsin leaving one of his dachas. 'This never used to happen in the Soviet Union. Now they make us wait for half an hour to allow Yeltsin a clear run into Moscow. It is quite disgusting,' complains Misha.

We park near the Red Square in heavier than comfortable rain. We walk round Red Square, but the Kremlin is closed as is St Basil's Church. Lenin's mausoleum is still there but without the guards outside it. GUM, the old communist apartment store, has been converted into a series of shops selling Calvin Klein and Boss clothes, but there are still stands selling the matryoshkas and I buy three of the small dolls for the girls. Otherwise the city looks shabby. The newspaper stalls only have Russian papers and that hallmark of the new Europe, the news vendor's stand or kiosk with the *International Herald Tribune* and a selection of foreign papers, simply doesn't exist, at least on the streets here. We walk on to the bridge that leads away from Red Square where there are magnificent views of Moscow. A huge new cathedral has been built in under two years and here and there are renovated buildings or simply large new ones. The effect is a city out of scale with itself, with none of the renewal or sense of architectural ease that one can see elsewhere in Europe.

Misha takes me to a supermarket, well at least that is what it was called, but it is like a rather cheap PX store that you see for UN officials in Nairobi or Latin America. I buy half a bottle of vodka for 25 roubles – about £3 – but the caviar is extremely expensive at 400 roubles for a small tin of good Caspian stuff and the days when one could pick up tins of caviar for $10 are long over.

Anne Applebaum and I go to dinner at the Dom Literatura, the Writers' House. It has been turned into a ghastly imitation Swiss or German restaurant with heavy linen and a wine list in exactly the same cover that one has in the House of Commons. The food is very expensive. Our modest two-course meal with a bottle of indifferent Georgian wine cost £100. Anne is now married to Radek Sikorski, who is deputy foreign minister in Poland. He is a Polish Catholic who was a refugee in England after Solidarność was shut down on orders from the Kremlin in December 1981. He graduated from Oxford, where he was in the Bullingdon Club with Boris Johnson and David Cameron. Anne is a Jewish American intellectual princess. It is a bizarre coupling. She lives in his country house a couple of hours from Warsaw with her small son, Alexander. Sensibly, she has retired from the London journalistic and commentator scene where she didn't really fit in with the New Labour dispensation, though she remains as ideologically driven as ever. But her story is anti-communism and that is yesterday's meat, despite the best efforts of people who only came to it in its last few years to keep the story alive. We have an enjoyable talk, but I am looking with horror at the hideous prices for a fairly tasteless borscht soup and a completely indifferent rabbit pie. The food I was given to eat at my conference hotel was ten times tastier.

At 9.45 p.m. Misha turns up with a driver and we sail back through the night to the hotel.

TUESDAY 14 JULY 1998

Dinner in honour of Robin Cook at George Weidenfeld's flat on Chelsea Embankment.

This was a collector's evening. The eighty-year-old Weidenfeld, accompanied by his new blonde Austro-English wife who must be nearly half a century his junior, was laying on a do for yet another Labour potentate.

The flat was a step back into the 1920s high culture of the Vienna or Berlin intelligentsia. Books rose from floor to ceiling in elegant teak and stainless steel bookcases. There were mixtures of different styles of furniture with giant busts either genuinely from Roman times or good eighteenth-century imitations. An oil painting – also eighteenth century? – of the Campo in Siena was there.

Two circular tables were set in the middle of two rooms knocked together and there was none of that ghastly chintzy English gen-teelness bourgeoisie. This was raw intellectual power, money made from ideas, everything set up for political and other forms of se-duction. Gaynor Cook was there and we had a very friendly chat. I think both she and Robin are simply more relaxed now and if they can just have two or three months without being in the news-papers, all will be well between them and for him and, I hope, the government.

John Lloyd was there as well as Tim Garton Ash and his Polish wife, Danuta, whom I had never met. She has a square handsome face mainly occupied by cheeks underneath nice blonde hair, de-lightful eyes and strong fingers.

Weidenfeld hustled here and there introducing me. There was a man who was over two metres tall who was the editor of *Die Welt*. His English was much better than my German, so I gave up. He said he had come to London to try to persuade Weidenfeld to do a column, but I expect George's success lies in never ever writing anything down whenever possible.

There was a weird man from Prague who was some kind of count with a little moustache underneath his snub central European nose, looking like a senior member of the Austro-Hungarian general staff. The Austrian ambassador, a statuesque woman, was there and we had a show-off discussion about *Kakania* – the word used to describe the old Austro-Hungarian kingdom and empire.

The food was excellent, loosely based on a theme of curry but just with far more tang and penetration than the official English cuisine which is so boring. As the waiter came round, I asked if I could take two bits of the curried chicken and he said, 'The Foreign Secretary's taking two bits, sir,' as if a regal precedent had been set which I could dutifully follow.

I was sitting beside Danuta Garton Ash. They now live in north Oxford and the two boys go to one of those posh prep schools there. She seemed surprised when I muttered a protest about private education, as if there was simply no rational alternative.

Weidenfeld made a gracious little speech followed by Robin, who referred to him as George as if they had known each other all their lives. I actually find this business of being taken up by the establishment – even if it is one I feel wholly at home with like the Weidenfeld network – slightly unpleasant. I would prefer some austerity or even attempts to create a new Labour salon of our own, but we have neither the time, the money nor, if we are honest, the style, and if Weidenfeld lays on all of these things, why not swig the champagne and enjoy it?

As we got up to go and were standing around to find our way out of the complex warren of rooms that Weidenfeld has created in his Chelsea Embankment flat, there was a woman of an indeterminate age but well into her sixties with a curiously unlined face and a kind of death mask of white make-up who was asking in a soft Irish accent if she could get a taxi on Chelsea Embankment to get her as far as Sloane Square. I piped up and said we could take her. She turned round to me and with her large bosom butted me, saying, 'There's no need, you know. I just need to get to Sloane Square, I can get a taxi.'

I insisted we could take her because I had realised that it was Edna O'Brien. 'You're Edna O'Brien, aren't you? I read all your books as a teenager and they turned me on to sex,' I said with a giggle.

She went into immediate seduction overdrive and kept jabbing me with her *poitrine*. Nathalie came up and I said, 'This is Edna O'Brien, darling. I have one of her books permanently in my bed,' and Nathalie looked a bit perplexed, not quite locating her in the running order of English literature, but said of course we could take her as far as Sloane Square.

In the car I couldn't remember the name of the collection of short stories which in fact I had got for 50p at a jumble sale at the children's school, but Edna rattled through them as we drove up through Chelsea across the King's Road to her house. There she insisted we should all come in for a nightcap. I was willing but Nathalie, who was tired, refused. 'Oh, come on. I've some very good champagne in the fridge, some vintage champagne just for you, Denis, come in and have a talk.'

I must check her age but the style and come-on was unmistakeable and certainly unmistakeable to Nathalie, who put her foot on the accelerator as we roared away. She protested that Edna O'Brien was trying to seduce me, which I felt she was, but even Nathalie can recognise the difficulties of a love affair with someone old enough to be my children's grandmother.

THURSDAY 16 JULY 1998

To a meeting in the morning organised by Patricia Hewitt. Through some link with the PSOE, the Spanish Socialist Workers' Party, she has invited Josep Borrell, the party's candidate in next year's elections, to a little seminar at the Commons. Borrell has made his pilgrimage to London to see if some of the Blair magic can rub off on him.

He is a very dry-looking professor with white-grey close-cropped hair, rimless glasses and a black jacket like an old Whitehall mandarin. He speaks goodish English and is a Catalan. His number two is altogether more Spanish-looking with that odd gene of red hair which runs through so many southern Spaniards. He hails from Andalusia – the old socialist fief of Felipe González – and doesn't speak a word of English. I bump into them outside Westminster Hall and practise my extremely rusty Spanish as they get a quick tourist look before going up to a committee room for the meeting.

What they desperately want to hear is how to become Blairites, however, they are not comforted by what they are told. An invitation to get the right-wing press on their side brings a protest from Borrell's deputy, 'What, even *ABC*?!' – the very right-wing monarchist paper. They are given a long lecture on the welfare state, which is pretty meaningless as their family structures are still much, much stronger than ours and what they really need to know is how to grow the economy and create jobs.

I tell them they must break with their past in the way that Jospin broke with Mitterrand, not even mentioning his name in speeches in recent years. The number two from Andalusia looks horrified at this *lèse-majesté* since Felipe González is still king of everything in Spain, especially on the left.

They are also not happy when I say that the next big challenge for Europe is enlargement to the east, to incorporate the new democracies of eastern Europe just as the Mediterranean countries emerging from dictatorship like Spain, Portugal and Greece had their turn to democracy and an open economy consolidated through EC membership. This, of course, will entail reform of the finances including the Common Agricultural Policy, and as I pointed out, we spent more on subsidising tomatoes, olives, wine and tobacco than we do on subsidising people. I could feel just a gentle political chill in the air.

FRIDAY 17 JULY 1998

Tribune published my take on the Derek Draper affair, when the odd chap was caught by an *Observer* reporter boasting he could obtain access for his clients to meet ministers and get legislation changed to suit a firm's needs. It was blown up into a 'Lobbygate' scandal, but it is no more than what many an ex-minister does to make money after giving up office. Once again, I argued for more public financing of political parties and the need to erect a Chinese Wall between corporate donations and party political activity. This won't go down well at No. 10, which wants to increase that source of financing, but I don't think our intense London-focused political system and media can take the strain of endless Lobbygate-type scandals. I tried to get Robin interested in democracy paying for democracy, but he dismissed the idea – which works perfectly well in many European nations – saying, 'The public doesn't want taxpayers' money to go to politicians.' He really can be very cautious and conservative without much effort.

I read the new biography on Gordon Brown by Hugh Pym and found it very thin. It is simply a list of self-promoting hero worship for all the players around Brown like Ed Balls and Charlie Whelan, though the strongest thing that comes out of it is the obsession with the United States and the policies and theories floating in the Harvard New Democratic circuit of the late 1980s and early 1990s. I am halfway through it and there is nothing about any influence from Europe at all. This is very worrying, as the evidence does suggest that the American model may now be getting into very rocky times indeed. If it is our only and exclusive reference point, we have got real trouble ahead.

WEDNESDAY 22 JULY 1998

To the Commons to hear Tony Blair's end of term pep talk.

Blair was in his white shirt, a dark tie and cufflinks. He has big hands which open and close all the time, coming together in the form of a prayer or being held in front of his firm waist with one hand pulling at the little finger of the other.

He was full of praise of Gordon 'and his colleagues' for the Comprehensive Spending Review. He uses the words 'New Labour' all the time, desperate to din this into everybody's head. He still has a good line in self-deprecating jokes. 'The right-wing papers say it is astonishing that Labour is spending anything on health and education. Some of you may be surprised as well.' He gets his laugh, but the 'some of you' accommodates a lot of people in the crowded room. He continues:

We are getting the state out of things the state doesn't have to do, but where government investment is necessary, we are ready to invest. However, the money comes with modernisation. It is a programme of reform. It is not just about spending money but about levering in money to achieve reform.

The historical roots of New Labour keep coming through his argument:

In the 1980s, we got every small decision we took right, but every strategic decision we took was wrong. We took tiny decisions on spending in opposition halfway through a government that seemed to be fair and then when it came to the election, we were nailed to a cross as all these tiny decisions showed up as giant spending plans and the Tories got us.

Where Blair works is that he is intensely political and that goes into the head and touches the heart of every new MP who wants to hold his seat.

We need to pin down the Tories to say which public spending is wrong. They are at sixes and sevens. Some say we're massively increasing public spending, but then others say it isn't enough and they want more for their areas. But if they start to say that public spending is wrong, we need to ask them which medical services will they cut, which schools will they close?

It was a good, solid, professional performance and with the pair of them, Brown and Blair, wrapping up the parliamentary year, Blair had achieved probably the best first year for a Labour government in living memory.

At 6 p.m. a drink with Giles Gordon, the famous literary agent, who is married to my cousin Miriam's husband's sister, so we are vaguely kinsmen in a very indirect way.

He is the most famous literary agent in the UK and has lots of big-gun authors like Peter Ackroyd, Penelope Mortimer and Fay Weldon on his books.

He is the literary agent for Margaret Cook and says that Robin has tried several times to persuade her not to go ahead with publishing her book on their life together.

'It is coming out in January with a big serialisation in the *Sunday Times*,' he said.

Oh dear, that just means a further six months of misery for Robin and then a ghastly two or three weeks as this drips, drips, drips its way through the system. He really will have to pull off some coups if he is to survive as a serious heavyweight politician.

MONDAY 27 JULY 1998

Today is reshuffle day. The worst moment of birth and death happening at one and the same time in the British political calendar. Thank God I was not involved. I neither have to die nor to be born.

I worked all morning on my article on globalisation and Europe, rewriting it for the *New Statesman*. By midday, the big news of the Cabinet reshuffle was known. Harriet Harman, David Clark and Gavin Strang are out. So too is Ivor Richard, who nobody had ever noticed was in the Cabinet as the Leader in the House of Lords.

Coming in are Peter Mandelson as president of the Board of Trade, save that he doesn't want to use the title and will be known simply as the Secretary of State for Industry. Stephen Byers becomes the Chief Secretary. He is Blair's man. Ever smiling, ever competent, ever right wing, but in essence grey and rather like Stephen Dorrell, a competent pair of hands who stands for nothing.

The other changes are simply a reshuffle in the literal sense – the same cards falling in different places. Margaret Beckett becomes Leader of the House. This worries me. She loves to spend her time in the Commons. She is always to be seen in the Strangers' Bar after the 10 p.m. vote with her husband Leo. They have no children to-gether and nothing else in their lives. Will they be prepared to push through the modernisation agenda? I have my doubts.

Ann Taylor, on the other hand, becomes the Chief Whip. The first woman to hold the job. I like her and we get on fine, but does she have the cojones for the job? Can she strike up a relationship with Margaret Beckett to modernise the Commons? Or will Mar-garet reject what she inherits from Ann and go her own way?

Nick Brown is sidelined into agriculture. The mischievous quip going round the place is that he has joined the sheep-shaggers, while Stephen Byers, who couldn't do simple arithmetic, has become the man in charge of adding up the nation's finances as Chief Secretary.

I go with Doug Henderson down to the tea room and have a talk. He says he has been told to stand by his phone and the word he has got is that he is going to be reshuffled sideways or dismissed entirely. I try to cheer him up, but he is adamant that he knows he is finished at the Foreign Office. 'You may get something, Denis. If they offer you something in the Whips' Office, will you accept?'

'Do you think I should? I'd rather do something on Europe directly.'

'Of course you should. If they offer you anything, take it at once.'

We shall have to wait and see, but my main purpose is to try to cheer Doug up and lift him from his misery. I suggest we go and have dinner tonight and he jumps on the idea. We agree to stay in touch on the phone.

At 7.30 p.m. I go over to the House and on to the Terrace for a drink where I see Nick Brown. I congratulate him and say that if I can help on Common Agricultural Policy in Europe, then I am at his disposal.

I bumped into Geoff Hoon and made a crack about 'heard any-thing?' and he just smiled in his rather cynical way and said, 'Who knows?' I realise with a thud that for people like Geoff, the pro-motion of Byers into the Cabinet must have been a bit of a shock. Geoff was the superstar of the Labour handling of the vote on the Treaty of Maastricht. But all that was five or six years ago and yes-terday's accomplishments count for nothing in the scales of who's up and who's down in today's politics.

Doug and I went for dinner to a restaurant he likes off the Fulham Road. He remained sanguine. He is still full of hatred for Mandel-son. 'Blair is incredibly cold and distant. He never smiles when you are with him. His smile is there for the media or when the public is around, but otherwise he never gives anything of himself.'

He rained dislike, not to say hatred, on Robin. 'I haven't spoken to him now for weeks. In the whole fifteen months I have worked with him, he has never really talked to me.'

Doug's driver came to pick us up close to 11 p.m. – what a luxury it is to have a driver at your disposal – and he told him to stand by for an early morning call, as early as 7.30 a.m., because that is when Blair apparently likes to read out his execution orders. What a life!

TUESDAY 28 JULY 1998

No execution for Doug. Instead, he is moved sideways to the Ministry of Defence to replace John Reid, who goes to the Transport Ministry though without Gavin Strang's place in the Cabinet.

Doug is replaced by Joyce Quin. She thus gets the portfolio that she had prepared for in opposition under Robin Cook and for which she has pined so much over the past fifteen months.

There are no other movements at the Foreign Office, so all my pathetic little hopes evaporate.

Instead, I have to watch my generation walk up Downing Street with a smile fit to burst her bulging eyes in the case of Patricia Hewitt and a manful 'I am Neil Kinnock's representative on earth' stride of Charles Clarke. Margaret Hodge also got a junior post at education with a little grin on her face as she knocked on the door of Downing Street. In effect, Blair has promoted all those who were the principal architects and bag-carriers of Labour modernisation in the 1990s. Patricia and Charles were all but ministers in name, save that they didn't have parliamentary seats, and now they will either prove themselves or be jettisoned. Ditto for Margaret, who has the administrative experience of running Islington Council. I am disappointed, but I can't really complain about those who have been promoted.

What is worrying about the whole reshuffle is that it is a reinforcement of Blair cronyism. His lawyer friend with whom he shared a house, Charlie Falconer, who has become a lord because he couldn't get a seat as his children are sent to private schools, now becomes a Minister without Portfolio.

In other words, someone who can walk into Blair's office in the way that Peter Mandelson did and just have a chat with him about anything. I am very unhappy (not just because of my own non-promotion) at this dishing out of great offices of state to people who have no political experience and who are in no way account-able. If Blair needs a fixer and an adviser, let them be appointed to his personal staff or let him keep Peter in the centre of things. Mandelson is a gigantic political operator. Falconer is no doubt a very smart lawyer who has made pots of money, but anything else? Oh, enough of these complaints. We'll see how it works out in the flesh. I just hope that the chemistry and balance is right.

There are some small changes, but completely idiosyncratic people like Kate Hoey have got a job at the Home Office. Given that she caused a lot of trouble on fox hunting, the message now is that loyalty doesn't get a pay-back.

Walking across to Parliament, I see Doug and Joyce talking together. I come up and I give Joyce a little hug and congratulate her, but she and Doug are already in deep conversation. On the big themes of the day? The future direction of European policy? No, not at all. Like ministers who have just got new appointments throughout the ages, they are discussing the respective size of and vista from their new offices. 'I've got a nice view of the Thames,' says Doug, who adds that Tony Lloyd's office is the best in the For-eign Office.

As I come out to get my bike to go home, I see Joyce looking helplessly around. 'Where's my car? Where's my car?' Thus, the only issue that really matters to a minister.

THURSDAY 3 SEPTEMBER 1998

There was no real political juice or gossip flowing. Everybody is surprised to see the large number of Cabinet ministers turning up to speak at the TUC. Peter Mandelson started the rush to Blackpool when he said that unlike Margaret Beckett, who had provisionally agreed to do a video, he would go there in person. John Healey told me that Nigel Stanley, his successor as TUC press chief, had told him that as soon as it was announced that Mandy was going to address congress, Gordon Brown phoned up and demanded a session.

I bumped into Peter Mandelson in the crowded tearoom, looking thinner and more svelte than ever. He is loving being a Cabinet minister and now is going to have to create a coterie of friends in the Commons. I said to him, 'I see you're going to talk to the brothers in a couple of weeks' time. If you want a few trade union jokes, let me know.' He smiled and nodded and we'll see if there's a follow-up.

After the vote, I was milling around behind the Speaker's chair when Harriet Harman came up with a big smile and a 'how are you?' We were beginning to have a chat when suddenly Tony Blair came out of the Aye Lobby with that rictus on his face which I'm afraid some of the cartoonists have got bang to rights, as everything is slightly rigid with bulging eyes beaming out from a head that's losing his hair. He spotted Harriet and came over to her with his face opening into a smile as he put his arms up on her shoulder. I looked at him, but he didn't even see me. I can't work out if he had seen me but hadn't clocked me or he had seen me and decided he didn't want to see me or, as I suspect, his mind was on something else and I simply didn't register, whereas Harriet he had to show love and friendship to after so brutally and cruelly dismissing her in the reshuffle.

Blair looked like a zombie from another planet. The immense pressure and wear and tear was awesome to behold. In Norway, the Prime Minister of the same age has been given a week off work after confessing to depression and stress-induced exhaustion. Blair looks like a man running a small textile factory with nothing but pressure from suppliers, employees, rivals and customers, and other than the knowledge that he is earning a good chunk of money and actually running something, where's the fun or satisfaction in it all?

I was glad to get off to bed.

SUNDAY 27 SEPTEMBER 1998

Up at 6.30 a.m. after a bad night's sleep and an easy drive from Rotherham to Blackpool. I do my television interview and a meeting with my steelworker friends. They are miserable and drawn and know that there are job losses coming up fast.

The conference opened with Blair doing an hour of question and answer sessions with delegates. As usual he is good, in command and in control. There are fifteen questions which I assume were taken at random but not one on an international or European theme. This great international party of ours is returning to its roots of indifference to the world outside little England.

Everybody congratulates me on the big win that Gerhard Schröder had in defeating finally after sixteen years Helmut Kohl in the German election on Sunday. Blair himself even turned to me as he went through the foyer of the Winter Gardens in the late afternoon and thanked me for the notes and work I had done on Schröder. But his voice and face have no warmth at all.

I told Jonathan Powell that I wanted to get a job and he grinned wickedly. I said that everybody I knew was putting their children into private schools and the little private preparatory school at Rotherham, Rudston, was oversubscribed. 'We've got to get standards higher in our schools because people are voting with their cheque books to go private,' I said.

'It's a ten-year programme, Denis. It will be all right for Jessica [his daughter], but it will take that time for it all to work through.'

I exploded, saying it may be all right for him but I had four children and there were millions of others who are constantly worried.

THURSDAY 1 OCTOBER 1998

At the Labour conference, it is the foreign affairs debate today. I sit at the front at the end of the foreign affairs team. So far I haven't been dismissed, but who really cares? I talk to the new Scottish whip in the Lords, a woman who used to be a big bee in MI6. I make the politest of polite conversations with her. George Robertson sidles in and sits beside me and it means that when Robin does his big denunciations of Kosovo, the cameras turn to George and I get picked up in the wash so I appear on TV news.

Afterwards, Robin tells us all to come into the general secretary's room behind the stage. Gaynor is there, dressed in an odd tweed suit. Earlier in the week, I had been chatting with her when Cherie Blair came by. She gave a big kiss to Gaynor and then turned and gave a big kiss to me, so somebody at No. 10 still remembers me.

Robin is full of himself and has had a successful conference speech with lots of applause and a standing ovation. It is the drug he needs. The royal jelly of endorsement by party militants that will keep him going. The newspapers are full of contempt. The new biography of him by John Kampfner, the *FT* journalist who now works for the BBC, has come out. It is pretty routine stuff but allows all the commentators to get their barbs out and hook them into Robin's not very thick skin.

The Labour Friends of Israel thing is fairly ghastly, with a long tedious speech by Israel's self-important ambassador. Derek Fatchett sweeps in and says that government policy needs to be such that everybody in the region can live in peace, so there is no more Israel, no more Palestine, just people living together. The applause is polite to put it mildly and I saw some of Labour's rich benefactors just looking at Fatchett with horror and asking who this man was. There is a real tension here between Tony Blair's own commitment to Jewish humanism and Jewish values and the huge amount of money that rich Jews have raised for the Labour Party, and the fact that UK state interests still demand a dialogue with, if not obeisance to, the much richer Gulf states whose flow of oil money is essential for keeping the economy turning over.

THURSDAY 8 OCTOBER 1998

Tomorrow I speak at a big conference organised by the Michel Rocard faction of the Socialist Party. Half the French Cabinet will be there.

I stay a night at the embassy in Paris. I turn up there at about 8.30 p.m. and the footman, or whatever you call the domestic servants, who is a young good-looking Englishman called Paul, takes me up to a room kitted out in the most luxurious way. There is fruit and whisky and a complete complement of shaving and other toiletries, so I needn't have bothered to bring a wash bag. He asks anxiously if I have any laundry that I want doing, but I wave him away and jump into the shower before going down to have dinner.

The embassy in Paris never ceases to amaze me in its sheer palatial luxury. Jack Straw is there with his wife, and Bob Ayling, the boss of British Airways. Michael Jay's lovely wife, Sylvia, is there as the most attentive host and it is actually a London dinner party transposed to Paris. Ayling is very nice to talk to and his wife is a peach. He is a great fanatic for the euro and really is quite easy to talk to, though a very big business player and, of course, closely tied in with the government which depends on him to put up lots of money for the millennium project and other schemes. He is on first-name terms with Blair, Mandy and Alastair Campbell. In a funny way, even though BA has been privatised, it is still utterly dependent on the state for so many permissions that Ayling can't afford to make enemies.

He is very funny about the Tory MPs who kept phoning up to get free tickets or upgrades. He said it all finished last year with the election of a Labour government. 'On 2 May, I got a memorandum from the girl who does parliamentary liaison who gave me a long list of all the Tory MPs who'd lost their seats and added at the bottom, "Hoorah!"'

Michael Jay turns up with another diplomatic colleague who is now the ambassador in Israel. We go into dinner, which is quite sumptuous. There is a French chef at the embassy who produces the most extraordinary meals. There was a pudding of mushrooms, which was excellent, followed by a fish stew called a souchy and then English cheeses which were as good as anything you could get in England and a giant mountain of a cake made out of fresh figs, which I tucked into heartily.

I can see why this is the prize job in any British administration and the sheer luxury of life must be overwhelming.

On my right was a Benedictine monk from Douai School and the extraordinary coincidence of having him there with all the common traditions and friends was remarkable, not that he had much to say for himself that was of interest.

On my left was Jack Straw's wife, Alice, a statuesque, imposing woman who had been private secretary to Brian O'Malley, my famous predecessor as MP for Rotherham, who had dropped dead at the despatch box in 1976 as a Health Minister – it was said because of all the work Barbara Castle dumped on him. Apparently, he was a chain smoker and was desperately overworked by Barbara Castle but was a nice man because he had appointed the young Alice as his private secretary when everybody said he wouldn't go for a woman.

She worked for a long time at the Department of Social Security and then had a few years at the Treasury. She must speak good enough French because she was seconded to two French ministries for a year – the *Trésor* and the Ministry for International Cooperation. She said she was known as the '*petite espionne*' – the little spy – and all decisions were taken when she wasn't there. She said the Ministry for Overseas Development was simply a giant slush fund to help French companies get contracts in West Africa.

SATURDAY 10 OCTOBER 1998

Up early and downstairs in this amazing palace to the breakfast room, where rather indifferent croissants were served with rather indifferent coffee. At least the orange juice was freshly squeezed. The English papers arrived – *The Times*, the *Daily Telegraph* and *The Independent*, but I suppose it is a bit much to expect Her Majesty's ambassadors to read *The Guardian*. People drifted in slowly. Michael Jay is full of a visit the Queen is to make with President Chirac to the First World War battlefield. He thinks it would be marvellous for British–French relations. It has potential, but it is at this level of royalty and protocol that these guys operate and it doesn't ever get down to *l'homme ou la femme de la rue*.

I beetled out to go to the French National Assembly for my conference. It was a pretty swish affair, with all the key players from the French government present. I made a very jokey speech saying it was now possible to mention the words 'reform' or 'social democracy', which ten or twenty years ago would have been absolutely banned from the vocabulary of any French socialist gathering. I gave them a good turn with lots of jokes before slipping in a few serious points quickly and made Martine Aubry laugh a lot, which, given she is such a sour puss, is no bad thing.

Basically, though, they aren't that much interested in what is happening in Britain. The animosity to Blair which was evident a year or nine months ago has died away as people are picking up on some of the left things he is doing. And there is a growing realisation that the crisis, or the difficulties, of world capitalism put all left-of-centre leaders into the same boat. Thus, it is better that they seek to get along than bitch and preen in mutual hostility.

Lunch was another sumptuous meal of lobster and pheasant en croûte with magnificent wines, which of course could only be sipped in order to avoid snoring siestas back at the conference in the afternoon.

Alain Richard was friendly but cautious about air strikes on Kosovo. I said I had seen a three-star general in a pullover rushing around as we came in and assumed he was planning for military intervention. Richard said that there had been ten significant crises in Europe involving conflict or potential conflict since the end of communism, and eight of them had petered out into some kind of resolution without requiring big military intervention. The two that hadn't, of course, were Bosnia and Chechnya.

'Are we so sure that Kosovo won't also resolve itself?' he questioned.

I did the usual litany about having to respond to public opinion and the horrible pictures of bodies being dug up of people who had been killed by the Serb troops. Richard said that Hubert Védrine was certainly not keen on military intervention. I said that Védrine should go and get himself elected at least once in his career in order to understand what public pressure was like. This produced a big roll of laughter from Laurent Fabius, the Culture Minister Catherine Trautmann, who was on my left, and Martine Aubry, who was sitting beside Richard. The point being, of course, that Védrine gives himself all the airs and graces of being a great politician but, in fact, is a pure functionary who has never once had to put his little bottom on the line and get himself elected by French voters.

The afternoon session had a good contribution from Dominique Strauss-Kahn, who argued that the new politics had to be based around the centre but 'a centre that incorporated and integrated the excluded'. He produced a set of reasons why the balance of political power chips to the left in France. His thesis was that Gaullism had been a centrist project that had driven a section of the right out to the fringes, which had constituted itself now around the National Front. As a result, France did not have a classic Conservative Party, and the left could reoccupy some of the Gaullist territory and exploit it.

This is a brief sketch of what was actually a much denser and interesting argument based on political geography and sociology and derived, of course, from DSK's professorial past.

However, he pointedly referred to European politics as being the 'second way' in contrast to American liberalism. Unfortunately, the French word 'liberalism' means what we would call neoliberalism and monetarism and the problems of vocabulary just get endlessly mixed up. He certainly wasn't offering any favours to Tony Blair, let alone Gordon Brown. It was a very pro-European and pro-euro speech – he was like all the others for whom the euro was a holy instrument of social democratic European salvation.

Alain Richard, in summing up, in contrast, went out of his way to praise Blair, saying he had opened up new possibilities in Europe and created opportunities for cooperation, especially in defence, that did not exist before. It was a generous and spontaneous tribute and he looked directly at me as he was paying it, so I was glad that I had stayed there and made the effort to make them laugh, which is always the best way of being remembered when you speak, all the more so if it's in a foreign language.

THURSDAY 13 OCTOBER 1998

Don Macintyre told me there was a do at Politico's for John Kampfner's biography of Robin Cook, so after putting the children to bed,

I took a taxi to Politico's and went in to catch the end of Kampfner's speech about himself and, boy, was it about himself! He was describing the perils of political biography as if he had written a major piece of work instead of a competent scissors and paste compilation. But he also made a reference to Margaret Cook and lo, there she was. I had never seen her before and she is much more petite and prettier than I had imagined.

Yet, what possessed her to invade this party or accept whatever invitation was offered to her in what clearly was a vulgar and rather demeaning publicity stunt? All the hacks there were agog and fixed on me as if I was the only representative of the Foreign Office present. But Derek Fatchett was there, as well as David Clark, Robin's European adviser, who was ranting at John Rentoul and Robin's press guy, David Mathieson. He was trying to control the story and all the tabloid hacks in particular were getting more and more excited about Margaret's presence and Robin's absence. It was all fairly ghastly and trivial and unimportant but how the London political scene fills up with these minor irrelevancies.

FRIDAY 16 OCTOBER 1998

To the House of Commons after some work. In the Members' Lobby, I bump into John Healey. He said that Mark Seddon has been nominated to go on the Successor Generation seminar in New Orleans next month. The Successor Generation Project is one of these right-wing operations funded by an American millionaire to pick suitable pro-capitalist MPs or Labour figures in Britain and their equivalents in America and mix them together so that they know each other. George Robertson, Liz Symons and John Monks have been on the do's from England and John Healey was himself one of the Successor Generation MPs last year.

'I got a wet weekend at some boring Scottish hotel while Mark gets an all-expenses trip to New Orleans. It's not fair,' he says.

We both giggle at the thought of the great left-wing leader of the Centre-Left Grassroots Alliance that had so shaken the Labour leadership being on the payroll of weird American right-wingers, but such is the gap between perception and reality in British politics that nothing any more surprises me.

MONDAY 19 OCTOBER 1998

More routine work after a run in the morning. Then down to the town hall for the launch of the Rotherham Cultural Strategy. It was full of people. I had worked hard on a press release with a quote from Ebenezer Elliott and an appeal for a cinema and a radio station in the town. I phoned up Martin Wainwright, *The Guardian*'s northern editor who lives in Leeds, and challenged him to get all this into *The Guardian* the next day.

As I was busy faxing my press release, I got a call from Ken Purchase, Robin Cook's PPS. Did I know there was going to be a statement on Kosovo that afternoon? The answer, of course, was no. Even though I had been in the Foreign Office the previous week, no one had thought fit to tell the rest of the parliamentary team that there would be a statement in the House. Again, I start the new parliamentary year feeling that politically, PPSs and indeed often ministers are simply seagulls floating on the choppy waters controlled by the permanent agents of the state.

I ran for my car, drove like fury to Doncaster and slumped into the train.

Eric Illsley, the Barnsley ex-miner MP, was on it and we had a brief chat, moaning about the new South Yorkshire organiser and the peremptory demand that we each pay £1,500 for his upkeep.

'I have got my youngest lass starting at university and have to fork out a fortune for her. There's no way I've got extra money to pay for Labour Party staff,' complained Eric.

As we drew closer to King's Cross, he suddenly looked up and said, 'Can I ask you a personal question?'

I said, 'Yes.'

'Is it true you once had an affair with Carol Barnes?'

I laughed and said: 'Far from having an affair, we lived together for a number of years, had a child, have remained very good friends and Clare, our daughter, is a big part of my family today.'

Eric grunted and I suppose was satisfied. But that is how the Westminster gossip machine works. He had been told of a little 'secret' and was being decent enough to tell me he knew. What, of course, he and the gossip merchants didn't realise was that Carol and I were, to all intents and purposes, married for about half of the 1970s and who really knows what would have happened had I not moved to Geneva and our paths separated.

I got into the Commons in time for a good professional Robin Cook statement on Kosovo. Michael Howard, as usual, was hopeless, full of bombast and claims that he had thought of sending in an intervention force first. But he is consumed by this pathology of anti-Cook hatred that just doesn't work. A gentle mocking style or even the occasional warm embrace and praise would be far more destabilising, but brute frontal attacks don't work.

WEDNESDAY 21 OCTOBER 1998

I have an adjournment debate in the main Chamber today on the steel industry. I sleep fitfully and wake up at 5.30 a.m. and go over my speech again and again and again, reading it out, timing it, not exactly memorising it but getting it clearer and clearer in my head.

At 7 a.m. I do a couple of short interviews over the telephone for radio stations on steel and then get on down to the House for about 9. There are a number of MPs in the tea room and the Members' Lobby waiting to participate, so there will be a decent crowd.

Somebody asks me if I have seen the statement that Eddie George, the governor of the Bank of England, has made headlines saying that job cuts may be necessary in the north to control inflation in the south.

I can't really believe he has been so crass and stupid, but I get hold of a copy of the *Yorkshire Post* and there it is on the front page.

I decide to start off my speech with a dig at him on this and furiously try to get my mind round a good riff of words. I am sure the story has been levered up. It looks as if Eddie just replied honestly but not with the professional guile of a politician to a question at a lunch with journalists. He spends an awful lot of time now doing political PR but none of it can replace the need to know when to speak and when to shut your mouth.

I glide into the Chamber immediately behind the Speaker and go through the prayers and then I'm off. There is a great cheer from most of the MPs in what is really a rather crowded Chamber for a Wednesday morning debate when I say that George should clarify his statement and, if he sticks by it, he should join the people in the north and resign.

The cheers continue and I can feel the Commons come around me as they realise I have called for the governor of the Bank England to resign.

As soon as I had sat down, the pager never stopped vibrating on me.

After the debate, I got congrats all round. John Healey said, 'You've pressed the panic button now with the call for Eddie to go.'

On the *World at One* and Sky, I quickly damped down the line that I was a brutal northern MP demanding the governor's head on a Commons' platter. Instead, I explained that I was in favour of Bank of England independence but that he needed to be aware of the needs of manufacturing.

In any event, the story just ran on and on all day, even up to the 6 p.m. BBC news where I saw myself gesticulating rather wildly left and right.

Charlie Whelan saw me in the lobby and came over with a smile, saying, 'Well done, Denis. We had to put up Patricia to defend Eddie.' But he didn't seem remotely fazed and from Gordon Brown's point of view a bit of kicking of the governor and a bit of pressure on the Bank of England is not necessarily a bad thing.

Diane Abbott and Alan Simpson, of course, congratulated me for having a go at Eddie, but the most interesting comment was from Enid Crausby, the wife of the Bolton MP David Crausby, who said when I bumped into her in the corridor going to my office, 'I'm glad you said that. Somebody has needed to say it for a long time.' So there is still this pent up anger that the values of the City and the needs of bankers are overdominant in our economy. Something is shifting underfoot and surfing and riding it will be difficult.

The whole day was blown away with TV interviews. On Channel 4, I was in the studio with Jon Snow, again ducking my way through difficult questions, trying to maintain credentials as a supporter of Central Bank independence and not loutishly wanting Eddie's resignation, while maintaining my integrity for being right in saying what I did. John Redwood and John Battle were in the studio in Millbank, slugging it out after me, and I can imagine the irritation of the spin doctors that here was a simple backbencher getting the media coverage, not a minister.

An interesting conversation with Lord Dahrendorf. He said that Patrick Neill, the warden of All Souls, who has produced a useless report on political funding, was well known on the Oxford head of colleges' circuit as a crashing bore in his hostility to Europe.

'His wife was a paid-up activist in the Referendum Party and they are both very anti-European. I am sceptical about EMU, but Neill is really anti-European,' said Dahrendorf.

This is interesting intelligence. People have wised up to the fact that Patrick Neill is hostile to Europe in a psychological way, but the extent of the entire household pathology hasn't been reported. I expect the whole Neill Committee report will disappear into the sands. Certainly, there is no support at all in the establishment for it.

MONDAY 26 OCTOBER 1998

Over to 12 Downing Street where Ann Taylor, the new Chief Whip, had organised a get-together for PPSs. I didn't recognise some of the people there and here we are, eighteen months into a new government, and I don't know my fellow PPSs, though it was nice to see young Chris Leslie, who is a darling sweetie, there with everyone else.

What was interesting was that a number of them obviously get to travel up and down the country and fill in for their ministers. One of them – I forget who – said, 'You know what it's like when you're in the wrong place, talking to the wrong people about the wrong subject,' and I quipped, 'Oh, you mean a GMC' (General Management Committee, the monthly meeting of a constituency Labour Party) and got a huge laugh. I must keep my tongue under control as this glibness just always does me down.

TUESDAY 27 OCTOBER 1998

After question time, I go back to the office and am working away at getting my papers under control when suddenly the TV headlined 'Ron Davies has resigned!'

The Welsh Secretary has resigned because he was involved in some kind of 'gay incident' on Clapham Common yesterday. I assume it was a 'gay incident' as I don't think there can be anything else that you can be doing on Clapham Common that would require a resignation, and the whole of Westminster springs to a febrile excitement at the thought of scandal, disclosure and humiliation.

SATURDAY 31 OCTOBER 1998

Surgery at 10 a.m., but it was over by 10.30.

On the train to London I saw Margaret and Henry Hodge. Margaret asked why I hadn't been made a minister and I said I simply wasn't in the loop or didn't have any powerful patrons.

'I was very pleased that Patricia got made up, she is seriously good, but they had to give a job to Charles Clarke because they couldn't give one to Patricia without giving one to him as well.' I couldn't quite follow this line of argument and asked how she was getting on with Blair.

'I never see him. I used to see him a lot when we lived in the same crescent in Islington and all our children played together, but he is now quite cold and remote.'

She said she was working longer hours than ever before, and she is a pretty hard worker. 'I am amazed at what they make ministers do. Margaret gets about five hours sleep a night and she's always under pressure,' confirmed Henry.

We had the usual moans about education and she said that her children had done all right at the Camden School for Girls, but Henry interjected to say that had they gone to private school, they probably would have gone to Oxbridge instead of to Bristol and UEA. As usual, I can't bear thinking about all these problems. I had a big row with Francis Beckett on the phone during the week when I forced him – a big critic of the government's education policy – to confess that he had sent one of his children to a private school. His excuse is that if all the schools were comprehensive, he would have been able to send his boy to a comprehensive, but I simply don't believe this. This is Jesuitical rationalisation and I started shouting at him. Apparently, Philip Gould has moved to be close to the Camden School for Girls, which just shows the hypocrisy permeating all of Labour's so-called modernising ranks.

MONDAY 2 NOVEMBER 1998

I change into a dinner jacket and go to the Reform Club for the London dinner of the Merton Society. Patrick Wright, Lord Wright of Richmond, the former Permanent Under-Secretary at the Foreign Office, had asked me to do the after-dinner speech. I had done a little research and found that Lord Randolph Churchill had gone to Merton, where Roy Jenkins said he had got 'a perfectly satisfactory second-class degree in modern history with the sustenance of a remark from his tutor that he could have got a first', which was typical of the insufferable pomposity of Lord Jenkins, who got one of those wartime firsts that were dished out with the rations.

Anyway, I cracked a few jokes and slipped away as early as I could. I like these threads of history that bind us all together, and who knows, the connection may come in useful one day.

WEDNESDAY 4 NOVEMBER 1998

A taxi picks me up at 8.40 a.m. to take me to Millbank where I do nearly an hour and a half on Radio 5 Live about the euro. The presenter is called Nicky something-or-other and is very lively and chirpy. There is a mad anti-European woman called Moira and *Newsnight's* sardonic economics correspondent, Evan Davis. We chunter round the houses with lots of phone-in questions or points. Most of them are frankly xenophobic. You get Larry from Manchester who says, 'Why should we trust the Germans or the French or the Irish?' and an old lady from Bournemouth who says that we didn't fight two world wars to be run by the Germans. This is all pretty disgusting stuff and these phone-ins on Europe bring out the worst of British xenophobia. I was a little too smart aleck and glib, but I also wanted to be lively and the time passed quite quickly.

SUNDAY 8 NOVEMBER 1998

Lunch with Andrew Brown, Gordon's brother, his wife Clare who is exceptionally nice and their two sons, one of whom, Alex, is a great friend of Benjamin's at the nursery school.

We all had lunch together in the China Garden in Soho and it was a great success both food-wise and friendship-wise.

Andrew talked incessantly about Gordon. He actually worked for him after leaving university until 1987. 'Even then Gordon was unhappy for me to leave, but I wanted to go off and do my own journalism.'

Each summer he goes off for a couple of weeks to have holidays with Gordon in Cape Cod. This Christmas the family will go up to holiday with Gordon at his house in the constituency and Gordon will drive up to Aberdeenshire to bring the parents home. It seems an exceptionally close-knit family, with Gordon needing this intense total loyalty around him, which is ultimately deliverable only by kin. I now see Gordon more as a Highland chieftain who can only trust his own blood or those who swear such permanent allegiance that nothing can make them betray their loyalty to the chief. I carefully avoided any obvious comments and was lavish with praise for Gordon, most of which was completely sincere, even though I detest his closed-in, clan-style mode of operation.

MONDAY 16 NOVEMBER 1998

An ordinary working day today save that I had to go into the Commons for a statement by Blair on Iraq. He was bellicose as ever, but I do not think tailing behind the Americans is a real policy. Once again, Saddam has outwitted the west. The bombers were in the air and ready to launch their missiles and he sent the appropriate form of words to the UN to stop everything. Basically, there is no foreign policy game plan on Iraq, and Britain is simply acting as a poodle for Washington.

I bumped into Doug Henderson. He is looking as dapper and debonair as ever. He told me an interesting story saying that the rivalry between Robin Cook and Gordon Brown goes back to 1981, when Gordon was seeking to become chair of the Labour Party in Scotland:

> I was helping to fix it for Gordon and I went to see Robin who could have got his constituency vote and one or two of his friends to vote for Gordon. He had always worked very closely with Gordon and they were seen as the twin leaders of Labour in Scotland, but when I asked Robin to back Gordon, he said he wasn't sure if he could deliver the votes. He was lying and Gordon has never forgiven him.

I suppose it's one source of this useless bitter enmity which corrodes the chances of the government working effectively as a team either at home or, above all, in Europe.

MONDAY 23 NOVEMBER 1998

I went to see Jonathan Powell at Downing Street today to discuss improving contacts and communication with European governments and political parties. He had said that he was drafting a note for the Prime Minister which was classified so he couldn't send it to me and I had to go over there.

I had a chat with David Miliband, who has a rather fine little office with a very neat little desk and a conference table. We chatted about Third Way problems and bringing everybody together and I said that there was no coordination on European policy or contacts. Yesterday, Peter Mandelson had had a meeting with Bodo Hombach, the chief fixer for the German Chancellor, Gerhard Schröder, to draft a joint statement on the Third Way. I said I hoped it wouldn't be published at the same time as the manifesto of the Party of European Socialists and David looked up and said, 'No, no, that won't happen,' but I bet he hadn't thought of it. I asked if there had been anybody in the British delegation who spoke German and he said, 'The interpreter.'

In other words, this is just a little cabal linked to Mandy and Roger Liddle of No. 10, but the Foreign Office and the Treasury and the rest of government are completely shut out. It isn't very serious.

Jonathan Powell gave me his paper, which was pretty good, and I added a few recommendations of my own and knocked out some of the sillier bits he had drafted. We were going over them line by line at his desk. To my surprise, he, as chief of staff to the Prime Minister, shares a small office with four other people. Secretaries have to come in and sit beside their masters to take dictation and it was all much more cramped and less grand than I imagined.

As I was hunched over Jonathan's desk explaining my points, a door to the left opened and Tony came out. 'Hello Denis, what are you doing here?' he said, in actually a very friendly way. Jonathan explained and he looked on approvingly.

We had a chat about secondary education in London since, of course, his daughter had gone to the Sacred Heart with Cherie at the same time as Nathalie and Sarah.

I made my usual presentation that we had a real problem with the elite of the wealth-creating, opinion-forming and policy-making classes all opting out of state education or using their financial power to move to a part of London where there was a guarantee of a reasonable comprehensive school based on some form of selection. I let him have it, saying that there needed to be a policy particularly for London and we had to get this right as parents simply weren't trusting Labour to improve things fast enough.

'Yeah, yeah, yeah,' he said in that half-agreeing, half-dismissive voice. 'Letting schools opt out of LEAs [local education authorities] will be a good step forward,' he said, turning away to go back into his office. It was obviously something he really didn't want to talk about too much and, of course, there is always his natural prudence to safeguard his own children from any part of the educational debate. He looked thin and well, dressed in a pristine white shirt which I noticed all the Blairites copy. Now I will have to buy more white shirts and throw away the pale lilac Jasper Conran number I was wearing with a red jumper underneath my blue pinstripe suit.

As always, close up, I was surprised at how uncharismatic he is, but he was perfectly friendly and I seem to be vaguely accepted as someone who can be there contributing gently to what is happening on the policy front.

TUESDAY 24 NOVEMBER 1998

A grey day, good for the execution of the hereditary peers. I watched the Queen's procession for the state opening of Parliament clattering by from 1 Parliament Street and then squeezed through the crowds with Ken Clarke to get into the Chamber for the speech itself. All discipline has broken down. When I was first elected – only four years ago! – there was a very neat queue that formed to leave the Commons. It was headed by the Prime Minister and the Leader of the Opposition, with all the Cabinet and their opposite numbers forming a double column which trooped off sedately while MPs waited in their proper place before joining the procession.

Now there is a great scrum of MPs in the Members' Lobby and while we all waited to allow Tony and William Hague to go by, people butted in as soon as Gordon Brown appeared and formed a scrum relegating the rest of the Cabinet to the general melee.

The speech itself was fairly boring until the Queen got to the bit about abolishing the rights of hereditary peers and I started a very gentle rumble of 'hear, hear'. It was taken up by others until it became a quiet but real noise. Diane Abbott, who was on my left, turned to me and said, 'You ruffian,' but sod it! A number of peers grunted their disapproval and sat bolt upright. The whole scene was electric as the Queen stopped for a moment and clearly looked uncomfortable at any interruption to her speech, which is normally heard in the most perfect silence.

I saw Naz Ahmed sitting against the back wall in his red and ermine and frankly it is not just hereditary peers one wants to get rid of, but the whole bang shoot of them.

WEDNESDAY 25 NOVEMBER 1998

I was on Radio 5 in the morning talking about the little scene in the House of Lords over the Queen's Speech. The *Daily Mail* has 'Labour insults the monarchy' on the front page, whereas the *Daily Mirror*, quoting me, has 'Peers snub the Queen'. I was on after Norman St John-Stevas and he was very funny, so I did the interview in exactly

the same light-hearted way, saying the commotion had all been started by the hereditary peers, which I don't really think it had, and we
were simply responding. Enough truth for the BBC at any rate.

THURSDAY 26 NOVEMBER 1998

I got a cab to Sloane Square as I had to buy a dress shirt for another official dinner tonight. There, in Peter Jones, I bumped into
Julia Watson who was looking dapper and pretty as ever. She was
just twiddling her thumbs before getting the train back to Brussels
and Martin Walker. She said she had bought a house in Parsons
Green and would continue to commute to Brussels. I suppose it is
a liveable arrangement, though it sounds pretty hellish to me. She
banged on and on about the monsters from Brussels dictating to
Britain and, of course, has completely swallowed all the *Daily Mail*
propaganda now that she is back there.

Back in the office, I picked up the phone and who should it be
but her husband, Sweetie, who was phoning up about a big story
they were going to run about Gordon Brown being criticised by
the German government over the handling of his European policy.
Of course, it is all completely true, though I waffled a bit to try to
locate it as much in German ups and downs. The basic fact is that
Gordon will not combine forces with anyone else and sing off a
common hymn sheet.

FRIDAY 27 NOVEMBER 1998

I walked down to Parliament and had kippers and toast before going
to sit behind Robin Cook for the foreign affairs and defence debate

of the Queen's Speech. The House was utterly empty. Mike Gapes, Jeremy Corbyn, Donald Anderson and a woman I don't know were the only speakers on our side. There were one or two more on the Tory and Liberal benches, but I don't think there would have been twenty out of the nation's 659 MPs willing to debate the security of the realm or our foreign policy and presence overseas.

The Guardian carried a front-page splash about a euro row involving Gordon Brown fighting with Oskar Lafontaine and two pages of analysis inside. It was all quite sound stuff and it's flushing this topic into the open, though to what effect I don't know.

Robin greeted me behind the Speaker's chair and I asked him if he'd seen *The Guardian*. 'I read all the papers every day, Denis,' he said frostily in his rather snotty, put-down fashion. I know the guy is under immense pressure, but he has all the courtesy of a moth-eaten rat and really isn't much fun to be around.

He thrust his speech and attendant papers in my hand while he went off for a piss and came back to take them just before going into the Chamber. Despite the empty house, he gave a good performance, bashing Michael Howard and announcing a lot of new money for diplomatic posts in Europe and around the world in contrast to the cuts of the Tories.

Howard was useless, full of ad hominem attacks on Robin quoting the now infamous BBC broadcast in which he said he didn't read his papers. I kept jeering and interrupting or chatting with people up to the point where Michael Martin jumped up and rebuked me, saying that a PPS should be silent behind his masters. Robin was actually quite cheerful and spoke up for me sotto voce, and the event was a non-event as nobody was there.

I went out and made several phone calls and bustled around

doing very little and certainly not doing anything like a PPS job at all. When Robin left at 11 p.m., I went too.

MONDAY 30 NOVEMBER 1998

Dinner with Tony Holden, his girlfriend Cindy Blake and Francis Wheen in the Commons. It is a good evening's gossip.

Tony described how last week he had been in New York at a dinner for some book that Harold Evans had written. The fare was only £148 return, which is pretty amazing.

He was sitting beside Henry Kissinger and the old monster protested at the idea of Augusto Pinochet being sent back to Spain for trial.

'What exactly has Pinochet done?' said good old Henry. 'They accuse him of torture and crimes against humanity and genocide. But the most he killed was about 6,000 people over two years. That's 3,000 a year. That's 250 a month. That's sixty a week. It's not even ten a day. I don't call that genocide.'

Tony tells it with an excellent imitation of Kissinger's accent but then confesses that although the entire table, which was full of New York and British liberals, was rendered completely stumm by Kissinger's amazing outburst, no one had the guts to challenge the man, empty a glass of wine over his head or tax him with the many more scores of thousands of deaths of Asian peasants in Cambodia that he was directly responsible for.

As we were beginning our meal, Bob Marshall-Andrews and Brian Sedgemore came in. They saw Francis and Brian said, 'What are you doing keeping such disreputable company?' Bob, whose grey and dirty hair is getting longer and lanker, just laughed.

In the lobby, I saw Alice Mahon, who came up and said, 'Oh,

Denis, Francis Wheen is such a hero of mine,' with that incredibly lovely smile that lights up her face and makes everyone love her. So I took her straight back to the Strangers' Dining Room and popped her down beside Francis so that she could be with her hero for a bit.

As we left, Tony thrust £50 in my hand and Francis £40. I tried to push Francis's £40 back in his pocket, but he was having none of it. How weird that these friendships are so strong and last.

WEDNESDAY 2 DECEMBER 1998

The big personal story has been where I get a tailcoat and white tie and all the clobber for the Guildhall Banquet for the German President tonight. I was hoping to borrow Keith Bradley's, as all the top whips have been given an allowance to buy this nonsense for their appearances at Buckingham Palace, but his wife had taken it home to Manchester. So I went up the Charing Cross Road to Lipman's and on the spot bought a tailcoat for £160. I can use dinner jacket trousers, apparently, and an ordinary shirt with a wing collar. All I had to do was buy a white tie and rent a waistcoat for £8, which makes sense since if I buy one I'll just make it dirty and I imagine they are a fortune to clean.

An interview on the *World at One* about the EU tax harmonisation row. The London press is claiming – quite falsely – that the evil Eurocrats are trying to force Britain to have the same taxes as the rest of Europe. I had had a small brainwave en route and got out from the taxi at Sloane Square and bought papers from France, Germany, Italy and Spain. As I thought, none of them had any of this europhobic British press tax harmonisation hysteria, and indeed the front-page stories on both the *International Herald Tribune* and the *Frankfurter*

Allgemeine Zeitung were about a huge row between France and Germany over common agricultural policy reform, the German contribution to the EU, eastern enlargement and environmental policy. So, in other words, there is a much bigger dispute looming over issues which need urgent consideration between France and Germany than there is between Britain and the rest of the EU.

I hit the poor *World at One* presenter with all of this and, I think, knocked him sideways, so he was left gasping, thanking me for my *What the Papers Say* review. No one at the BBC ever does any research before swallowing some anti-European line from the *Daily Mail* or *Telegraph*. I had gained some initiative and felt reasonably happy about the points I made.

The Commons in the afternoon was unbelievable. I was awaiting a row over tax harmonisation in which Hague would knock bits off Blair, but instead the idiot stood up and ranted about some agreement which would leave some hereditary peers in the House of Lords as part of an agreed deal to reform the place. Obviously, he wanted to get Labour MPs all tizzed-up, but it backfired completely when Blair said yes there was an agreement and it was an agreement with the leader of the Tory Party in the Lords and did Hague support it or not. Hague was completely wrong-footed and started stuttering and Blair pressed home viciously, simply asking again and again if Hague would endorse the deal agreed to by Lord Cranborne in the Lords.

I couldn't believe myself as Hague dug himself deeper and deeper into a hole with all of the Labour MPs cheering and his own people in sad, stunned silence. What a contrast with the Queen's Speech last week, when he really had scored a lot of good debating points.

Then back to my office to change into the *Full Monty* rig of tailcoat and white tie. I stole a towel from the dressing room in Westminster to take over to 1 Parliament Street to use in a shower which is in the gents' toilet on the second floor and which has plenty of soap but no towel. This freshened me up a bit and I struggled into all the gear, along with Nathalie who had turned up direct from work.

We were both stressed and rushed and as we came out of the office, she slipped badly and fell on her face. She was suddenly fragile and vulnerable and held on to me very hard all the way to the Tube in a grumpy and uncertain mode. Just before we got to Westminster Station, a voice said 'Hello' and it was *The Guardian*'s Simon Hoggart, who saw me in the full white tie rig and burst out laughing. Oh dear, this will appear somewhere, and not to my credit.

It was the first grand dinner I had been at and it was very grand indeed. There were trumpeters and yeomen and immense luxurious warmth as well as silver and candles in the Guildhall. I hardly know this German President, Roman Herzog. Funnily enough, Nathalie kept bumping into people we knew from the Foreign Office or others like Quentin Davies's wife Chantal. She spoke to her people and I spoke to different friends as well including Tim Garton Ash, who was wearing two decorations, his German cross and a rather more handsome Polish decoration. I pulled his leg about these shiny gongs which he sports with immense pleasure and he took it in good spirit. Margaret Beckett was there, but there was also rather a lot of Conservative MPs – from grandees like Edward Heath, Douglas Hurd and Geoffrey Howe to anti-Europeans like Bernard Jenkin, who was wearing the £ symbol badge in his lapel as if it was a military decoration.

The dinner wasn't bad and the speeches were to the point. There were two boring old dossers who sat on the City of London Corporation telling me how wonderful it all was and how dreadful it would be if ever they were merged with the rest of London. I just let this reactionary self-interest wash over me and took no notice.

It was all over by 10.30 p.m., including the speeches and a good hour of standing around having a chat in the reception beforehand, which wasn't bad going at all and let us get out and catch the Tube to Victoria, where we got a taxi home.

The papers are full, full, full of Hague's suicidal behaviour. He has now sacked his leader in the Lords, predictably a Cecil, and has completely wiped the ghastly tax harmonisation row off the front pages.

MONDAY 7 DECEMBER 1998

A good run in the clear, cold air. Stryker McGuire, the lovely *Newsweek* bureau chief, came in for a chat. *Newsweek* is going to make the European left its 'man of the year'. McGuire interviewed me about all the connections that he thought I was responsible for. I both gave him some but slightly downplayed my role, though I suppose it has been as important as anyone else's in London.

TUESDAY 8 DECEMBER 1998

Lunch with Andrew Rawnsley and Patrick Wintour of *The Observer*. I first came across Andrew when he was Vincent Hanna's assistant, always gently mocking Labour's leadership, while Patrick has been so long on-message and loyal to New Labour that it no longer shows. I made them buy me a bottle of Mersault, which Andrew downgraded to half a bottle, which I drank with some rather fat oysters and some defrosted lobster, but at least it was a light meal. Conversation lasted until 4 p.m. but actually was indifferent with me asking them as many questions and not getting much info on who was up, who was down, who was in, who was out. They had spotted Michael Wills as a coming person but knew nothing about him. I just don't click on to all these millionaires who are fabulously rich and have popped themselves a seat in Parliament at least for this parliamentary period.

Dinner with Matthew d'Ancona and Sarah Schaefer, the German lobby correspondent for *The Independent*.

Matthew, of course, is easy to talk to and likes both history and speculation, so I enjoyed our conversation. It focused on William Hague. 'I am very fond of William,' said Matthew in a proprietorial kind of way, 'but he is leading the party to extinction. Take this Pinochet business. Of course he should be extradited to Spain, but William cannot shake off being the son of Margaret Thatcher and so has to do anything that Mother says.'

He believes that Hague will go after the next election to be replaced by Portillo:

Portillo is the only one who can lead the Tories out of the wilderness over Europe. Until they get it right on EMU, which can only happen after EMU is up and running and seen to be successful and Blair has a referendum and takes Britain in, then and only then can the Tories start to do anything again.

I wonder if the period out of power will not last longer. Are we in for a long period of Conservative wilderness, such as they suffered from the Corn Laws to the 1870s?

Matthew agrees with me that Portillo is the only one who has something of the style and breadth of Disraeli.

The big news, of course, is that Jack Straw has decided that

Pinochet can face extradition charges. There is a real zizz about the place on this and it is the only story in town when I get back to the Commons for a vote. There has been some pretty drivelish stuff in the papers about Straw as a potential future Prime Minister. I must say I cannot see that happening. You can take a man out of the National Union of Students (NUS), but you can't take the NUS out of a man. Jack is still a student politician – technically competent, a clear speaker and good at picking up causes and running with them – but in the end you don't really know what he believes in or stands for. I also suspect he is anti-European and I don't think the party would go for someone who is organically hostile to Europe.

I arranged to meet Matthew and Sarah in the Strangers' Bar after the vote and went down there to find Matthew drinking a pint of beer – really quite the manly thing to do – with Liam Fox, whom I just am unable to take seriously. I saw Ewen MacAskill and took him out to the Terrace where we had a chat with Claire Ward, the young Watford MP who everyone likes loads. She has been attacked in *The Independent* because Ken Purchase organised a jolly to Bahrain and everybody was given a very expensive Rolex watch. It was front page of *The Independent* with a big picture of smiling Ken as Robin's PPS. Frankly, I found it all very embarrassing and I wish MPs just didn't have to get involved in these grimy little exercises.

SATURDAY 12 DECEMBER 1998

I biked up to the Institute for Contemporary Arts (ICA), where I was to speak on democracy and the media at a big Charter 88 conference.

Hardly anybody was there and the ICA – where I haven't been for years except for parties – was pretty much empty of the event.

Anthony Bevins, the paper-hopping political editor at Westminster, spoke. He is extremely priggish and moralistic and basically said all politicians were rotters and that all journalists were in their own tiny little lobby groups and were incredibly lazy, with the sole exception of his good self. He said that he was going to get Geoffrey Robinson. 'I have got my teeth in his ankle and I'll never let go. This is a man who made money from money that Maxwell stole from pensioners and I am going to get him.'

However, this model of honourable political journalism asked me when we were having coffee during the break if I would table a motion for him that would mention Dominic Lawson, who has been named as an agent for MI6 while editing the *Sunday Telegraph*.

I muttered something about not being allowed to do motions as a PPS and Bevins just jabbed me in the chest and said, 'You're a coward, just another coward, I'll find someone else.' Well, I suppose I am a bit of a coward, though I'm not really prepared to get into a parliamentary fight over Dominic Lawson, but what was extraordinary was the presumption of Bevins that I should use my parliamentary privilege to help him write his story. My reward would have been a mention, but it is just as corrupt as any request to an MP to ask a question in exchange for money. I didn't bother probing him on this as he suffers from no little self-importance, but I shall make sure the story gets well told.

TUESDAY 15 DECEMBER 1998

Up a little after 6 a.m. to go for a run. Then a taxi to 1 Carlton Gardens, Robin Cook's residence, for a political breakfast. Under the urging of David Mathieson, Robin had invited quite a variety of

MPs. There were ministers there like his own Derek Fatchett and Peter Hain but also Charles Clarke. Bill Rammell and David Lock were there as were Lorna Fitzsimons and Hazel Blears. Clive Soley and Jean Corston represented the older PLP establishment.

The food was average – a fruit medley and then some over-cooked bacon, sausage and scrambled eggs – but we had a good talk for an hour or so. Robin was remarkably accessible. He greeted me at the door as I arrived and I told him I was pleased to see he was being his own butler, which got a smile. When he's willing to be friendly, he really is very nice indeed, but he doesn't know what to do with it.

He was lavish in his praise for Tony Blair:

Tony has got this remarkable relationship with middle England, the *Daily Mail* readers. He understands them in a way that no one has in the past. But I think he is pulling the wool over their eyes to a certain extent. He is bringing in all sorts of taxes that are actually quite redistributionist. The rhetoric and the careful cosseting of middle England and the *Daily Mail* readers disguises the fact that a lot of his actions actually help our community.

Charles Clarke taxed him on Europe, saying that all of the business community were accusing politicians of not showing any leadership. He said that in Norfolk, farmers were switching to being paid in euros.

Cook refused to get enthusiastic. 'If the euro succeeds, I have no doubt we'll be in after the referendum and everything else,' he said. Again my heart sank. 'If' not 'when'. You can take a man out of the Labour committee on safeguards in Europe, but you can't take

twenty-five years of Eurosceptical discourse, especially about the
EU's economic and monetary arrangements, out of the man.

WEDNESDAY 16 DECEMBER 1998

I had to go on television with George Galloway about the forthcoming attacks on Iraq and we had a real ding-dong. He is a marvellous polemicist and one of the best speakers in the House but is
also arrogant and a bully beyond any reasonable limits.

He kept calling Clinton a liar and a fornicator, which I thought
was a bit rich on his part. I gave as good as I got and the BBC Two
viewers had a ding-dong that was a cut above the usual boring
exchanges around question time. Actually, I didn't like it and I
won't do any more interviews which mean going on television with
Labour MPs.

I went over to the Foreign Office for Robin Cook's Christmas media party. It was a pretty big bash, with lots of big names
there. Mary Ann Sieghart introduced me to David Yelland, *The
Sun*'s editor who comes from Harrogate, so we had a good laugh
about Yorkshire folklore. I could even find myself warming to
him and I didn't get the feeling that he had a strong view in his
bones about anything. Trevor Kavanagh, who stood alongside him
like a grey-bearded cardinal advising a young headstrong prince,
bet me at dinner that the whole euro project would fail. I took
him on.

Robin came in and made a strained little speech full of jokes that
went down half-well. He said he would have a drink on New Year's
Eve for every wrong story that had been told about him. He also

said that he had to pay for the chocolate biscuit he took with his coffee, 'which is how it should be'. I must nose around about this. I have noticed that Chevening has fallen off the agenda and I wonder if it is because he got a big bill for its use and simply doesn't have the money or is too mean to splash it out.

Anne McGuire, who was at the breakfast yesterday, told me later that she had known Robin for thirty years and he had been the most arrogant and cocky of any of the Scottish politicians she had worked with. 'And he's no better now, though he is learning a bit.' I must find out more.

At 9.30 p.m. Margaret Beckett comes in and announces a special statement and debate tomorrow. The House is subdued and uncertain. Most MPs have either gone back to their constituencies or are planning to do so.

I cycle home and watch Blair come out of No. 10 live on *News at Ten* to announce that bombing raids have started on Iraq. The lighting is bad. He looks drawn. The determination is there, but where is the strategy? In the United States, Congress is about to impeach Clinton for having sex with a young female intern. I know US Republicans are right wing, often extreme and always partisan little politicians, but he has brought so much of this on himself. He has been a good President in many ways, but there is some deep – 1968ish – flaw in his character. Roosevelt he ain't. I don't think most Americans will support the right in their witch hunt against him, but there is no bedrock, gut-deep support or enthusiasm for a man who has manipulated, twisted, lied and cheated, and for all the very good things he has done as a politician, he has left a trail of slime and corruption about him.

THURSDAY 17 DECEMBER 1998

So, we are now bombing Iraq. I see little point in it. There is no strategy for the region. Saddam is a bastard and I suppose we have to knock him back a bit, but there is something pathetic and tiddly-winks in all this. George Galloway and Tony Benn are making hay on all the airwaves, denouncing Clinton and Blair as launching a crusade and killing innocent people. My bile rises, but what can I do?

I go on French and German television to blather away about the war, but I don't really feel convinced myself.

I go into the Commons for Blair's statement on Iraq. It is OK. He delivers it in that firm but 'gosh, it is really hard for me to take such historic decisions' sort of voice. Hague backs him up and apart from Tony Benn, there is no real opposition. Robin then opens the debate and is competent. Howard comes back with a lot of quite good questions about what the strategic aim is and the fun starts with George Galloway and Tony Benn making long ranting speeches. Chris Leslie, the young MP from Shipley, beautifully punctures Benn. He stands up and asks simply, 'What actually would the right honourable gentleman take to disarm Saddam Hussein?' He sits down and Benn barely has time to catch his breath, as he was expecting a more aggressive type of question. He patronises Chris to begin with as a young man who knows nothing, but from all over the Chamber come calls of 'answer, answer' and Benn says he would lift the sanctions. The reply is so ludicrous and inappropriate that the whole place bursts out laughing and he is completely deflated. It is one thing to be shouted down or shouted at by hostile MPs from all sides of the house; it is another to say something so absurdly ludicrous that people just laugh at you.

Into the Members' Dining Room, where I sit down with the Chief Whip Ann Taylor, Mike Hall, Tom Pendry and Bob Ainsworth. It is excruciating. They are talking about their holidays in France and the wines they like to buy. It is matey and saloon bar and utterly worthless as a conversation between a Cabinet minister, two intelligent whips and me. I order an extra bottle of wine to share round and have no idea how to wrench the discussion to a higher plane.

Back in the Chamber at the end of the debate, the left try to pull a stunt by calling for a vote on the adjournment. About fifteen, maybe twenty of them are there, though the only stars are George Galloway, Tony Benn and Jeremy Corbyn, for whom I have a lot of respect and who has not been trying to grandstand his way throughout the unfolding events on Iraq this week in the way that Galloway and Benn have. With three minutes to go, they call the vote and there is some disorder. What they needed to do was to put their own tellers on the 'Aye' as well as the 'No' lobby, but they waited for government whips to go and stand at the lobby doors. When none did, there was no vote and Galloway exploded like a monkey on Super Pep pills. He stormed up to the Tory benches and started shouting at the Speaker. His claim was that the government had denied him a vote, but it was pretty obvious to everybody that a vote could have been called if he had got two of his chums willing to act as tellers. I think it was all completely phoney and they didn't actually want to register their names. At any event, Galloway kept screaming at the Deputy Speaker, Michael Lord, and it was also obvious to anybody there that what he wanted was to be named and thrown out of the Chamber. Thus, he would have guaranteed his headlines the next morning. Lord is a shrewd old bird and spotted this rather cheap little trick and was having none of it. In the end, Galloway spluttered out of steam and the evening finished on this foul and silly note.

In the Members' Lobby, Dennis Skinner was absolutely contemptuous of his colleagues. 'Everybody knows that you have to put tellers on if you call for a division. You can't rely on the government. They should have known that.' I wondered who he meant by 'they'. He, Tony Benn and Tam Dalyell have about 100 years of parliamentary experience between them and usually know the ropes by heart. It reinforced my view that the whole thing was just a stunt and I'm glad they didn't get away with it.

TUESDAY 22 DECEMBER 1998

After Iraq now we have the Mandelson scandal. Apparently dear old Peter took a £375,000 loan from Geoffrey Robinson to buy his swish house in Notting Hill. The loan seems to have been without interest and is on the front page of all the papers. It is a monumental misjudgement. Robinson is being investigated by the DTI and it puts Mandelson in an impossible position. I presume the story was leaked by the Treasury gang who will do anything to crucify either Mandelson or Robin Cook. But with Iraq, it is a double blow and simply makes the government look like A. N. Other government.

Why do these people have to try to live as if they were as wealthy as the people they like to cavort with? I suppose Mandy did this in 1996 when it was safe to do it in the sense that he wasn't yet a minister and so there would not be any corruption or smell of sleaze involved. I always wondered why Geoffrey Robinson was made a minister as he was pretty useless in the Commons and I just didn't see what talent he would bring to the job. Now, in addition to this scandal, questions are being raised by journalists as to all the money he has provided to Gordon Brown.

Even if Gordon hasn't in any way profited from it in the way that Mandy has, there are still going to be questions asked. It was about the same time that Mandelson started to disconnect from all other MPs. He was given the use of a chauffeur-driven car by some wealthy discotheque owner in London as if he was already a minister. It clearly has gone completely to his head. It is an awful blow to Blair because Mandelson is the left side of his brain and I think this will mortify him.

Back home it is Mandelson, Mandelson, Mandelson, taking up all the news bulletins. It is a gift from the Gods for the media in what otherwise would be a dull Christmas week. The only small advantage is that it has completely wiped Iraq out of the news and comment pages. I don't think we could take much more of the post mortem on what was a very unhappy instance of British foreign policy.

WEDNESDAY 23 DECEMBER 1998

Out for a run and I go down and get all the papers. It really is big bad news for Mandy. Trevor Kavanagh in *The Sun* rounds on him and says he has to go. All the papers are dumping massively on him and it really is a groundswell of pressure such as I have not seen about an individual Cabinet minister since the Ron Davies affair.

I call Mandy a little after 9 a.m. to wish him well and he sounds very dejected, though defiant, blustering to me that it was not him but his officials at the DTI who would carry out any inquiry into

Geoffrey Robinson's affairs. Yes, I thought to myself but didn't say anything to him, that's all very well but not the point. The point is that democracy power has to be separated from money power. Robinson got so much of his money from people like Maxwell and then splashed it out in such a crude influence-buying way. It reinforces my belief in state funding and the need to just get money out of party politics.

Then a bit later in the morning comes the news that Mandelson has resigned. It is an immense blow for Blair and although lots and lots of Labour people, including a number of his fellow Cabinet ministers, will be gloating like mad, it is just bad, bad news and starts the mid-term off in a horribly negative way. I call up Don Macintyre who says the resignation was a 'class act' and thinks it will actually be the saving of his book. The papers seem to suggest that the story may have emerged as a way of trying to spike the main selling point of Paul Routledge's biography of Mandelson, which had as its main revelation the fact of this big loan from Geoffrey Robinson. Everybody names Charlie Whelan as a spider in the middle of this web and I imagine Gordon will have a fight on his hands to save his neck. How loathsome and appalling these venal personality squabbles are, but there is hardly anyone at the top of the government who can escape from them. The sooner that old gang go and are replaced even by inexperienced but team-playing individuals like Stephen Byers and Alan Milburn – the former who has got the DTI job and the latter who takes over as Chief Secretary – the better.

I get calls from a lot of the press in the afternoon and say some nice words to the effect that 'nothing became Peter's holding of high political office as the manner of his leaving it. He'll be back.' Which is a bit rent-a-quote, but what the hell. I also do an interview on Radio Sheffield where I am fairly breezy, saying there is nothing in my financial cupboard that would cause any trouble. Who knows?

Sarah and I go down to Marks & Spencer and buy a lot of party food for a party for the Executive Committee of the Rotherham Labour Party tonight. Most come round and we have a very nice and friendly evening. Mahroof Hussain was bang-drumming about Iraq and I gave him a copy of the letter I had written to his brother Tariq. I simply hope we can hold the line on this. But even with Stan Crowther there, who can be quite grumpy, the mood is friendly enough and we have a very enjoyable three hours of talking, drinking, joking, gossiping.

THURSDAY 24 DECEMBER 1998

Christmas Eve but the only political story is that of Peter Mandelson. I am quoted in *The Guardian* and the *Financial Times* picks up my quote saying that he might have some future on the European front, but the stories are all bad news for Blair and Labour. It now appears he may have failed to fill in properly his application form for a mortgage from the Britannia, which technically is illegal, so he may get into even more trouble. Last night none of the party friends had any sympathy for him. I suppose if I am honest, I think that his contribution has been exaggerated. There is a European and, if you include Clinton's election in 1992 as part of this process, a worldwide move away from the right in recent years and it is that trend that has taken us into power.

Blair certainly accelerated the trend, deepened it and articulated it beautifully, but the plain fact is the right were and are being kicked out of office everywhere and it is not a miracle solution on the part of Peter Mandelson and New Labour that is responsible for all this. And yet Mandelson did speak a lot of truths at a time when few were willing to say them and many of his judgements have been spot on, hence the wonderment about that most crucial judgement, the decision to take so much money from Geoffrey Robinson, who has fallen like Lucifer from the heaven of the Treasury to the edge of history's dustbin. I am on the record as saying Mandelson will come back, but politics now moves on at such a fast and furious pace that this may not be the case and Blair will have to rethink some of his modus operandi, as there may simply be no room for the Mandelson of the 1980s and early 1990s as we move into the next century. I suppose Blair could always offer him a job as an ambassador or European commissioner when the next British vacancy comes along. But Peter is 200 per cent a political animal and needs to be at the centre of British politics.

It is a lazy day and I have been sleeping marvellously long hours, doing very little. Rotherham steel union leader Austin Senior comes round and picks up the two cartons of House of Commons whisky for himself and Terry Butterworth. He doesn't seem too pessimistic about steel, thinking they can hack their way through the next few months or even year without a major plant closure, but nobody knows which way the economy is going, where orders might come from or what the nature of constructional manufacturing will look like in a year's time. I must say I am pessimistic.

The children go to bed and we put presents out for them around the tree. What bliss it has been to have this Christmas week just consisting of the family and no one else. We take life very easily, watching too much television, lying around, doing none of the work I had said to myself I would try to do, but how refreshing and relaxing it all is.

MONDAY 28 DECEMBER 1998

I write some letters to David Mathieson suggesting groups of MPs who could come and have breakfast with Robin. I don't know how far it will go, but it is worth a little political effort to maintain my interest.

Drinks in the evening down the street in Pimlico with Peter Bingle and Liz. Peter is a political lobbyist and Liz was the BBC's political editor in the north-east. They live and breathe politics 24/7 and are a good source of political gossip. They are both adamant that No. 10 fed, or rather fuelled, the story about Nick Brown being gay. I wasn't sure about this, but they insisted it was all organised from No. 10 to damage and diminish Nick.

TUESDAY 29 DECEMBER 1998

I phone up the press gallery to talk to somebody at *The Independent* and end up talking with Paul Waugh. As we were chatting about nothing very important, the other phone rings and he picks it up and comes back to say it was Peter Mandelson looking for Andy Grice.

We both giggled at the old spin-master unable to kick his habit and turning to his favourite conduits to get a story into the papers. Paul says Andy is going round openly bemoaning the fact that his career is over since Mandelson will no longer leak through him.

1999

FRIDAY 1 JANUARY 1999

So the big story today is that the euro has arrived. Its launch yesterday only amounted to the permanent fixing of rates but was done with tremendous panache in Brussels and other European capitals. Here in Davos, far from England, one can sense the surge of confidence at the currency's arrival and its heralding a new era in European history. I notice that Britain simply isn't a player and fear and feel for my country at its self-imposed marginalisation.

MONDAY 4 JANUARY 1999

Charlie Whelan has been forced to go. I have known and liked Charlie since he was a young leftie activist working for the engineering union, the AEEU. He moved to work for Gordon Brown and was a brutal but brilliant bully of the media to promote his boss, nearly as good as Alastair Campbell. But after the leaks from the Brown camp that forced Mandy's dismissal, the Blair camp want their pound of Brown camp flesh. This is open revenge for

Mandelson's dismissal. You have one of ours so we will have one of yours. It is pretty rough stuff.

I had a good talk with Hugh Bayley, the MP for York, today and he was moaning about his lack of prospects. 'I nursed York for seven years until winning in 1992 and have worked pretty hard since, but I am not remotely in the loop or anywhere near the loop and I just wonder if it was all worth it?' he says miserably. I agreed with him, feeling pretty much the same way myself, though of course I did absolutely none of the hard work to win a seat like he must have done during the 1980s.

TUESDAY 5 JANUARY 1999

We go on to do a long off-piste ski. This involves climbing up from a T-bar for about twenty minutes to a ridge and then breaking the crust of the snow to plunge into the other side into quite thick, heavy snow which becomes thicker, warmer and more sticky the further we go into the valley. I felt I couldn't even get to the top of the ridge, since side-stepping on skis up to what seemed to be a narrow slope quite close to snow that looked as if it might avalanche was both nerve-racking and utterly exhausting. On the other side, the snow is simply too heavy to be able to ski through it properly unless you are a great expert, which I am not.

Towards the bottom, we thread our way through trees before finally hitting a road and ski down to the restaurant. When I stop, I am soaked in sweat and am shaking for at least ten minutes – both my body and my head going thud, thud, thud as if I had no control over either. I have never experienced this after physical exertion, but everybody else is pretty shattered so I hope it isn't old age.

Back in the hotel, we go to dinner to find everybody jumping up and down because Hugh Bayley has been made a minister. Tony Blair phoned him up from the Seychelles and promoted him to be the junior minister at the Social Security Department. Stephen Timms has moved up to be Minister of State and John Denham goes across to be Health Minister in place of Alan Milburn who becomes Chief Secretary in the Cabinet.

THURSDAY 7 JANUARY 1999

The euro seems to have been an even bigger success than people imagined. All sorts of money is now appearing and coming in to be invested in different euro funds or accounts. Britain just has been left to one side as Europe ploughs on ahead. When are we going to have the confidence to do something to remake our country?

SATURDAY 9 JANUARY 1999

A long and tiring journey home. Looking after three noisy children by myself is a bit much. Luckily, David Montgomery, a viscount, was with me and he was very kind, helping carry the suitcases, which, given his age and the weight of them, was no mean feat. He was upset because his father, the famous Field Marshal Montgomery, had been exposed in the papers as having written the most filthy racist diatribe following a visit to British troops stationed in Africa in 1948. He described the Africans as 'savages' wholly ill-equipped to govern themselves. The government had to pigeon-hole his report because of the political stupidity of its argument and conclusions. I don't have much time for field marshals, but, of course, he is vital for David's self-esteem, so I just sit quietly while he complains about his father's memory being traduced. I don't know why anyone bothers to pretend that the British Army in its imperial heyday was anything other than disgustingly racist.

SUNDAY 10 JANUARY 1999

Up for an early morning jog and I go in to buy the papers and every one of them from the tabloids to the qualities is full of Robin Cook, based on his ex-wife Margaret's book. He stars on every front page as a man who has had six mistresses, drinks and loathes and hates his fellow Cabinet colleagues, notably Gordon Brown.

The wall-to-wall coverage looks awful. There is almost shock in seeing it all displayed like a remorseless avalanche advancing towards its cowering victim.

I had received a message in Davos to call David Mathieson and phoned the Foreign Office to get the number at Chevening where he was staying with Robin this weekend. I tried one number and there was no answer and then tried the next and to my surprise, Robin picked it up himself. I asked him how he felt and he said it was pretty grim at Chevening. I tried to cheer him up by saying that six flings over decades of marriage is hardly going to condemn him as a Don Juan womanising fornicator, the drinks thing was improbable and nobody would believe it, while the crucial difference with the other scandals was that there was no hint of financial impropriety. Indeed, the *Sunday Times* carries two stories about Jack Cunningham using a private jet to whizz around Europe on official ministerial business and a story that Geoffrey Robinson had via the *New Statesman* given lots of money to Sarah Macaulay's PR firm. Sarah is of course now seen as Gordon Brown's intended. Of course, we all knew that, in that she organised the parties for the *New Statesman*, but it is interesting how a commonplace piece of knowledge can be cooked up into a political scandal by a twist of the media ratchet.

Robin was quite chatty and said I was succeeding in cheering him up. I suppose actually he was very isolated in Chevening and it must be a very strained relationship with Gaynor as he works eighteen hours a day on big issues surrounded by officials while she just has to twiddle her thumbs in those cavernous official residences.

I watch the David Frost programme on television because Blair is going to do an interview and he is remarkably good in defending Robin as doing a 'superb job' in Europe. It is not quite true, but it sounds very strong and well beyond just a routine defence. Blair also makes a plea for cooperation with the Lib Dems and an end to 'tribalism'. Again, he is taking head-on the resurfacing by John Prescott and David Blunkett and to a lesser extent Gordon Brown of the Old Labour 'ourselves alone' *contra mundum* set of beliefs. Here is a possibility for Robin if he becomes the interpreter of the Prime Minister's wish for a more plural politics in Britain.

But it all means that his fate now completely depends on Blair's goodwill. I think short of a miracle, he has come to the end of his political career. He can keep the Foreign Office for as long as Blair wants him in there and might shuffle here and there to another Cabinet post, but awful and vicious and termagant as his ex-wife's book is, it is going to be hard for people ever to forget it.

MONDAY 11 JANUARY 1999

When I went into the Commons at about midday, I found people quite ready to go in and support Robin. Helen Southworth, the nice Lancashire MP, said, 'He may be a bastard, but he's our bastard.' In the event, there was a good solid clump of people behind Robin, and I manoeuvred to ensure that there were plenty of Labour female MPs, including Gillian Merron from the ski trip, right behind him.

He made a sombre statement about the troubles in Yemen, where some British-Yemeni men have been arrested and accused of being Islamic fanatics connected to the attack on British tourists that ended in four being killed a couple of weeks ago. Yemen is a basket-case place and will remain so, and Robin can be statesman-like, sad and serious at the same time.

Luckily, Michael Howard came to his rescue. Howard compared Robin's strong words on terrorism in Yemen with what he claimed was softness in releasing IRA terrorists and everybody exploded because of the false comparison. Then he said Robin wasn't on the job – which of course is the very thing that he has been on in all senses of the word – over the past three or four days. The *sous-entendu* is that the newspaper allegations have taken up all his time. Even backbenchers behind Howard look pretty sick at the cheap shot and this has allowed Robin a dignified exit line about Howard demeaning himself.

WEDNESDAY 13 JANUARY 1999

I work in my office during the afternoon and watch a score draw between Blair and Hague in the first Prime Minister's Question

Time of the New Year. I was meant to have gone to Paris today, but the Liberal Democrats have organised a debate on Europe and Joyce Quin has to reply to it so her trip is cancelled and mine with it.

I came in to take my place behind Joyce Quin and Alan Milburn, who is leading for the Treasury. He looked up with half a smile and half a sneer and said, 'Oh, I see the euro freaks have arrived.' I said nothing, but that off-the-cuff snide remark, even if it wasn't meant deliberately sneery, commends him to no one, certainly not me.

The debate is fairly pointless, exposing as usual the divisions on the Tory front bench. David Heathcoat-Amory made it quite clear he wanted nothing to do with the euro or Europe of any sort, a point reinforced by John Bercow, who seems to swallow an anti-European pill each morning. But I am not interested. I come back for Joyce Quin's wind-up speech. Robin came in to sit beside her, which wasn't a bad show of solidarity and a necessary demonstration of his presence.

THURSDAY 14 JANUARY 1999

Up at 5 a.m. to go to Paris. This is for the Franco–British *colloque* which is being held in Versailles. Joyce had told me that there were party political meetings beforehand and asked me to come along. I had asked her to get authorisation for me to accompany her as her PPS, but Nick Hopton, her private secretary, phoned up to say she didn't really want to approach Downing Street on this. Downing Street has to sign off on any of these trips and she obviously wants to save her credit rating at No. 10 for something more important. So I had to hustle to get a ticket from Eurostar, which I will have to record in the Register of Members' Financial Interests, which is a bore.

At the embassy, I go in and have a chat to the ambassador's wife, Sylvia Jay, who is busy cleaning and polishing her aspidistra plant in the little office where she sits next to the library in which her husband works.

We have a very good chat about David Montgomery, whose wife is the daughter of Daphne du Maurier and who has lent a huge picture to the embassy dating from the Duff Cooper times. My mobile phone rings and a woman announces herself as 'the ambassador's secretary' and asks how I propose to get to Versailles. I said I assumed I was going in a car with everybody else, but she says that there is only room for three passengers in the ambassador's Jaguar. I think this is a little pompous and say, 'Well, isn't there another car?' She says, 'No, no.' I say, 'Well, don't worry about it, I'll get a train or make my own way.'

I felt royally pissed off and once again the way the wretched embassies treat MPs, even those with a tiny position at the Foreign Office, as pieces of shit really managed to get up my nose.

Joyce comes out of her interview and Sylvia rushes up to say how good she was on French television the previous night. The charm and praise are unfeigned and although I am sure Lady Jay is probably more at home with the bourgeoisie of the Conservative era, I think she genuinely wants Britain to be more Europe-friendly and having a fluent French-speaking minister like Joyce makes a big difference.

We get into the car and go to the Quai d'Orsay for a party political lunch with Pierre Moscovici. He is the saturnine Romanian who is the French Minister for Europe. The lunch is splendid and Nick Sigler and Clive Soley join us along with Henri Nallet, the former French Agriculture Minister who is the Socialist Party expert on Europe.

There is some contrast between Britain and France here. Moscovici can throw a swish lunch in the Ministry of Foreign Affairs for a purely party occasion, whereas we would have to take them all for sandwiches somewhere. Clive Soley apparently has been named as the international affairs member of the National Executive Committee (NEC). He is a most likeable man and is thoroughly grounded in British politics, but in his speech yesterday in the House, he said that the only thing coming from Europe in his view were German bombers and he has the worst of Old Labour suspicious reflexes about Europe.

The French want Tony Blair to come over for a big electoral meeting on Europe along with other European leaders. Nallet is working jointly with Robin Cook to produce a manifesto for the European elections. 'We argue over every comma, but we are making good progress,' he says cheerfully.

Now that the parties of the left are in power in thirteen out of the fifteen EU states, there is no desire for a combative or visionary European manifesto.

We explain that we are going to lose a lot of MEP seats because of moving to a regional list system elected on a proportional basis. It is a very bad scheme cooked up by Jack Straw, who probably wishes Labour MEPs didn't exist. We will lose lots of seats and as it's PR, the racist right will win seats. This dismays the French, who realise that the Party of the European Socialists will stop being the biggest single party in the European Parliament. Mind you, they haven't even decided who will be on their list or who will lead it and although the European Parliament is having a great time this week threatening to pass a vote of censure on the European Commission – a proposition that our French comrades just dismiss as silly and not going to happen – there is still no organic sense that the European elections are that important.

FRIDAY 15 JANUARY 1999

Into the seminar proper and I have to be the rapporteur for the workshop on 'A New Transatlantic Partnership'. This is almost completely dominated by Sir John Kerr, the Foreign Office Permanent Under-Secretary. He is bright and clear, intervenes and knits everything together. His game plan is obvious. He wants these powerbrokers to accept the idea that Europe should have its own independent but not anti-American foreign policy that could be backed by arms. The dread of these men is that Europe is going to be simply a greater Switzerland on the world stage. He makes a lot of persuasive sense.

The only sharp difference is over Iraq, where the French just shake their heads in cynical disbelief that the British should be so foolish as to blindly follow the Americans in an air strike that is not connected to any strategic goal that anyone can recognise for the region.

Kerr bounces up to defend the UK, as he must. He says that during the November crisis, the US Cabinet, including all the key players on the defence and foreign policy side, were ready to bomb Saddam and the planes were already in the air:

Prime Minister Blair made seventeen or eighteen calls to President Clinton over that 24-hour period to try and stop the Americans. He extracted from Saddam an absolutely clear and binding promise to abide by the UN resolutions, so when he broke that promise no one should have been surprised that in effect the November decisions and air strikes were simply carried out.

Despite his polished justification, Kerr tells me later that the French were absolutely right and that there is no strategy. He is very cunning and contrasts the St Malo Agreement on Defence, which in his words was 'our idea and concept but we let the French draft all the language so they had pride in what was said', with Maastricht, 'which I helped negotiate and we all know what a disaster it is. We don't need the wiring, we simply need more vision.'

I go for a swim in a very nice pool in the basement of the hotel with Adair Turner of the Confederation of British Industry (CBI) and then there suddenly appears Peter Mandelson.

He has a rather spindly body with little bits of black hair on his chest, slightly less than me a few years ago, and has rather over-developed upper arm muscles from his gym workouts, which don't really fit on a Lytton Strachey profile.

He bobs around a bit swimming and then I notice him standing still and go up to talk to him in the middle of the pool. When I ask what he is doing, he looks at me with amazement and says, 'Stretching, of course, don't you do it?' So I spread my legs and move my body left and right in what is a faintly pleasing business, though I would much rather be swimming.

I ask him how things are going and he says, 'I've been very surprised at the very warm reception I have had from the PLP. I've spent the last three days going into meetings, into the Chamber, or at the PLP meeting and apart from people like that ghastly Gwyneth woman, everybody has been very nice and very friendly.' If Gwyneth Dunwoody is his only problem in the PLP, he's OK. She snarls at any vaguely pro-European MP and has been banned from the Members' Dining Room as she never pays her bills.

Peter is still a member of the club – he's been kicked, he's down, but I hope he isn't over-reading the natural friendliness of MPs to one of theirs who is down on his luck into organic support for himself. I'm not going to give any advice, but a period of silence and quiescence from Peter would be useful.

There was a message up on my TV screen in my bedroom to phone Robin Cook, but when I tried the number it was David Mathieson.

'Denis, Robin would be very grateful if you could come to Swansea to fill in for him on Sunday.'

I didn't know what he was talking about, but it transpires that this thing called the National Policy Forum is meeting in Swansea over the weekend and Robin is meant to reply to a discussion on foreign affairs on Sunday but wants to be excused so he can be with Gaynor in order to hold her hand in Chevening as the second extract from the Margaret Cook memoirs hits the papers and the public.

I protested, though, of course, I was just a little bit flattered at being asked – no, not a little, quite a lot – and said surely there were other MPs present who could reply to the debate, which is a pure formality but of symbolic importance to say that somebody from the Foreign Office team is there.

No, no, Robin specifically wants you to be there and would be really grateful if you could do it. I know it's a dreadful imposition, but if you can get back early, the Labour Party will cover all your costs and everything. He explicitly didn't mention Ken Purchase or anybody else.

So, there we are. I told David to keep trying to find someone else but said that of course if it was important, I would do it. It means leaving the *colloque* a little earlier tomorrow, but that's no bad thing to get back to London before the evening.

SATURDAY 16 JANUARY 1999

A car took me to the Gare du Nord and I jumped out just before we arrived to buy two tubes of harissa so I can start making couscous again. I was back home by 12.30 p.m.

Then I left at 7 p.m. for Swansea and I ate two filthy sandwiches and half a bottle of bad French Chardonnay en route. It was an hour late in getting in, which meant I didn't get to the rather grubby little Marriott hotel in the old Swansea docks area until just before midnight.

There was a dreadful whiff of a Labour Party conference there with John Spellar, Rosie Winterton, Mike Gapes, one or two of the No. 10 policy people and some trade unionists. Apparently Robin had announced that I was coming, so everybody knew what I was doing there when I turned up, but there were one or two glares on the faces of people as if to say, 'What the hell is he doing here?' as the National Policy Forum isn't something I have ever been linked to and it is one of those private little clubs within the Labour Party run by the elect for whom any outsider is unwelcome.

Ian McCartney, in particular, always seems cold and distant and I might amuse myself for two seconds to find out why he doesn't like me.

In my room, I found a very nice note from Robin, full of gratitude, which I shall perhaps have framed so that my grandchildren can see one day how their ancestor worked closely with a man who still has the capacity to be a big Foreign Secretary if he chooses to concentrate his mind and reinvent himself.

SUNDAY 17 JANUARY 1999

Up for a nice cholesterol breakfast and into the plenary session. There are about sixty people there.

Ian McCartney introduces me with a snigger as sitting on 'his far left but on your far right' and makes lots of little jokes about everybody having got drunk the night before and needing paracetamol this morning. It is like the worst kind of union, or indeed student union chairmanship, and although heavily folksy, it just doesn't match the seriousness of the job he has got.

I tell Ian I ought to have a word to explain that the BBC World Service cuts are as a result of their own internal decisions to move resources from broadcasting on short wave to Germans who are totally uninterested and don't listen, and spend more money on other resources around the world. *The Guardian* has blamed Cook for the cuts, as the BBC World Service budget comes from FCO money.

I have a little second to defend Robin and put the BBC story in context before Ian starts to use his chairman's right to cut me off, so I shut up, but somehow there was bad chemistry there which I didn't properly understand.

That was it. One minute's speech and about fifteen minutes on a platform for this entire wretched trip to the far west of Wales.

The *Sunday Times* stuff by Margaret Cook in many ways is worse than last week's because it is all about what has happened in the last year, not just Robin's girlfriends and political ambitions. It is excruciatingly unpleasant about the rows over the divorce settlement and the letter that Tony sent her which she felt was cold, cynical and uncaring about the break-up of the marriage. She has a real grudge against the Labour Party. She blames Blair and Campbell and Mandelson, who acted as a divorce broker, scuffling between London and Edinburgh or talking to her on the phone to try to calm her down. She says Robin told her he could not lose his job, so she feels she was free to write this vicious and awful biography, which has more than a feel of a female Samson pulling down the temple around her.

It damages Cook and I have to ask myself whether his appeal to me yesterday was because there was simply no one else he might turn to. Professionally, he goes on, but everybody will be sniggering behind his back.

Alan Watkins, in the *Independent on Sunday* which I never bother reading, predicts that Labour may not get a second term. And he is meant to be a serious political correspondent?

MONDAY 18 JANUARY 1999

In the division lobby at 7 p.m., Robin greets me warmly, clasping me with both arms and thanking me profusely for going to Swansea yesterday. I actually quite enjoyed it and it was fun to get back a bit into the Labour policy swim. As I went down the corridor afterwards, Ian McCartney said, 'I see you were telling fucking lies yesterday about the World Service.'

I told him I wasn't.

'Well, everything I have been reading in *The Guardian* means that you were telling a bunch of fucking lies yesterday.'

The Guardian, of course, has a big story saying that there will be World Service cuts and in it is the line that the BBC hasn't got all the money it wanted from the government. In fact, Robin has negotiated an extra £44 million out of the Treasury, which means a real above inflation increase for the BBC, but McCartney doesn't know the details and has just taken his news from *The Guardian* which implies it is the government's fault that World Service language services face the axe.

I explain all this to him, but he just snorts in disbelief. There is a naive belief that *Guardian* journalists can never get anything wrong and are sympathetic to Labour. If only.

I think I will get a letter out to all National Policy Forum members explaining the truth.

TUESDAY 19 JANUARY 1999

To the Foreign Office for a very quick meeting on Foreign Office questions. Robin turns to me and tells me to say to Joyce, who didn't turn up for the beginning of the meeting, that if anyone asked a question about Peter Mandelson's role in the Foreign Office she was to say, 'He has no role, no post and is not an envoy in any way.' This follows all the stories in the papers about a meal Robin and Peter had together and a new job for Peter as a special envoy acting on behalf of Robin to build relations in Europe. I talked about this yesterday to Andy Hood, Robin's special adviser, and he told me that it was a very good idea, it was going to happen and it would bind Robin more closely to No. 10 and that Peter would work very well with the Foreign Office. So what has led to this remarkable reversal of position? It is, I think, that in the tea room yesterday, Robin was got at by Ken Purchase and his friends, all of whom loathe and abominate Mandelson and are rejoicing in his fall and taking great pleasure in continually kicking him while he is down. Why shouldn't they? He was so foul and mean to them over the years.

However, I don't think it will do Robin any good to get publicly into a position of slapping down Mandelson. At the end of the twenty-five minute discussion, I mentioned the World Service cuts problem and everybody looks up and realises that this could be raised this afternoon as it is running as a big story in *The Guardian* and *Independent*. We desperately hunt up and down the order paper looking for a question which will allow one of the ministers to say some positive words about the World Service. We light on one about Burma and I have to go out to find Gillian Merron and get her to mention the World Service in her questions so Derek Fatchett can bang out a reply praising the new money that the government has found for the World Service.

I go back into Joyce's office, but there is no preparation to be done as she has simply the one question to answer. I say that in my judgement, she should on no account slap down Mandelson from the despatch box:

> If you do that, Joyce, it will be the story. And in any case, everyone's confused because twenty-four hours ago the line was that Robin and Peter had got on famously and that Robin was delighted to lend him the support of the Foreign Office to carry out bridge building exercises in Europe.

Joyce replied:

No, Denis, I'm not having any of that. I will not have Peter operating as an unofficial minister. He really tried to shaft me in opposition, putting horrible stories in the paper because he wanted my job. And then when I was in the Home Office, he put stories in tiny paper saying I was no good at the job and was trying to get me fired.

This was a very un-Joyce-like outburst as she suddenly showed claws and fangs of real hate. I guess she must have also added to the pile of complaints to Robin about any idea of Mandelson having a role in the Foreign Office. 'I was amazed when I went into the lobby yesterday and I was greeted by so many people, a queue of them, saying they didn't want Mandelson in any way to come into government through a side door,' she added.

So that's that. Mandy is going to have to bide his time.

In the Chamber in the afternoon, question time in fact goes very smoothly with none of the Tories and no one on our side mentioning the word 'Mandelson'. He slipped into the Chamber just as Joyce got up to speak and I saw him out of the corner of my eye and wondered if that might spark a sly question. Had it done so her language would have been interesting and there might well have been a little story if she followed Robin's line and slapped him down hard from the despatch box. But, of course, the question you fear never gets asked.

THURSDAY 21 JANUARY 1999

Over to the French Embassy where Jack Lang is to bestow a French decoration for arts and literature on Salman Rushdie. We arrive after the ceremony to find *le tout Londres littéraire* is there. Tiny Martin Amis, tall Michael Ignatieff, fat Richard Rogers, bubbling Kathy

Lette, granny-glassed Ian McEwan and others whom I vaguely recognise but not all of whom I could put a name to. Jane Wellesley,
Melvyn Bragg's blue-blooded number, once an NUJ activist and
proud of it, was there, but the longest conversation I had was with
John Diamond. Conversation isn't the right word, as he can't talk. Nigella Lawson came up to us and said that the cancer had come back
and all they were offering was more chemotherapy. She didn't say it
but the implication was clear it was game or life over... So I talked
and talked to John and he replied by scribbling points or asking a
question on a little pad of white paper using a brown ink pen. It was
awful and all I wanted to do was weep at this man of unbelievable wit,
whose mouth was his most prized possession, reduced to scribbling
on a pad of paper and occasionally grunting a 'yes' or a 'no' which
one could hardly understand. He can't eat or drink and it is a modern
tragedy made cancer-ridden flesh before our eyes. He told me that
the family had been invited down to Chequers for Boxing Day and
I twigged him on promoting my merits to become a minister, but it
was just impossible to sustain a conversation so he gave me his email
card and I will try to write to him every day until it is all over.

THURSDAY 1 APRIL 1999

April Fool's Day but no one is cheerful. The bombing of Serb military positions goes on. War has its own logic. There is no glory in
this. Slobodan Milošević is a bad man, but the whole of Yugoslavia
from top to bottom has been a disaster for ten years. Events un-
leash themselves. Passions that Hobbes said required a strong state
to control take off. I suppose there is a good side and a bad side in
this, but I fear it will all end badly.

No matter. The family always endures. This one was up at 4 a.m. ready to leave for France.

We drove to Bayeux, as I wanted to show the children the Bayeux Tapestry. It is utterly remarkable when you see it in real life. It is about fifty metres long and about twenty inches deep and everything is so clear in a very simple stitchwork with the Latin captions as easy to read as if they were in a cartoon strip. It was quite different from all the pictures I had seen in the different history books over the years and brought to life the awesome adventure that the conquest of England by the Norman duke had been.

We bought sandwiches to eat in the car and hurried on down to Bissin, getting there for about 3.30 p.m. The house was empty as no one expected us so early and certainly this route through Normandy seems much quicker than going via Paris.

We went down to the beach and plunged our toes into the warm and wet sand and ran into the sea. After a nice rich dinner and kisses from their grandparents, we were all safely asleep by 9 p.m.

FRIDAY 4 JUNE 1999

It really does look as if the Kosovo War might be over. The Yugoslav Parliament has agreed to accept the NATO peace offer. I won't be convinced until there are democratic troops in Kosovo.

TUESDAY 8 JUNE 1999

Into the Fabian Society at 10 a.m. for a round-table discussion with Mary Kaldor, Jeremy Corbyn and some peace campaigner about humanitarian intervention and the new forces deciding what a legitimate use of military force might be to uphold international law. We have a good thrash at it with Mary being very supportive. Afterwards we chat and she wants to talk about Robin Cook.

How is he? I used to talk to him before the election, but is there anyone he talks to now? He doesn't seem to have any close friends. I think his marriage to Gaynor has been good for him, but I hear they just sit alone at home watching television and eating take-out food. Who on earth gets things moving in the Foreign Office? The problem is he has never run or managed anything before he became the Foreign Secretary. At least at Sussex I had run a big department, but he just doesn't know how to manage.

This was interesting stuff from a good pro-Cook friend who had spotted his vulnerability even though he has come well out of the war to end the Milošević decade of death squads, ethnic cleansing and terror. She added an interesting thought, which was that Robin was much more at ease with women than men.

I went to my office and then to the House for Blair's statement on Kosovo. It was measured and completely untriumphant. There were no real cheers from our side and the Tories only got going about Europe as Blair had to cover the well-nigh irrelevant European Council meeting in Cologne last week. He dealt with aggressive questions from Tony Benn firmly and I think emerged in the House, as he has in the country, as a real quality leader. On Europe, he again got passionate and warned Hague that his anti-European politics might bring short-term tactical advantage but were going to do damage in the medium and long term. I hope that is true and certainly Blair sounded as if he meant it.

Then on my bike down to Millbank, where I had been asked to swell the crowd for a joint statement on the Third Way and the *Neue Mitte* by Blair and Gerhard Schröder.

It was awash with serious business leaders, the bosses of GEC, Vauxhall, KPMG, Northern Foods and bankers and bigwigs from the City whose names I didn't know. Ken Jackson from the AEEU and Margaret Prosser from the T&G were there to provide union balance.

Blair and Schröder came in and read out their document. It is top heavy with right-wing New Labour stuff about cutting public expenditure and lowering taxes on business. But at the same time, it has plenty of good social democratic language and advocates a role for trade unions. But the message is clear that they are committed to a right-wing reformist path.

Blair reads out his speech and Schröder gets up, leaving his notes on the table, and talks off the cuff. But he doesn't go on too long and then sweeps away while the rest of us go for a drink upstairs. The media are kept out of this and I just beam and burble generally about how well we are doing in Europe. I say hello to Blair as he is going out and start to talk to him when Jonathan Powell comes across to say: 'Sorry, we're off to see the Queen.' I had forgotten the Tuesday evening chat at Buckingham Palace. Blair seemed relaxed and on form and not as tired as many of the papers say. But the Kosovo War, as well as these new initiatives on Europe, leave him as the man who carries everything forward himself.

WEDNESDAY 9 JUNE 1999

I do a television interview for French television on the Blair–Schröder statement. All hell has let loose in Paris. The newspapers are treating this as a deliberate British–German attack on Jospin and he has come out fighting, saying the Third Way isn't for him and France must retain its socialist specificity. I have fielded calls from newspaper journalists all day and try to present the Blair–Schröder declaration as being at one with much of what Jospin is doing. But in my heart, I wish there was something that was left of the left in all our policy pronouncements.

MONDAY 14 JUNE 1999

I am in Brussels having flown here yesterday to represent Labour at a Party of European Socialists press conference after the European Parliament election. Turnout for our vote last Thursday was below 20 per cent. No one is interested in MEPs except MEPs. They are a good bunch, but UK domestic politics only operates around the Commons.

I stay with Martin Walker and Julia Watson. They have bought a big estate in the Dordogne to which we are warmly invited. 'Martin simply doesn't want to live in England any more,' says Julia. I know the feeling.

He then joins us and we have a rather bad croissant. He is openly contemptuous of Blair. 'The Third Way has been defeated. Blair and Schröder came out with it and they are the biggest losers,' he said. Labour, which had 10 per cent of all MEPs in Strasbourg in 1994, is down to just twenty-nine. The Tories won more. Turnout was 24 per cent, the lowest of any EU member state. UKIP, a nasty, racist, right-wing identity party, has won three MEP seats.

Martin says he is going to write a column attacking Joyce Quin as the 'invisible minister for Europe'. I protest and defend her gently, saying that she really knows her business and it is actually an impossible job in the British government. If you come out with strong positions on Europe, you will annoy all the others who think that European policy is their preserve – Blair, Brown, Cook or anybody else around who is a big cheese. Martin can't quite believe how limited and technical the job of being a minister in the Blair government is.

We walk out and catch a tram and then I buy my Eurostar ticket and twiddle my thumbs for a bit before having an easy ride back to London.

Just before going into the Chamber, I spot Hilary Benn, the new MP for Leeds Central, and I join him for a photograph outside St Stephen's entrance. When I stood there equally proud five years ago, it was John Smith who met me. Now all Hilary gets is Ann Taylor, the Chief Whip.

TUESDAY 15 JUNE 1999

I work in the office in the morning and get a call from the *World at One* to ask if I would go on to talk about Peter Mandelson coming back as a campaign and communications supremo. Actually, I think it is a good idea, but I checked with No. 10 first. The next move was a call from Phil Murphy, the new Labour Party press boss, who is an old mate who said that he had talked with Lance Price and the instruction was to go onto the programme and, as Phil put it, 'hose down this idea about Mandelson coming straight back'. The metaphor of 'hosing down' was a new one and I discussed what I should say with Phil quite carefully. Basically, the orders from No. 10 are not to give a lot more credence at this moment to a swift return of Mandelson.

At the studio, I listen to the programme and just before me, Bill

Cash is in a triumphant mode declaring that the new shadow Cabinet, which contains out and out anti-Europeans like Bernard Jenkin and Iain Duncan Smith, is 'Eurosceptic'. He is immensely satisfied and smug and says that Hague has to break with the European People's Party at once and go for full renegotiation of all the treaties. Thus, Hague, in pandering to his Europhobic right, has created a monster that drives the party further and further to a right-wing nationalist position. Then, even more amazingly, Cash announces that he is seeing Hague this afternoon to tell him all this.

This gives me my chance when I am interviewed to talk about the very right-wing shadow Cabinet and how William Hague is now taking his orders from William Cash.

David Mathieson comes in for a talk. Robin is in an ebullient mood after the praise in the press and Blair apparently describing him as 'brilliant' on television. But we both agree that a new campaigning mode is needed for Europe.

David said:

Robin wanted to campaign in the election but Kosovo just took away all his chances. He insisted that any visit had to include a speech at a workplace. He prepared a speech which referred to the gains for workers from signing the Social Chapter, including the Working Time Directive, but when it was sent over to No. 10 for approval, they took all that out.

WEDNESDAY 16 JUNE 1999

I drive the car in early and have a kipper breakfast in Bellamy's. The sun is shining and a London summer looks like arriving.

Unfortunately, my *World at One* interview yesterday still rumbles on. The *Daily Mail* has a quote saying I am opposed to Mandelson coming back to a top position in the party. Later in the day, he glares at me and scuttles past.

To lunch at *Private Eye*, where I get very little gossip and am sat beside a publisher from Orion, the company that now covers Weidenfeld. They have just brought out Gyles Brandreth's diaries as MP for Chester 1992–97, which I am reading at home and finding very entertaining and interesting. Gyles was amongst the most talented of our generation at Oxford and yet seems to have frittered an entire life away. That is my pompous over-political judgement. He no doubt feels he has had a good time, written lots of jolly books, made tons of dosh, brought up a nice family – and the devotion to his wife, Michèle, is one of the finest things in the diaries – and completed life with a good stab at being an MP and ultimately a government whip.

I ask my neighbour if there are any Labour MPs keeping diaries in a similar fashion. He doesn't know of any, but I keep my counsel.

Downstairs in the Strangers' Bar, I have a chat with Ian McCartney, who is quite friendly. Tomorrow's newspapers are running a story that he has been appointed head of a special inquiry team into why we did so badly in the European elections. He is ready for a chat and I give him my thesis that we should park the euro question for a bit but at the same time get out and gauge much more solidly on European issues with the public.

I told him:

After 1992, Labour had an extremely clear and unambiguous position on Europe – we were in favour of a full engagement in the EU. Whereas, in contrast, the Tories spent the whole time sitting on a fence worried about their Europhobes and giving no clear message to the public. Now William Hague has a very clear position – he is against Europe. We mustn't make the mistake of looking for a fence to sit on as the public always punishes waverers and fence-sitters.

His hooded eyes blinked in acknowledgement but I don't know how much of the message was getting across. He is a former agent himself, so he knows how it works on the ground. But you can almost feel the palpable desire of so many MPs for an end to the European debate. They simply want it to go away and never come back. If only it were that easy.

THURSDAY 17 JUNE 1999

There is a debate on Kosovo today which is a huge bore but it gives me an excuse to cancel all the planned lunches – I had a clash between a lunch with two journalists from the *Telegraph* and the Taiwanese ambassador, neither of which I wanted to go to.

The Chamber was thin, very thin. Robin made a good combative speech. He is much more relaxed and self-confident. I thought he would miss Michael Howard as his opponent, but although Howard cranked him up, there was always that lurking danger that he might land an effective punch. John Maples, Howard's replacement as shadow Foreign Secretary, is much weaker. He effects an air of studied reasonableness and has a nice speaking voice. Listening to him is a bit like listening to John Major. It's fluent, coherent, every idea in its place, but no words with any weight or punch.

Cookie has a go at the SNP and a turn at those who criticised the government's handling of the war in the 'dark days' when the news about NATO bombing mistakes filled the front pages.

I think good as Robin has been in helping keep all the different bits of the coalition together, there is some puffing up in all of this. History will record a sub-colonial military sortie to put an unruly tribal chief back in his place. We have been lobbing our shells into the heart of darkness and finally the wicked head of the Serb tribe realised he couldn't take on the empire any longer and slunk back to his mountain fastness. Robin is putting this two-month campaign on a par with the Second World War. I suppose if you are fighting it yourself, you have to rev up your internal motors to present a solid face to the world, but I can't quite buy it. Nonetheless, it is a competent speech and goes down well.

I drift in and out for the rest. There is some windy bombast from the 'told you so' brigade and no little jeering and self-indulgence by those who have supported the conflict. Alice Mahon is brave and stands up to defend her position that it was all a ghastly mistake and the Serbs are equal victims to the Kosovan Albanians. Really, with all the news coming out about atrocities, torture chambers, mass graves and other evidence that the Serbs are not just being beastly but inhumanely brutal and murderous, I think she might have had just a little more discretion. But she is a plucky Yorkshire girl and battles on against wind and tide and I admire her for it.

I am still reading the Gyles Brandreth diaries. They are getting better and better and provide a real insight into the Tory government. He records all the ambitions and hopes and disappointments that I feel. What a funny life it is to come into this place too late to make any real impact. But what kind of impact does one make, since the ministers he records working with – like Stephen Dorrell, who was at the head of the Department for Culture – obviously hate the job and are completely indifferent to it, leaving lots of stuff for Gyles to do. I like Dorrell and he comes over as a decent chap, but there is simply nothing in what he has to say that has any real impact. Gyles records the dog days of Toryism when nothing was going right. I wonder when this will start to happen to us.

SUNDAY 20 JUNE 1999

In the evening, we went over to Martin Rowson's house in Lewisham for a party. As usual, we got lost. Once you turn off from New Cross, all the roads have little Berlin Walls at the end of them to stop rat-runs. That's fine if you have local geography, but we were blundering backwards and forwards, up and down and sideways, until we arrived at his house, which was a nice early twentieth-century villa with magnificent dark-stained wood staircases and panelling.

Martin and his lovely wife, Anna, are great hosts and the food was spectacular. A Polish woman came in with fresh ham and chorizo from Spain and I ate too much. I didn't really link up with anybody there. They mainly seemed to be his mates from Cambridge of about twenty years ago, i.e. ten years after my generation. It's funny how one clusters together in blocks of years from Oxford and Cambridge.

Fiona Mactaggart came in for a little while but then went off to go to Slough for a meeting or an event she had to be at. The Slough Labour Party is in complete turmoil with dozens of members being expelled or forced to leave and it must be pretty miserable for her. She is loud, bright and, despite her money, always badly dressed in black. I just don't get her at all, but there is a good, interesting woman there I need to know better. We didn't stay long and it was early to bed.

MONDAY 21 JUNE 1999

I am off today on an odd little mission. All last week, I had been pestered to go to Moscow and finally said yes, so here I am in a comfortable seat on the British Airways flight there. The fellow MPs are a pleasant bunch. Sylvia Heal, George Robertson's PPS, is there with her very precise, neat, clearly articulated Welsh voice. She is an embodiment of JP-ish common sense. George Stevenson, the ex-bus driver and ex-MEP from Stoke, is also there. The last Labour MP is the Tory transplant, the smooth, good-looking, white-haired Peter Temple-Morris. He comes up to me and says he has met with the other people in the group and decided I should be its leader. Wow! Leadership at last!

The Tory is Sir Nicholas Lyell, the former Attorney General who had been a minister for years before that. I had always found him rather wooden and unconvincing in the House, but he is actually pretty decent and liberal to talk to. He carries a small sketchbook and does brilliant quick sketches on our meetings, catching the key features of the speakers. It is much better than the copious notes I write down in my notebook.

Finally, there is David Chidgey, the Lib Dem MP who chain-smokes little Hamlet cigars. He is rather overweight and a little self-important but no fool and one of the rare MPs with a proper engineering qualification and background. At any rate, it is a fairly happy group and we rub along well.

The airport at Moscow was pretty scruffy, but the city seemed cleaner and more modern than on my last visit even a year ago, let alone on an earlier trip. We stayed in a luxury hotel right opposite the Kremlin and were taken a few hundred yards to the embassy for dinner.

The British Embassy, of course, is the most famous nineteenth-century building in Moscow and its internal decor apparently has not been changed since the Revolution. There are lots of heavy wood panelling and brocaded wall furnishings. It is more like what one imagines a luxurious country dacha to be. The architecture from the outside is conventionally Italian, though there is no classicism inside but I suppose a Russian equivalent of Biedermeier.

The ambassador, Sir Andrew Wood, is a dapper little figure full of energy and has assembled the usual gathering of policy wonks. We have a very good discussion over a very bad meal. Almost without exception, they are hostile to the NATO attack on Milošević. No ground is given. It was aggression, it was done without UN sanction, it was disproportionate, it resulted in far more humanitarian tragedies than it sought to prevent, the attack on the Chinese Embassy was deliberate, Russia thought it had a partner for peace in NATO but now finds an outfit that is bombing European cities. When will it start bombing Russia? Russia will now have to re-evaluate its defence posture and look to China, India or Pakistan. And so on and so on and so on. We were pretty strong and kicking back, but there was a very dead hostility that the bonhomie of the occasion could not disguise. Back to the hotel in a depressed state.

TUESDAY 22 JUNE 1999

It didn't get any better. We had an hour or so off in the old Arbat for tourist shopping. I bought one of the matryoshka dolls of Bill

Clinton, which had inside Monica, then Paula, then Hillary. One of the nicest of the economists I met said that America was the only country capable of accepting socialism as everybody there obeyed the law, whereas in Russia everybody was an individual and potential anarchist. The Russian's cynical contempt for authority is a joy to behold but must make governing the place impossible.

The meetings today were with the International Affairs Committee and the Defence Affairs Committee of the Duma. In both cases, our principal *interlocuteurs* were generals. They were both identical. Hard faces, trim bodies without spare fat and penetrating eyes. They wore blue short-sleeved shirts with just a single star as a giveaway on their shoulders. Both repeated the message we heard last night that the bombardment of Belgrade was a crime and an aggression and was perceived as a threat to Russia. I took lots of notes, but it is pointless repeating them all in the diary. We were talking past each other, but at least we were there talking face to face. I asked the chairman of the Duma's International Affairs Committee to give me three things that Britain or the west should do to help restore relations. His name is Vladimir Lukin and he had a sharp little face and is actually one of the more reform-minded politicians in the place. 'Three things? Well, that's difficult, number one – let us win a victory at Wimbledon. Number two – let Russia host the World Cup and number three: send the Princes Will and Harry to stay for a bit in Russia.' All this with a twinkle in his eye, but then he made three serious suggestions. Firstly, that we should disarm the Kosovan Albanians. It is as if Srebrenica never happened. But I guess most Russians think Katyn was a western lie. Secondly, that we have to prove that NATO is a strategic partner of Russia. And thirdly, that the debts dating from the Soviet regime which Russia is paying should be written off.

The latter point is the sensible one, save that most of the debts are owed to German banks and they can't rewrite their balance sheets that easily. It would be good to find something to do jointly with Russia. The real problem is that Russia keeps measuring itself against the United States and when it was a global superpower between 1945 and 1989. Somehow Russia has to come to terms as have the other ex-European superpowers like France and Germany and, I suppose, Britain, and start behaving as a big European power. That has to be the way forward.

We had dinner in the house of the number two at the embassy, which was more average food and more Russians moaning and groaning about NATO. Afterwards, we went for a beer in the Red Square area and I showed them all the gravestones behind Lenin's tomb where Russian and international communist bigwigs are buried. The tomb itself still stands there, black, forbidding and inaccessible.

WEDNESDAY 23 JUNE 1999

Meetings this morning with Gennady Zyuganov, the head of the Communist Party. In pictures, he comes over as a typical fleshy, sweaty Soviet bigshot bureaucrat. In the flesh, he is very good-looking with nice blue eyes, blond hair, good hands and dressed in a well-cut lightweight suit. His office, like the rest of the Duma, is now housed in the old Gosplan office and it is a bit like the Treasury with long gloomy corridors everywhere and a fusty, out-of-date feel to it.

He was quite urbane, saying that Russian history consisted of Stalin's cruel measures necessary to modernise the country and defeat Nazism but it then all came to a dead stop in the 1960s when economic reform should have been introduced.

Gorbachev and Yeltsin were both the archenemies. In fact, several of the people we met expressed a visceral loathing for Yeltsin that was quite remarkable in its intensity.

Gorby and Yeltsin between them had destroyed the Communist Party, the Soviet system of administration, the economy and public control, so the big ship of Russia had no steering mechanism. Yeltsin was under pressure from his family, and the outside Mafia. 'If the Mafia group get power, they will have missiles and Kosovo will look like a school outing,' we were told.

The main enemy, of course, was the United States. 'A country with only 200 years of history cannot rule the world. The history of Europe is much more subtle and it must stand up for its own interests,' Zyuganov proclaimed. He complained that Europe was pushing Russia in the direction of Asia and the Islamic world where new alliances could be made. It was necessary for Russia, the Ukraine, Belarus and Kazakhstan to come back together and form a united power.

All this was delivered freely for more than an hour, with lots of friendly questions from our side. He was fluent and coherent. Beside his desk was another little table with ten white telephones on it. He had an aide who would jump up now and then when one of the phones rang, though how he decided which one was ringing I don't know. There was a heavyweight feel to him but not, I would judge, a real figure of destiny. A competent open communist – at least when he meets international visitors – but a future President of Russia? I doubt it.

On to Grigory Yavlinsky, leader of the Yabloko group of deputies.

He is one of the west's preferred reformers in Russia who got 15 per cent of the vote at the last Duma election. His sister party in the UK are the Liberal Democrats.

Despite his pro-western outlook, he was equally strong in condemning the war in Yugoslavia:

People now think that NATO could attack Moscow. You say it can't happen? Look, I never believed we would bomb Grozny in Chechnya, but it happened. We didn't believe you would bomb Belgrade, but it happened. Now the Caucasus is becoming Balkanised. Does that mean that NATO will come to enforce the peace in the Caucasus? In previous elections, I said I was for European values, but you have let me down. I have to defend international law. Madeleine Albright said that NATO was a peaceful organisation when it expanded to our borders, and then we put on the radio and this peaceful organisation was bombing the hell out of Belgrade.

He was bitterly critical of the simplistic economic measures proposed in the early 1990s:

The Economist was full of wishful thinking. Russia was far more complex than the west realised. It is difficult to know which western economist has done more damage to Russia – Karl Marx or Jeffrey Sachs. People have low expectations, which is good. They want a little bit of improvement and that would do. We see there is a new government in the UK. We need new ideas and young people. We need to fight both the robber barons and cronies' capitalism. Last August, the banks stole the people's money [through the defaults and closures] and people expected western banks to be very tough, but it didn't happen. The western banks cosied up to the Russian banks and looked after them. We have seen a 4–5 per cent fall in GDP, 10 per cent fall in production and a 10 per cent fall in agricultural output. Wages have been cut and people are very nervous.

It was all gloomy stuff and yet in Moscow itself the people looked young and bright with a spring in their step and a laughter in their eyes, far different from the sullenness I first saw when I first went there under Gorbachev. Russia, I suppose, will muddle through. We need to encourage it to think of itself as a European player. What Sir Henry Tizard said of Britain in 1950 applies to Russia. 'Britain is a great nation but no longer a great power. If it pretends to be a great power, it will cease to be a great nation.'

We had a quick show round the Kremlin grounds, paying an extra 600 roubles – about $25 – to jump the queue and go in with the guide. She was pregnant and had qualified as an engineer but there was no work for her and she could earn more money by being a tour guide. We looked at the churches and the famous cracked bell and had a sense of the great European history that is bound up with Russia. Which way will it go? To become like an India or perhaps a Brazil – *sui generis* – hostile to the rest of the world and proud of its own culture and national identity, or can it find some common cause with the rest of Europe and finally overcome a Russian exceptionalism to become a major European nation for the first time in its history?

To lunch at the commercial attaché's flat with some British businessmen. I sat beside a man from BP who knew Nick Butler well, so we had a friendly chat. According to the official statistics, Britain is in the top three or four investors in Russia, but I could see no evidence of real factories belonging to British firms. Obviously, BP and the energy and raw material extractors and traders are here because that part of the Russian economy still is vital on the world stage. There are lots of accountancy firms which just act as middlemen for Russians who want to park some of their money in a Swiss bank account and need legitimacy in Moscow and in the west to get the money out, and I suppose they can be counted as part of the UK financial operations in Russia, but what Russia needs is a lot more foreign direct investment especially outside Moscow, lots of little firms to show good western management examples and skilful use of new technology, but I don't think these guys are providing much of it. At any rate, it was a perfectly pleasant lunch and one felt one had done one's duty for our export trade, whatever that is worth.

I agreed to draft a note on behalf of the team and we flew back to London allowing me time to scribble, scribble on the plane.

THURSDAY 24 JUNE 1999

Into the Commons for Treasury questions. The Tories have made the mistake of appointing Quentin Davies as one of their Treasury frontbench team. It is logical as he knows finance stuff backwards, but of course he is notoriously in favour of the euro. This means that Gordon Brown has a field day for twenty minutes as he knocks the Conservatives left and right on Europe and the euro. Our cheers get louder and louder and the Tories look shamefaced. Francis Maude shrinks into his seat. He sits between Quentin, who tries not to smile and looks completely ill at ease, and Oliver Letwin, the clever-dick young Tory who is hostile to Europe. He is one of these John Redwood/Keith Joseph All Souls types who can write the most mystifying rubbish that disappears up its own fundament while being very urbane and charming. Anyway, it was a triumph for Brown and cheered everybody up.

I run to catch the train up north. There is a fundraising dinner at Bradford to which I must go. The train is full of MPs. There is a BBC *Question Time* in Leeds and I sit opposite Nick Soames who is going up to it. Then Decca Aitkenhead walks past. She gives me a big grin and 'Hello' and Soames swoons with excitement. 'Cor, God, what a smasher! Tell her to be nice to me on the programme tonight, Denis. She mustn't be beastly. God, how can I get to meet her?' he burbled in excitement.

I have a chat with Decca who, of course, is all fired up on *Guardian* themes like freedom of information and the asylum bill and the uselessness of Blair. I try to steer her gently to be more positive, but *The Guardian* is now utterly one-dimensional and doing as much damage to Labour as any Murdoch paper.

Alistair Darling was also on the programme and we had a brief chat as he read through his immensely long briefing notes on it. I never watch *Question Time* any more and I don't know anybody who does. It has ceased to be an important part of the political week.

Hilary Benn was on the train and as he was going to the same fundraising occasion as me, I offered to drive him up from Doncaster, where I had a car, which would give us the chance for a chat.

He seems a very good egg. He has to play himself into his Leeds seat, where he narrowly won the selection by ninety votes over eighty against a very popular party chairman and local councillor and woman, to boot. We had a chat about office costs and other arrangements and didn't really grapple with any political issues save a general sense of the party's unease about aspects of the Blair project. We all know that unease but what to do? Strident leftism is no answer and it just has to be managed while we get on with incremental improvements. Not very exciting but better politics.

There is no overarching political vision for people to get to grips with, as he knows as well as I do. He lives in Turnham Green with four children so, like me, won't be moving to the constituency. It is remarkable how the Yorkshire seats now are filling up with academic and professional types who are full-time political animals. I don't think a proletarian has been chosen now for some years.

MONDAY 28 JUNE 1999

To south Harrow for the funeral of Screaming Lord Sutch. It was a wonderfully British event. The church was full and his agent and friend pulled me into the front row as I think I was the only MP who was there. There was an excellent tribute with all the best one-liners from the Good Lord's political career. On his coffin was his trademark top hat and outside everybody was wearing his extravagant clothing with funeral wreaths in the form of the green and orange top hats he loved to wear. 'Why is there only one Monopolies Commission?' was what he asked, and we need more of these brilliant fools to ask questions about what we are doing and why. It was a wonderful send-off and I was pleased to link up briefly with his eccentricity, which is one of the best things about our benighted country.

TUESDAY 29 JUNE 1999

I have offered to speak on a debate on passports today. The passport office is in complete chaos. Queues stretch for hundreds of yards in London and Liverpool. The row has been rumbling on for weeks now and ministers have not got any grip on the problem at all.

My only interest is to try to promote the idea of identity cards, which we could carry in our wallets and use for travelling around Europe without all the inconvenience of a passport.

I get a couple of ID cards – one from France, *celle d'Emilie en occurrence*, and a German *Personalausweis* from a German friend. Armed with these, I go into the Chamber to find Ann Widdecombe roaring and panting in an utterly manic way. She has tons of Tory MPs behind her who cheer her on. She is a most wondrous creature. Little birdlike in size but with the most gigantic bosoms and very funny teeth that seem to pop out of her mouth at moments of high excitement, like a vampire descending its fangs. She is on a roll and she knows it. Jack Straw does his best but is on weak ground.

My speech aroused plenty of opposition from the Tory benches, who started shouting about Geneva endlessly. It didn't put me off my stride and if anything it was rather flattering that I was the object of so much attention. I got my demand in for ID cards, but in the wind-up, Mike O'Brien forgot even to mention the Labour speakers, which was extremely discourteous of him. He was completely thrown by the wall of opposition and barracking coming from the Tories who cannot believe that their militant organ, the *Daily Mail*, has been caning the government so hard on this.

WEDNESDAY 30 JUNE 1999

To Salzburg to speak at the summer version of the Davos World Economic Forum. The summer version brings together all the leaders of central and eastern Europe as well as Russia and the successor states of the Soviet Union.

At the reception, I bumped into a few journalists, including Andrew Nagorski, the *Newsweek* columnist. He has written great stuff out of east Europe. We started chatting and found that our respective fathers had been in the Polish Army and had come through France to land in Scotland after the defeat in 1939. His parents, however, had moved on to America so he grew up an American, unlike me. There was *The Economist's* Moscow editor, Ed Lucas, who is a bit know-all, though enjoyably cynical and witty with it.

I cannot understand why I am the only British representative here other than the usual PWC consultant gang and one or two PR flacks from some of our big companies. There are more heads of government, real powerbrokers (including some of Yeltsin's oligarchs from Russia) and businesspeople here gathered under one or two roofs than one could imagine. Why the hell aren't we here networking, shaking hands and getting to know people? I bumped into Grigory Yavlinsky who I met in Moscow last week and so suddenly we become two people who know each other instead of passing visitors in the night.

SUNDAY 5 SEPTEMBER 1999

Blair has given an interview to *The Observer* in which he calls for a more moral Britain. This is in response to a twelve-year-old

Rotherham girl who gave birth to a child followed a day or two later by a twelve-year-old in Sheffield who gave birth as well. Rotherham is now branded as the child mother capital of England. Blair's stuff on morality, though I personally happen to agree with it, since Britain has become an utterly value-free nation in recent years, sits at odds with the somewhat less than moral profile of many of his Cabinet members and the utterly immoral and amoral behaviour of too many of the media and business tycoons he finds so much time for.

I mow the lawns and just wallow in an incredibly hot Sunday. My doctor brother Martin, his doctor wife Linda and son David come over for dinner later on and it is simply an easy family day.

WEDNESDAY 8 SEPTEMBER 1999

Alan Clark has died and the papers are full of him. Clearly his brain tumour operation didn't go well and there he is at seventy-one, just about the most interesting Tory MP I have seen in action in Parliament itself, now dead. Damn! The place will be so much greyer without him. He was always very nice to me and about me and his charm and desire to be liked were utterly infectious.

FRIDAY 17 SEPTEMBER 1999

Off to Siena for an agreeable little conference. We fly on an odd Italian airline called Meridiana from Gatwick to Florence. Harriet Harman and Jack Dromey are on the flight plus a loud Treasury civil servant who is wittering away like a schoolboy on his first excursion to the seaside. There is the nice Charles Grant, who is wearing an anorak like a sensible Englishman going abroad. Paddy Ashdown and his wife, Jane, are there too. He already seems strangely smaller. The moment you give up position in British life, you give up power. There are braying English Hooray Henrys and their womenfolk on the plane talking about how much money they make from management buyouts. Their voices carry loud and arrogantly the length and breadth of the plane.

A coach takes us to Siena and the Jolly Hotel near the main bus station pick-up point in the town centre. Over how many years have I seen this hotel and never put a foot inside it? It is actually a pretty low-grade place without even a bath in the bathroom.

Into the city centre and I buy a blazer and a pair of trousers at Upim and some mortadella from Morbidi to eat greedily, greasily rolling the pistachioed ham with fingers direct from the paper on the way into the Campo. We bump into Jack and Harriet. Jack is on a suit-buying spree and has already bought two, plus shirts and ties. They take the mortadella from the wrapping.

But all good things come to an end and it is time to put on a tie and go to the university for the first set of speeches. George Robertson is our star speaker. I am afraid I don't take any notice of what he says. Transferring from being a Cabinet minister to being secretary general of NATO is like going from the White House to a state administration. I would like to have George's money but otherwise the job seems pretty hellish. The NATO headquarters are parked next to Brussels Airport and he will have to spend his whole time travelling around Europe going to dinners with the military. Military dinners sound a bit like military music or military intelligence, nothing but an oxymoron. He has in attendance a general with lots of curly things around his shoulders and red badges on his lapels who brings him a drink at the reception that follows. I also fear that removing somebody as good on Europe as George Robertson from the British political scene may turn out to have been an error.

TUESDAY 21 SEPTEMBER 1999

Up to Rotherham and I drive over to Wigan for the by-election there. It is a safe Labour seat. I go and canvas a few streets. There is no anti-Labour hostility. There is an anti-politics hostility.

'I am not bothered voting this time. It makes no difference. You're all crap,' is one typical response.

I pull out a few of the Liberal election addresses from the letter-boxes. These show a podgy barrister from Manchester who comes over as a rabid Tory ranting about crime rates. Charles Kennedy, the new Lib Dem leader, has just made a passionately pro-euro speech but his man's election address in Wigan contains no reference to Europe. That's not quite true. There is a sentence that says, 'Europe: the Conservatives voted to support proposals which would do away with pounds and ounces in British shops.' Pathetic. There is a real gap between the cosmopolitan and European and stylish politics of the Lib Dems at the top of the national tree and ghastly guttersnipe Little Englander Lib Dems who are no different from Tories in the north of England.

SUNDAY 26 SEPTEMBER 1999

Down to beautiful Bournemouth for the Labour Party conference. On the train I talk with Jim Murphy (like Jack Straw and Charles Clarke, an ex NUS president and now a Scottish MP), Ben

Bradshaw (the Exeter MP) and an easy-going *Times* reporter, James Landale, whose father, he says, is really angry about the fox-hunting ban. Why are we bothering?

Europe seems set to dominate the agenda. Blair has allowed briefings to be given out that he wants to win three elections and beat Margaret Thatcher's term as Prime Minister. Let it happen, but why announce it now? It seems arrogant and hubristic. In *The Times* yesterday, Philip Gould had an article saying that the Conservative Party was finished. God, those whom the Gods wish to destroy, they first make cocky.

Blair does a competent question and answer session. Mo Mowlam is there but already the incredible popularity she had last year is wearing a tad thin. She reads out a letter from Ian Mc-Cartney attacking the press following his son's heroin overdose and death. Emotions are being milked and I find it rather unpleasant.

The usual round of evening meetings. Robin Cook talks about enlargement in almost messianic terms. He is sounding more and more euro-fanatic by the day. I whisper to Jan Royall: 'Why wasn't he saying this fifteen, ten or even five years ago?' Jan is Neil Kinnock's assistant and works in Brussels and is pro-European. David Clark, Robin's assistant, overhears this and sniggers, 'Better late than never.'

The *New Statesman* party was full of hacks and I had the usual jolly time, bouncing like a pinball between them. Martin Ivens said he had had lunch with Martin Walker and I told him to hire him. Peter Stothard also came up and said that he was going to give some work to Sweetie, so *The Guardian*'s attempted destruction of him doesn't seem to have worked.

Cherie Blair comes out of one of the hotels in a rather *décolleté* number and I greet her and she gives me a big kiss and a hug. She always seems so friendly, but why do I have no personal contact with her or her husband?

MONDAY 27 SEPTEMBER 1999

As usual, Gordon Brown made a brilliantly competent speech. He is technically the best orator, other than Robin Cook, in the Cabinet. What was in the speech? It was all 'you've never had it so good', but we're only just beginning. It is part of this pattern of hubris that worries me. We are a success, but we should stop shouting it from the rooftops.

He made an impassioned call to end child poverty and so say all of us. Whether adopting American tax and social policy will do this remains to be seen. But I was fast up on my feet and don't begrudge him a minute of his standing ovation. The newspapers are full of war between Brown's aides, principally Ed Balls, and No. 10 on the euro. Very dangerous stuff.

Lunch with Matthew d'Ancona and briefly at the end his girlfriend, Sarah Schaefer. Sarah wants to play a role in the party and is going to get on the Young Fabians executive. Matthew is full of admiration for Blair and full of contempt for the Tories. Given that his politics really are on the right, it is amazing that he has nothing positive to say about his Conservative Party at all. Maybe, after all, we can indulge a little hubris.

THURSDAY 30 SEPTEMBER 1999

Hooray, I can go home today. I tried to speak without success, but at least I stayed in the conference hall listening to most of the speeches. Frank Dobson was the best. Unflashy, calm, sincere, he somehow managed to convey a style of politics that is quite different from the competitive, vying-for-applause one gets from Blair, Brown, Prescott and the others. Prescott has made a complete ass of himself. To go and make his speech yesterday, he took a Jaguar 300 yards down the cliff path from the hotel to the conference centre. When he got there, he told everyone not to use cars. And when questioned about it, he said he did it to protect his wife's hairdo. It is all unbelievable. I talked to Rosie Winterton and asked her why on earth he hadn't got a spin doctor or any kind of half-witted adviser who could point out that on that day of all days he should have walked to his speaking venue. She shook her head in misery. Prescott is ceasing to be anything other than a figure of fun. That's a shame, as he is a much more effective politician than he is given credit for.

I went down to the conference hall, but the speeches are all so boring. The replacement generation of Alan Milburn and Stephen Byers make speeches that are like lighting matches to heat and illuminate the whole room. They are just beyond belief in their nothingness. Steve, at least, had a mention about putting core labour standards into discussion at the World Trade Organization conference in Seattle in December. I bumped into him and said that that was a good line and he said, 'Yes, and it was quite a struggle to get it in.' I wonder when No. 10 will realise that the world is moving into anti-globalisation mode and simple neo-liberal free trade evangelism won't work any more.

TUESDAY 5 OCTOBER 1999

The bad news this morning is that Jörg Haider has come through decisively in Austria with his quasi-Nazi Freedom Party. This is a massive shock wave through Europe. Does anybody know what it means? Everything evil this century has come in some way or another from Austria. Haider is a raving xenophobe and a deeply bad man. I am beginning to feel that Europe is looking shakier and shakier. Schröder has said on German television that his joint manifesto with Blair that Mandelson wrote was a great mistake. So there goes the Blair–German connection. Jospin is banning our beef and the German Chancellor is trashing the Third Way. What's left?

MONDAY 11 OCTOBER 1999

Everyone is feverish about the reshuffle. The big story is that Peter Mandelson is back as Northern Ireland Secretary. I think this will have been a genuine surprise to him. Certainly, in all our brief conversations in recent weeks and months, he gave the impression of being a man who had accepted a goodish period on the back benches. He had taken a job as deputy chairman of the British Council, chairman of the Anglo-German Foundation and other little titles and positions that certainly were good for a year or two. It is a great job for him. It keeps him out of the London gossip machine. It allows him to focus eighteen hours a day on a task to be accomplished, at which he is superb. I recall my conversations with David Trimble in which he revealed himself as being quite homophobic, so I wonder if that will appear and influence their relationship.

I can't quite see Peter giving up his camp mocking style and, adorable as that is, to many it won't go down with the rigid Orangemen of Ulster Protestantism who probably still believe that God created the world in 4004 BC.

But it shows how desperately dependent Blair is on Mandy and how he can't live without him. It is an interesting snub for Gordon Brown. His spin doctor over the water, Charlie Whelan, was viciously unpleasant about Mandelson the week before last in his columns and appearances at the Labour Party conference. Whelan had also gloated about Mandelson in his self-important film that went out just before the conference started. The old hatreds are there. I wonder when they will simmer back to life? It's also a blow for Robin. Next stop after Northern Ireland has to be the Foreign Office in Mandy's game plan.

The reshuffle is much bigger than expected. Jack Cunningham has been fired to make way for a bunch of technocratic, managerial Blairites. Above all, Geoff Hoon has been promoted to take over as Secretary of State for Defence. I faxed him a short note pointing out that I had now served under three Ministers of Europe and had seen them all off. It's a great shame as Hoon had really started to motor at the Foreign Office and I felt a good grip and a positive relationship and a chance to do some real work. It's good news for him and I wish him well, though there are some horrible defence issues to resolve in terms of Blair's ambition for Britain to be a global interventionist policeman of world law and order and the fact that we haven't got the money or men to carry it out. There are also horrible decisions to take about big-ticket orders for missiles and other equipment where we will have to make a fundamentalist decision to go broadly with Europe or to maintain our subordinate status to the United States.

Mo Mowlam comes back to run the Cabinet Office with Ian McCartney as her number two. It's a funny choice to put two of the party's most loved characters into the same department. They remain government ministers so can't spend all their time cheering up the troops, which is what they should be doing. Alan Milburn goes to the NHS hell, which Frank Dobson has escaped from. A high-level job for Alan but utterly thankless with the problems that the NHS faces. At least as the former Chief Secretary, he knows where the money is hidden.

Andrew Smith – who is utterly faceless and grey, nice, caring and intelligent but boring – finally gets into the Cabinet. He first worked as Blair's number two in some shadow spot years ago, and Blair likes to reward his loyal supporters. Except for me. Jack Dromey phoned up and said that I should expect something tomorrow, but I don't. I will leave for Rotherham as planned at 6 p.m. and although my pager will be on, my plans will be to assume nothing. I just hope that whoever gets the Minister for Europe job is someone I can work with and don't feel too humiliated by the appointment.

Overall, the government becomes very Blairite, very techno-cratic, very uncharismatic. It's a reshuffle for loyal, do-as-No.-10-says types. Apart from Mandelson, it is not a reshuffle that implies significant new political changes. Cunningham and Dobson have gone, so bit by bit Old Labour is being chipped away at. I may be wrong but my judgement is that none of the new ministers have really significant support in the PLP or in the party. They are all Blair's creatures. More and more of the passed-over backbenchers will be looking at them to trip up. I expect the ones who have had their two years and have been packed off will actually look back on it as quite an easy time as decisions will get harder, the opposi-tion will get tougher and the pressures from the party, Labour MPs, constituency activists and the press will relentlessly increase.

TUESDAY 12 OCTOBER 1999

Well, nothing has happened. Keith Vaz is the replacement Minister for Europe. It is a surprise, as I can't think of any reason why he should be transferred from his just-achieved foothold at the Lord Chancellor's department. I'll make one or two enquiries. I am disappointed and it is bizarre that I am now serving under the fourth Minister for Europe in barely more than two years. He is a nice enough guy and a good public speaker and very energetic. The two other people promoted are Yvette Cooper, who becomes a health minister, and Jane Kennedy, who leaves the Whips' Office to take over Keith's job. Given that the Lord Chancellor's post is pretty much a legal job, I don't know what Jane is doing there. I wonder if Geoff Hoon has some influence, as, of course, he is a big – very big – pal of Jane's and may have picked up David Lock's vibes that certainly were not friendly to Vaz. David Mathieson phones up to say he is in despair and that everyone in the Foreign Office concerned with Europe can't make heads or tails of it. He doubts if Robin was consulted but merely told whom he was getting. 'Roger Liddle didn't even know the appointment was going to be made,' which speaks spades for Liddle's influence at No. 10.

WEDNESDAY 20 OCTOBER 1999

Early in the morning to the Foreign Office where Robin Cook wants to meet all the PPS team. We sit in the large leather armchairs and sofa instead of around his table. His first question is, 'What's the point of a state visit?' and I am not sure if by that he means the rows in the press over the police behaviour against pro-democracy campaigners upset about the Chinese dictator having the red carpet rolled out for him, or the sheer tedium of having to dance attendance. He tells a good story about trying to take salt from a very heavy gold salt cruet on the table at Buckingham Palace last night:

I had been fascinated by these solid gold cruets in the form of Neptune and wondered if they actually had any salt in them. So for this banquet I decided to find out and asked my neighbour if she would like some salt. When she said yes, I leant over and pulled the cruet towards me and dished out salt for her and myself. I then tried to put the cruet back and found it was tilting over. I thought it must have been an extension leaf of the table, but as I pushed it to another place it still was about to topple over. I then saw that in its original place there was a little cardboard ball. What had happened is that one of the four gold balls on which it stood had simply been lost or perhaps had been nicked by a previous diner, so they made do with a bit of rolled up cardboard in its place.

Thus, for Robin, the shabbiness of the royal rituals which we are all meant to admire.

I go over to the Foreign Office to get a lift with Keith Vaz to the French Embassy, where he has to speak. He is very courteous in the car and asks me if I am disappointed about not getting a job.

'Just bide your time, Denis. Look what happened to me. I didn't get a job in 1997 and you just have to be patient.'

He reads out the first sentence of his speech, which has been written in French for him to practise his French. Every possible bit of accent and pronunciation is wrong and the look of horror on my face must have told him that he shouldn't do it, but he is quite cocky and doesn't really like the advice.

We also have a sharp exchange on the fact that he has taken over responsibility for issuing visas in Pakistan and India. I think he is insane because there is a real conflict of interest, especially as he is a number one champion of the Indian community.

'But MPs have to have a say. What do you do if you have a reselection vote or a key vote on your GC and the swing person is desperate to get a relative in from India or Pakistan? You have to help them out.'

I am amazed to hear such nonsense:

Keith, you're quite wrong, that is exactly the moment when you mustn't give someone a visa in order to secure a favour. If we go down that road, it will explode in our faces. Of course, there are horrible stories and great unfairness and racism, but there are also the cheats and the con artists. I don't speak Urdu, nor do you. How the hell can an MP act as an arbiter in these cases?

It was a both-barrels onslaught and although the conversation was conducted in a reasonable tone of voice, I could sense the ears of both his private secretary and the driver prick up. Oh dear, I hope to God all this doesn't end in tears, but I certainly don't want to get involved in political decisions on who comes into the country or not.

To the Polish Hearth Club in South Ken for the launch party for Francis Wheen's magnificent new biography of Karl Marx. Without knowing a word of German, Francis has written an Englishman's approach to Marx and finally has got the old bugger taken seriously as a great Soho eccentric.

Nick Cohen comes burbling up to me saying I must go and defend him in front of Roger Alton, who is also there, about a column he wrote in *The Observer* last week attacking Geoff Hoon. It was a pretty vicious attack but not, as far as I could see, defamatory. I go up and say hello to Roger and ask him if he is interested in running a column about my preparing for the marathon and he nods benignly, though I am not sure anything will happen. I say Nick's very worried about that Hoon column but don't worry, Geoff Hoon can take it and will have to take a lot worse.

SUNDAY 31 OCTOBER 1999

The *Sunday Times* has a front-page story about diaries kept by Lord Richard's wife whom I have never heard of. It is all good bitchy stuff that sounds true to form about Derry Irvine's arrogance and fondness for the booze and John Prescott's anger about the freezing of Cabinet salaries. It is too early and too inconsequential to really grab hold of public opinion. But it is the first – no, the latest – breach in the dyke of Blairism. They really do hate each other at the top.

MONDAY 1 NOVEMBER 1999

An office meeting with Keith Vaz in his office at the FCO – full of spooks, generals and FCO Balkan experts – on what to do next in Kosovo. They all chunder away and it's clear Keith hasn't the faintest idea what they are talking about. After ten minutes, he looks up and asks plaintively, 'Before we go on, could someone draw me a little map and show me where Kosovo fits in?' His private secretary duly obliges and the Balkans wallahs keep their heads down to avoid sniggering.

Over to No. 10 where I say hello to and shake hands with John Sawers, who is the Prime Minister's new private secretary on foreign affairs and sounds just like Jonathan Powell. David Miliband has written to me asking me to go to Florence for the Third Way summit with Clinton, Blair, Jospin from France, Schröder from Germany and D'Alema from Italy – five left leaders of G7 countries. But I have to pay my own way, as government funds can't justify my presence at a political occasion. What a creepy business. But I suppose I'd better go.

In the afternoon a French TV crew from Antenne 2 arrive and interview me endlessly on the Third Way. Then at 6 p.m. their rivals from Arte arrive to do exactly the same thing. They are both here because of the Socialist International congress, which is seen as the moment that Blairism and Jospinism confront each other. I don't give them the raw meat they want, but who cares?

To Politico's for the launch of Melanie Phillips's book. This is her usual rant against feminists, though I am sure it is much cleverer than that. I simply was there to allow the French TV crew to arrive and do some more interviews and get some flavour of British politics. But the place was crawling with Tories and only Martin Linton turned up as a Labour MP.

David Mathieson asks me to organise drinks for Robin Cook in his office at the Commons. It was going to be at 1 Carlton Gardens, but with the heavy three-line whips, it will take place now in the Commons. But David won't be there and I will have to get Lesley and Susannah, my new German intern, to do the work. I am not even sure Robin will pay for the drinks, so I wonder what will happen in the end.

TUESDAY 9 NOVEMBER 1999

To the Commons for Gordon Brown's pre-Budget statement. It is full of tricks and presents like free licence fees for OAPs aged over seventy-five and the announcement of lots of funds for childcare and venture capital and regional development. There are things close to my heart, like an announcement on employee share ownership, where he has been quite bold, and on reducing substantially the threatened tax under the climate change levy, so the steel companies should be a lot happier. I ask a question about both issues and get a very friendly reply and dash off to do a quick press release.

Francis Maude, poor, poor man, gets up and is utterly lost. His voice is thin, he has a complete inability to bite or get a hold of Gordon and everybody just keeps shouting Portillo at him. The entire Conservative front bench look miserable as Gordon announces a great Budget for enterprise, otherwise known as capitalism. It's very much an orientation towards the United States. Supply-side trickle-down economics with a more active engagement at the labour market end than is the norm in America but the state steadily shrinks and as the rich get richer, by some miracle the poor are meant to get less poor. We'll see.

WEDNESDAY 10 NOVEMBER 1999

In the afternoon Prime Minister's Question Time starts off well for Hague when he says, 'On Monday, you went to Paris and gave the French the Third Way and today they give you the two fingers.' It is a good line and the House knows it. I stand at the bar beside Charles Clarke as Charles Kennedy gets up to speak. He has a soft unimpressive voice nagging away about tax breaks for the rich while the disabled face cuts. Clarke turns to me and says, 'He's not doing it at all. He's turned out to be very disappointing.' But although Tony slaps Kennedy down, I later hear Kennedy on radio and he comes over as a voice of quiet reason, gently but emphatically making his point in contrast to the scorn and shouting of Blair and Hague. The audience in Parliament counts for nothing. A Liberal leader will never hack it in the Commons, but Kennedy may be getting through to a wider public.

Back in the Commons, it's all over for hereditary peers. The key amendment on the Lords, which is to allow the ninety-two hereditary peers who remain as quasi life peers, is actually supported by most of the Conservatives. In the division lobby, Michael Ancram takes my arm:

This bill is designed for me. When my father dies, I can be the Marquess of Lothian MP. The first one to benefit will be Douglas Hogg, who won't have to give up his seat. We're going to go right back to the nineteenth century and have plenty of earls and viscounts in here as MPs.

He is being ironic, but there may be something in what he says. Maybe our aristocracy will resurface as a political elite now using their style and money to command the place that once their great-great-grandfathers had in the Conservative Party. Or will Labour ensure that the first earl MP is actually a Tony crony?

In the Members' Lobby, I see Nick Soames and start to chat to him but he shuts me up saying, 'I don't want to talk to you tonight, Denis. This is sheer bloody vandalism. There are good men up there who are emptying their desks and saying goodbye to Black Rod for the last time. This is a dark, dark day,' and off he sweeps.

I, on the contrary, feel almost more cheerful than I have since I have been an MP. Actually casting a vote to put an end to all of this is just sheer political bliss.

As I walk away down to the cloakroom past the Cabinet ministers' offices, I see that the door to Margaret Beckett's office is open. Leo Beckett spots me and calls me in. Inside there are just a handful of her civil servants and champagne being opened. She herself had stood in front of the tellers' desks in a long red tunic like the proud captain watching her troops finally storm into the citadel and crush the enemy. She has to be given some credit for this. We all drink champagne and I don't quite know why there isn't a huge party of MPs, just little me and her PPS, Ivor Caplin. I bike home happy.

WEDNESDAY 17 NOVEMBER 1999

Up to the ISTC executive council. I make a short speech to everyone's welcome and disappear quickly to go and see Anne McElvoy. She has just had a new baby, Benjamin, and I want to salute him. He is tiny and perfect as all small babies are, with a protruding upper lip just like his father. I lounge around as she deals with the health visitor and her cleaners and a nanny. It is a mocked-up London life based on endless staff. I sit in her bedroom as she feeds the baby and watch the Queen's Speech. It seems dull and incremental without any bill that provides real bite or produces that indrawn breath that you can hear even on television if something strong is said in the speech.

Anne and I have a lunch of a pizza and some very salty salad cooked by her Turkish maid. We talk a lot about foreign policy, as she has to write a *New Statesman* article. I have no doubt it will be a knocking job on Cook. But I just see Cook now as finished. He is on the downhill slopes. Mandelson has got an eye on his job. Anne is doubtful. She obviously isn't sure about Mandelson. 'I don't know. I don't think he is very bright. He has made no difference in Northern Ireland. I think he will implode. There simply isn't anything there.'

I half-listened to all of this without any real interest. Anne adores all this high-level gossip. The who's up and the who's down stuff? I know I should be more interested. She says she is going to some event involving Helena Kennedy, but she doesn't want to. 'But she's a director of *The Independent* and a girl needs all the help she can get to move on in that dreadful paper.' I tell her to praise Helena's choice of faces for the 'Portraits of the Century' exhibition I had seen last night.

'Yes, who did she choose for her portraits?'

'Oh, you know, the usual feminist pictures that they all choose for the twentieth century. I am sure you can waffle your way round it if you see her and she'll be so flattered that you went to see her choice,' I said.

How I wish I could liberate myself of this cynicism, but it is there as corrosive now as it was when I was in the lower sixth.

I get a taxi back to the Commons and watch the Queen's Speech exchange on television.

Jack Cunningham makes the veterans' speech, moving the humble address. It is competent and has an early impact because of its shock effect. Here was a great Cabinet minister and figure in the party now brutally dismissed by Blair and given this sop. He made a joke on it to begin with but then drifted off into bathos about his constituency and I stopped listening.

William Hague made, in terms of sheer wit, his funniest ever Commons speech. It was a tour de force. He laid into Blair on the complete shambles of choosing a London mayor, saying that Blair could have both his 'day mayor' (Frank Dobson) and his 'night mayor' (Ken Livingstone). On and on went the jokes, including some vicious ones about Prescott which made Blair burst out giggling. And yet there was simply nothing in Hague's speech. A momentary presence in the Chamber and for those like me watching on television, you could enjoy it all. But to the outside public whose impressions are defined by an odd set of icons and signals, it would have been rubbish from this weirdly shaven-headed man.

Blair responded with a dull drone of a speech. He simply isn't a natural Commons performer. But he had the most effective argument of all that one can deploy at the despatch box. Success, success, success. Success in what he had achieved so far. Success in his mastery of his party and of politics. Success in arguments and statistics that were heavier than those of Hague. He rather pathetically turned to the Labour backbenchers to get them all cheering like in a pantomime on his side, but it was not worth lowering his dignity. The facts for the moment are with him and not with Hague and that's an end of it.

I chatted at a dinner for the ISTC steel union to Keith Bill, the union media fixer who was sitting beside me, who said, 'The asking rate for a peerage is about £300,000. I was present when one of the two officers – I won't tell you which ones – handed over £250,000 for Tony's blind trust.' I don't bother to probe him. The unions have always provided lots of money to the Labour Party or to key

Labour chieftains to help them run their offices, but the arrival of all these peerages and the handing over of lots of cash leaves one with a rather sick taste.

FRIDAY 26 NOVEMBER 1999

Nigel Sheinwald, the chief Europe man in the Foreign Office, had produced his own paper. There were just the usual neo-liberal economic bullet points – more market opening, more flexibility, more entrepreneurship, more e-commerce and a rubbishing of social values. Culture wasn't even mentioned. I thought it was completely dismal, but I assume it's just a tactic to put in a crap paper now and then to come back with something much more sprightly at the next meeting. I hope so anyway. I have the feeling that Vaz just isn't interested in the intellectual to-ing and fro-ing. At the end of each meeting, he always asks for a 'timetable', as if that gives them structure and leadership. But he knows that all this will be decided in No. 10 and his group is simply footling around.

Over to the House, which was completely empty, for a Friday debate on arts and culture. I would have taken part and given some real thought to it all, but I just am snowed under with work I must do and am late with.

I bump into Ed Balls, who congratulates me on having changed government policy on the energy tax. 'I didn't know PPSs were allowed to attack the government so directly, but I hope you're happy.'

I didn't really understand what had provoked all this. When we had been talking about the steel industry and he had said that I had been acting as a lobbyist on behalf of industry, I had snapped at him, 'Now, now, Ed. You're looking for a seat and when you get one you'll realise there's something called constituents who expect you to lobby on their behalf and in Rotherham I've got plenty of steelworkers who didn't like your energy tax.'

'I'm not looking for a seat, Denis,' he said quite firmly. Was this it? Is the great and powerful Ed Balls – ever written about in the newspapers as the Chancellor's right-hand man and the architect of Britain's economic policy – actually miserable because he would always be number two and never be a number one in his own right? Is this what he and Yvette fret about as they pacify their baby during the night, that far from being the rising stars and the future commanding heights of politics, they are condemned always to be captains and colonels because the generals and marshals are so young they will hold all the positions of high command for as long as Labour is likely to stay in power?

WEDNESDAY 1 DECEMBER 1999

A good, hard run around Battersea Park and then I walked the children to their school with Emilie and Benjamin taking it in turns to ride on the bike. Laura said rather pathetically to me this morning, 'Daddy, why do we never see you?' I was away last week and in Rotherham earlier this week and have to go back there again tomorrow and then to Berlin on Monday. Why do my children never see me? It's a killer question and I have no answer.

In the House, Michael Portillo greeted me and I said that I was pleased to see him back in the House and had always enjoyed exchanges with Alan Clark. I then said that I had enjoyed very much the book *Burying Caesar* by Graham Stewart, which had been written in a cottage lent to the author at Saltwood Castle, where Clark lived.

'Yes, I had plenty of time to review books and I like that one. He had the same tutor as me at Cambridge, Maurice Cowling, who believed in the idea of high politics where what counted were the decisions taken by about fifty to 100 key people.'

The Cowling quote is in fact at the beginning of the Stewart book and the idea of politics as a game of personalities desperately matters both to Portillo and to all the Tory right since the huge personality impact of Thatcher. I muttered something about being in the low five thousands as far as influential people were concerned and Portillo had the grace not to demur.

So, no Portillo in the European debate but instead a crotchety, bad-tempered speech from John Maples. Full of smears and no grace notes. He is being pulled harder to the right and has to become more and more aggressive against Cook in order to keep the place which many feel he is simply keeping warm for Portillo.

Archie Norman did the wind-up for the Tories but must be one of the worst speakers in the House. He stutters and repeats words and reads through a script nervously with zero impact or punch. He just can't hack it in the House at all. In contrast, Vaz was rather good with some nice jokes about Archie being his own candidate for enlargement as he now had three jobs – shadow Minister for Europe, chairman of Asda and boss of this new investment fund called 'Knutsford', which has suddenly shot up in value – and then went on to take apart other criticisms or pay compliments to other speeches. It was a completely empty, flat House, but Keith spoke well and he is undoubtedly a good performer.

I wandered into the tea room and sat down with Chris Mullin and we had a bit of a talk. I asked him what it was like being junior transport minister and he said he had just spent three hours working on his box:

I'm not sure I would have taken it on had I known what being a Parliamentary Under-Secretary is like. I told Blair I didn't want it, but he insisted and came back to me again and again with the promise of better things to come. I told him that I would sink without trace and he said, 'Oh no, I won't forget you.' But all I do is accept the speaking engagements of people like Michael Meacher and Gus Macdonald, who I have to stand in for at all their engagements they cancel at the last moment. I got an invite the other day and Michael Meacher's private secretary had written on it: 'This is not very important, let Chris Mullin do it.'

The worst thing is I don't know anything about my brief. I keep having to mug up on incredibly complicated subjects. Even at question time, I have to prepare for all the possible supplementaries. I had John Redwood having a go at me the other day and I didn't know what he was talking about. The Tories started saying, 'Give him some help, give him some help,' but I didn't get any. It's very hard work. I think I'll take it through to the election and that'll be it. I'll come back, start looking for some select committee work again. Being a Parliamentary Under-Secretary just isn't worth it.

Chris asked me about the Foreign Office and said that he assumed Robin would be replaced by Peter Mandelson – again this now-established wisdom that Robin goes and Peter comes. He also asked me if it was true that Robin never had team meetings. I muttered about it being difficult to get ministers together and then lowered my voice as I saw Tony McNulty sitting behind us. He got up and walked away and I said to Chris I didn't want to say anything in front of the Foreign Office whip.

'Oh, is that the man from Harrow? He's a real nark. Nobody likes him.'

I asked him about Beverley Hughes and Chris said that she was very good. I suppose she must be, but she is a complete piece of blank paper as far as I am concerned. He looked rather sad and lonely. His neck seems to have shrunk and got more wrinkled and his collar floats around it as if what he was wearing was of complete indifference, which I guess it always was. I told him I had written an essay on political thrillers where I had been nice about his books and that cheered him up a bit. He thought that Tony would certainly stay for a few more years and then Gordon would take over.

'Otherwise, I think Steve Byers is looking very good. Everybody likes him. His rise has been effortless. He's made no enemies.'

I told him my story that I had been listening to Byers on the radio the other week and thought the voice was that of John Major – classless, accentless, competent but not abrasive.

'Yes, he's never abrasive, but he does get his points across,' said Chris, who is no bad judge of these things.

I got on my bike and cycled home and as I biked past Pimlico School, I saw a familiar bulky figure and focused my eyes and it was Charles Clarke. He was walking with Gisela Stuart, who had her arm firmly through his and was leaning on his shoulder. It was a touching sight to see these overlarge middle-aged politicians linking arms to – what? – let us just say keep warm together as they exchange their politics on a bitter December night.

THURSDAY 2 DECEMBER 1999

Down to the Commons where Ruth Kelly sat in the Strangers' Dining Room with me and asked for my thoughts on how to help the family. She is so serious. I said that one of the best things we could do to help teenage pregnancy was to make available the morning after pill on sale in Boots. She shook her head. 'I don't agree with that.' What she means is that as a staunch Catholic she just doesn't like the idea of contraception for children under sixteen. She'll learn. But on everything else, she seemed to be listening to what I had to say about the family. She asked about the *Daily Mail* article in favour of the family I had written that had provoked Polly Toynbee's ire. I tentatively suggested we might do a book together – but a pamphlet would do. I wonder if we might hack something out. I really like her and she has the future, whereas I just have the present.

I talked to both our ambassadors in Paris and Berlin today. The first one, Michael Jay, to arrange a quick trip to Paris on 13 December to brief journalists about our trade union and social policy in Britain. I don't know why, given how fed up I am, I am continuing to carry the Blair water all over Europe, but there we go. The second conversation was with Paul Lever, the ambassador in Berlin, who won't be there next week for the SPD congress at which I am to be a delegate. But I arrange a car to pick up myself and a Labour International officer. While one is the governing party, one might as well take advantage of the odd perk.

I arrive in Greasbrough in blinding rain, cold, chilly, dark, to help the by-election campaign team. I drive out with Neil Hamilton and with John Healey to pick up people to take them to the polling station at the Old Town Hall in the village centre. There was a good gang of people gathered in Lindsay Johnston's house. Pork pies, chicken legs, plenty of tea and, as the night got colder, a little glass of whisky.

The count was over quickly. The Conservative candidate, Susan

Smith, got just sixty-seven votes. A catastrophe for the Conservatives in William Hague's home ward. His parents had signed the
nomination papers for the Conservative. The Liberal also saw her
vote slump from 253 last May to just ninety-four.

Jubilation all round. Everybody went across the road to the pub
and I bought a round for £25 as we cheerfully celebrated a pretty
good Labour night.

I went home and quickly dashed off a press release hailing not so
much the Labour victory as the terribly bad showing by the Tories
and whizzed it out on the fax machine.

FRIDAY 3 DECEMBER 1999

My press release trick worked. The *Sheffield Star* had on its front
page 'Tory poll catastrophe for Hague' and published my press release almost word for word. It's all about morale, morale, morale,
and we need as much as possible to cheer ourselves up. It really
is quite different from the same period twenty years ago, when
we were losing every council election seat in sight under Jim Callaghan. Blair is popular and, my God, are the Tories just nowhere.

THURSDAY 9 DECEMBER 1999

The French have reimposed their beef ban. *Quels espèces de merde*!
Jospin is doing this for purely internal political reasons, but it is
a massive slap across Blair's face and indeed across my face as
someone who has constantly argued for good cooperation with the
French. How the Tories are gloating with their horrible little right-
wing anti-European friends in the media. God, it is all so utterly,

utterly useless. The Americans, Canadians and Australians – all our English-speaking friends – won't accept any British beef for their own consumers, but all the attention now will be focused on the French. We have mishandled this from top to bottom. The plain fact is that despite our assurances, no one really quite believes that Britain has eradicated BSE because we didn't destroy enough animals. The Scots and the Welsh won't sell beef on the bone and the whole thing stinks but plays right into the hands of the foulest anti-European mood in the country.

SUNDAY 12 DECEMBER 1999

In Paris, it was grey, raining, windy and icy cold. I wandered about looking at shops for a bit and got into a taxi to go to the embassy where I was staying. Christine Ockrent had booked me to go on her Sunday night current affairs programme with François Hollande, the Socialist Party general secretary, to debate about, oh God, beef.

In the studio a very dense make-up – more so than one gets on *Newsnight* – and the rather heavy, brutish, Serge July, the great founding editor of *Libération*, was there and in came Hollande. He was amiability itself and clearly is an exceptionally nice man. He is much shorter than his pictures and has a rounded little stomach and rolls on his heels as he walks. It reminded me slightly of Mitterrand, who was short and had *embonpoint*.

In the programme, we had a good ding-dong for six or seven minutes on beef but neither Hollande nor I got shirty, even if I think I made some pretty good points. But it's all over. The decision has been taken. I tried to get Hollande to agree to see negotiations to get the ban lifted before the French presidency next year, but he ducked his way out of that and I doubt if anything much will happen. Christ, it really is gonna be a problem to solve.

Afterwards we had champagne and a glass of wine and he gave me a lift back to the rue du Faubourg Saint-Honoré.

'Tony isn't really very cross with us, is he?' he said.

I repeated as clearly as I could that it really was a huge problem and the beef ban had been marvellous ammunition for the anti-European right in Britain. I kept nagging him on it while trying to be as positive as possible, since he is in the modernising and re-formist grouping of key European leaders. But I think despite his smiles and gentleness, it will come to nothing.

I hadn't eaten anything other than bad food all day and went off looking for a couscous. A waste of time. I settled for six oysters and a delicious onion soup with a heavy cheese and bread topping. Perfectly adequate and perfectly self-indulgent. At the embassy, I found myself in the Soames Room. All the rooms on that floor seemed to be named after ambassadors and this was a huge room with two large beds in it side by side and the usual immaculate selection of fruit, drinks and bits and pieces that make staying at that embassy a wonderful treat. The only drink was a rather sweet sherry, but water was all I wanted.

MONDAY 13 DECEMBER 1999

Up to some fruit and a good shower and breakfast with Michael Jay. We talked about the continuing anti-European poison in British politics and I said that I thought it had started with Jacques Delors's speech at the TUC in 1988. I noted:

If only Margaret Thatcher had embraced Delors's speech and said it was exactly along the lines of her policy and her thinking on the need for responsible trade unions, then the TUC and the Labour Party would have been snookered, but because she attacked him so violently, they suddenly decided that Europe had all the merit because Europe was hostile to Thatcherism.

I asked Michael about his role in securing the opt-out for the Social Chapter at Maastricht, which further tightened the screw between the Conservatives as anti-Europeans and Labour who could be supporters of the European ideal. Jay said that Major had no idea what to do about getting out of the Social Chapter obligation but clearly didn't want to sign up for it.

'Well, if a Prime Minister doesn't want to do something, then it's our job to help him not to do it, so we went off and came up with the idea of the opt-out,' said Jay. However, he revealed that Major's famous phrase that he had come back from Maastricht having won 'game, set and match' over the Europeans hadn't been said by Major at all.

'It came out in some briefing at 3 a.m. but was never Major's phrase and Major never said it, but it was always hung round his neck. It's just like Douglas Hurd, who never said that Britain was "punching above her weight". I was astonished as I had always assumed that was a pure Hurdism. 'No, no. He hated the phrase and it really wasn't him at all.'

A bit like 'ethical foreign policy', which Robin Cook never actually said but has been forever hung round his neck.

To *Le Monde* to talk to Henri de Bresson. He is their foreign pages European political editor. Professorial in a ramshackle way. We have a very good talk about what is happening and he takes plenty of notes about my argument that Britain has got a coherent and justifiable social policy as part of the new Labour government's approach. Of course, as I hear myself talking, I feel split down the middle. Part of me loves the idea that finally my party, to which I have always belonged and which has always been the governmental carrier of my hopes, even if its personalities and policies can be oh so tedious, is now definitively in power and is behaving as if it wants to stay in power. On the other hand, its radicalism is that of a snail's approach to making a journey. I wish it was between the tortoise and the hare, but I have never known a snail to get from A to B.

Anyway, it is good simply to be in the heart of the French media establishment and to have a chance to talk.

Then on to *Libération*. Its modernist building in an old internal car park allows a view from its top floor which is quite magnificent over all of Paris. My friend François Serjeant is there, but I am interviewed by two of his colleagues who aren't really interested in the social policy stuff I have come to sell but instead press me endlessly on British beef. I give them a few lines. A woman fusses endlessly, taking a picture, but when it is published I just look like a bald frog. Actually, as far as I recall, frogs don't have any hair.

We rush on to the Gare du Nord to get the train to Brussels. I buy a couple of sandwiches but on the train find a delicious lunch is served. Of course, the journey is between France and Belgium, so there are no border controls. What a difference it all makes.

I called round to see John Palmer and his lovely wife who had a smashing new haircut. I adore their art deco flat in the *Square Marie-Louise* and he got out a bottle of champagne to salute an old friend and comrade. First, the Palmer rant about how great Ken Livingstone is and how useless Blair and the Labour Party was and is. I let that wash over me serenely, because the day John stops being a Trot denouncing social democracy is the day he is no longer worth talking to. But he knows so much and his analysis is so shrewd. Give me a journalist that had one hundredth of his engagement as opposed to the cynical tired cliché producers that control most political reporting and commentating in London.

He is particularly scornful of Gordon Brown:

I know where Gordon's problem started. It was the first time that the euro committee was formed. It was agreed that there would be a meeting of Ecofin [the EU Finance Ministers' Council] and then all those who worked in the eurozone would leave and just the eurozone ministers would stay. When it came to that point, the Greek and the Swede and the Dane got up, but Gordon wouldn't budge. Everybody looked at him and at each other and then finally, gently, as he was chairing the meeting, he was told he had to go. He left with great ill grace and has been hostile to the euro ever since.

Si non è vero... But I am sure that Gordon needs psychological interpretation as much as political and policy understanding, and John may well be right.

Only a short stay with him and then the train back to London. As I settled into my seat, Peter Riddell, the political commentator for *The Times*, appeared and we spent the rest of the journey together.

He settled into the quiet gossip about Westminster. 'Robin Cook is nearly finished. I have never seen a reputation eclipse so quickly.

Who would have thought he would have been so low in the parliamentary stakes so quickly.'

I demurred, advancing my usual pro-Robin arguments, but Peter obviously has consigned him to a political past and waits for his friend Mandelson to become Foreign Secretary.

He agreed with me that the Cabinet that met on Thursday had no real power and that the real shadow Cabinet consisted of people like Charlie Falconer, Philip Gould, Lord Michael Levy, David Simon and, of course, Jonathan Powell and Alastair Campbell. Peter is always flattering about Charles Clarke and Patricia Hewitt, but, of course, he loves high civil servants. Both Patricia and Charles are the children of senior mandarins and have inherited from their fathers that rather urbane judgemental search for a middle way which marks a good civil servant but is not the sign of a great politician.

Peter has been at the centre of things for a number of years. He told a lovely story about being with Margaret Thatcher at a Camp David gathering with George Bush. Thatcher made a complete fool of herself denouncing Europe and drunkenly waffling on about the English-speaking world. She was taken away and then Douglas Hurd had to get up and, without in any way being disloyal, was quite masterful in restoring the view that the leadership of the United Kingdom had sensible views to put to the President and his top advisers. She clearly was quite batty before she even left office.

TUESDAY 14 DECEMBER 1999

To the Foreign Office for a meeting that John Kerr had set up for Robin Cook's private office of high-flying officials who form his personal secretariat to talk to the MP PPSs about how to make more time for their ministers to carry out parliamentary and political duties. The shock comes from Sherard Cowper-Coles, who says that the real problem is Gaynor:

> She is very insistent that Robin is at home in the evenings and available for the weekends. She doesn't want to travel with him or accompany him anywhere. He is very conscious that it's a new marriage and really enjoys it, but all the time when we suggest things, he just looks up and says he can't do it because he has to be with Gaynor and she doesn't want to share him with anybody else.

I really thought it was a bit off for Robin's private secretary to put what was more or less known information on the public record in front of (a) MPs, including Tony McNulty who will take it straight back to Ann Taylor and the Whips' Office, and (b) all the little dips from the other private offices who run Whitehall's best gossip network.

I made my own blunder by reporting what Peter Riddell had told me last night that Robin's stock is very low in Parliament and needs to be raised.

Outside the meeting, John Williams, the ex-*Mirror* political editor who is a FCO press guy, comes up with a frown on his face. 'For God's sake, I hope nobody repeats what Sherard has just said. I'm waiting for the "Gaynor is a dampener on Robin's work" to hit the newspapers. He really shouldn't have said it. Can you have a word with him?'

I tell Sherard not to talk publicly about the problems with Gaynor and he asked me who had been the correspondent I had quoted as saying Robin was on the way out and I told him Peter Riddell. 'Yes, I thought it was. I like him very much. He is a good man.'

My heart sank as I realised Sherard would repeat this back to Robin and who else besides? Damn. Will I ever learn to button my lip?

Later Robin came over with a smile-snarl on his face. 'So Peter Riddell tells you that I'm finished in Parliament, does he, Denis?' His tone is menacing, but I am not going to be browbeaten.

'He said that your standing had been very high before the election and now you weren't seen there and not making an impact, Robin.'

'You mean Peter Riddell doesn't see me there. I do more time in Parliament than I ever did before – committees, statements, questions, debates.'

'Yes, you're there a lot, Robin, but you're not seen. You know the difference. If you don't want me to tell you what people say, I won't, but we need to do something to get your stock up.'

He looked more and more bitter and grumpy, but he knew I was telling the truth, not that there is any thanks for the bearer of bad tidings.

'Look, I'm gonna spend the next four days out of the country. That's my job, to be travelling. To meet people...' he whined.

I interrupted him:

I know all that, Robin, but we're now on the downhill slope to the election and the next government. I want you to stay here, but you've got to recreate a political base. There's a new parliament and a new party. They don't know the old Robin Cook. You've got to get out there and re-establish a domestic political base.

'I can't do that. I don't have any time.'

I exploded. 'Make time. Do some speeches on domestic things...'

He cut into me. 'I can't do that, that's all Blair's territory. That won't work. I can't go off the Tony Blair line. It would be impossible.'

I realised just how much he had to look over his shoulder all the time at Blair.

'Just put the Third Way into the speech and say you're extending Third Way ideas and thinking and he'll be all right,' I said rather breezily.

The snarl returned to his face. 'I can't do that, Denis. I just can't go off what Blair wants. I'm trying to do my best.'

Again I hit him:

Look, I bought Cook shares a long time ago and I don't want to see them lose any more value. If you don't want to hear it from me, fine. There's no team work here. There's no sense of people grouped around you. You've got to start working in a different way if you want to survive.

He looked more and more bad tempered, but already by this stage one of his assistant private secretaries, Andrew, had come over to tell him he had to get a plane to disappear to somewhere in Europe and he just looked at me with one final look of hate and disappeared into the crowd to do his official business.

I looked at the crowd. Not one of them was going to act on Robin's behalf behind his back. A handful close to his office would be loyal and report that he was – as he is – a good negotiator, but this was the London conservative establishment par excellence and they were just panting to have a right-wing admirer of the City and the Thatcherite capitalist system from which they had done so well and which was making my country poorer and progressively less important in the world. Why the hell wasn't Robin with his own people? What was he doing spending all his time hoping that sucking up to these turds would make any difference?

SATURDAY 18 DECEMBER 1999

The big story is about Shaun Woodward defecting to us. I don't really know him. Apparently, he is very pro-European, which is a surprise to me. He read out a long speech in support of reducing the age of consent from eighteen to sixteen in the debate a few months ago. He started off by quoting Oscar Wilde very pompously and then read out his speech, which was very much a written affair, in a slightly mannered way. Otherwise I just see him patrolling around the corridors looking slightly self-satisfied and slightly self-important. He wears very expensive clothes because he married a Sainsbury heiress who is frightfully rich and now he can live in a grand Tory manner.

His defection is a blow, a huge blow, to William Hague, but somehow I am a bit uneasy. I wish we could have some poor people who decided to join New Labour, not all these rich celebs just throwing in their lot with whoever is in charge.

We had the Rotherham Labour executive round for drinks tonight, which was a friendly enough affair, though not everybody turned up. I must plan these things earlier and give more adequate notice. But for the size of the house, it was a good crowd. People weren't delighted with the Woodward defection. It's all a big London clatter and chatter and doesn't affect people at the base in Rotherham.

MONDAY 20 DECEMBER 1999

In the evening, dinner with Marius and Spiv Barron – friends since we were at Oxford – and Sophia Lambert, a senior official at the Department for Transport (DETR). She said Chris Mullin was turning out to be hopeless as a minister there. 'He doesn't focus. He lets everything go over his desk and just agrees with what civil servants want. Civil servants love somebody who just wants to do two or three things. A Parliamentary Under-Secretary can get things done if he just decides to focus,' said this most senior of senior civil servants at the DETR. It was an interesting bit of advice and if ever I get a job, I shall appoint her my private personal adviser on how to handle the civil service.

WEDNESDAY 29 DECEMBER 1999

In Davos for the parliamentary ski races with Swiss parliamentarians. Jonathan Powell and I go skiing together in fairly bad weather today. He and Sarah Helm have come with their two little children, but to my amazement Davos seems incapable of finding them a decent babysitter and there doesn't seem to be any kind of kindergarten or crèche organised in the town for children under the age of three.

We have a chat about my constituency and Jonathan explains why Kevin Barron, the neighbouring MP in Rother Valley since 1983, did not get a ministerial job. 'He is a super loyalist, but he just wasn't going to go very far and so we couldn't give him a job.'

I always feel Kevin has never much enjoyed my arrival in his home town and me getting loads more publicity and making a bigger splash. I'm sure he would love to see me leave politics and then he would have the profile he thinks he merits. 'John Prescott is nagging us to put Rosie Winterton on the Intelligence Committee,' Jonathan continued. 'Tom King [the Thatcher-era Defence Secretary who chairs it] will have a fit, but we never give John anything so King will just have to put up with it.'

I said that ministers came and went and spent all their time looking over their shoulder waiting to be fired. I mentioned Joyce Quin's misery when she was sacked last summer.

'Yes, she always looks at me with real hate and won't talk to me, as if I was responsible, but I wasn't,' insisted Jonathan:

> She just wasn't making it in the European job. She can stay a minister as long as she likes. Doug Henderson was only given the job because Gordon Brown played games at the beginning of the government. He should really have gone after the first year. Tony Lloyd had a very grumpy interview with Tony and protested at being fired.

FRIDAY 31 DECEMBER 1999

The last day of the year, the century and the millennium, though apparently a hundred years ago the new century was not thought to begin until 1 January 1901. Who cares? I have lived through half of this century and it has been for my generation a most wonderful time. Lucky enough to be born in a rich country with our health and our education and at least in my youth our chances for jobs and a career guaranteed. We have all been given the possibility of building a home and making a family and living in an open democratic world full of travel and surprises. That we have wasted or been unable to use so many of these opportunities is something I think future historians will judge us harshly over. But there have been magical moments like the end of communism and I think of my poor father who died in exile because his land was not free. Now it is. And the end of apartheid in South Africa, which began when I was born and ended when I was forty. I had a chance to play a small spear-carrier's role in both those great movements of history. And then to be a Labour MP at the moment of the greatest electoral triumph in the party's history. I have a family, which every day fills me with awe at the richness of their existence, and I have still, I think, with all the frustrations and unfulfilled ambitions, one of the best jobs that anybody in my country can ever have.

2000

SATURDAY 1 JANUARY 2000

If anyone can define a better way of spending a New Year's Day than skiing on fresh snow under the brilliant sun of the Swiss Alps, I'd like to know what it is. A glorious day's skiing.

In the evening, dinner with Ralf Dahrendorf and his wife, Ellen. The great German professor and lord and sociologist is staying in Davos at a house they have borrowed from a musician from whom they rent in the summer but who is away this year and lent them his house for the New Year. Dahrendorf, as always, is deeply intelligent, sceptical, liberal and open. Jonathan Powell cross-questions him all the time about what Blair is achieving. Dahrendorf obviously thinks not very much.

At the end of the dinner, Jonathan looks across at him and asks if it does make sense to define the twentieth century as the Tory century because the progressive forces – i.e. the Liberals and the Labour Party – had split at the beginning of the century. This is an Andrew Adonis thesis, which lies at the heart of a lot of the historical underpinning of the Third Way.

'No. That is complete nonsense,' replied Dahrendorf:

The Labour Party was set up as other social-democratic and socialist parties were set up, to respond to clear material needs which liberal parties denied existed. They were formed in opposition to the fact that the liberal parties were allied with the Conservatives. The parties of the left at the beginning of the century represented a real material interest. It wasn't an artificial split. In any case, it hasn't been a Conservative century. The welfare state has been introduced and a lot of the things that the parties of the left called for have been achieved.

Dahrendorf's rigorous dismissal of a core element of the No. 10 history line dismayed Jonathan, but he had no real answer to the uncompromising analysis of the famous German professor. Dahrendorf asked if a coalition with the Lib Dems would be possible in the future. 'Maybe after the next election, or the election after that when we have a majority of just one,' replied Jonathan.

I said the difficulty with that would be that forty or fifty Labour MPs would be voting against the government, since in the north the Lib Dems were now the real enemy and had replaced the Conservatives. Dahrendorf nodded vigorously at this and I caught a flicker of dismay in Jonathan's eyes as part of some huge strategy seemed to be put into question by the reality of local politics.

Dahrendorf asked him about the chances of a coalition. Jonathan was dismissive of the account that appeared in the press based on Paddy Ashdown's diary that two Cabinet posts had been offered to Liberal Democrat MPs. 'I was there. I was at all those meetings. Tony made no such pledge. Paddy simply over-read the signals and allusions that Tony was making, but there was absolutely no commitment given. Paddy's diaries are completely wrong.'

'Yes,' said Dahrendorf. 'The distance between memory and history is enormous. Even if you write down what you think was said and what you think you have heard straight away, it is only memory. History has to sift other sources to find out what really happened.'

So much for my hopes that these diaries might be a footnote to history.

WEDNESDAY 12 JANUARY 2000

A talk with Ken Purchase today in Robin's large but somehow depressingly scruffy and unused room in the House of Commons. So many Foreign Secretaries will have sat in this room, taking so many decisions over the century or longer. And yet, it is like a second-rate university gothic-style common room or perhaps a waiting room at Edinburgh Railway Station thirty or forty years ago. The furniture is all heavy, pictures lie against the wall and there are dirty glasses and coffee cups. Ken is miserable:

> I am fed up being his PPS. I don't see any point in me going on. It's useless talking to Robin. He is incapable of working with a team. He now seems to have fallen in love with Caroline Flint, as he gets excited at everything she says. I am simply wasting my time. Robin is finished. He won't survive the next election. Oh, I know he has to stay in the Cabinet. He really needs the money with his outgoings. But he will just do whatever Blair tells him.

Poor Ken. He is the salt of the old Midlands industrial working class. Aged sixty, he must have thought he would help to contribute to make this a transformational government. Instead it is a principally transactional government, managing brilliantly, achieving significant progress in areas like Northern Ireland and the House of Lords but on the core issues that matter to Ken and his world values – jobs, public services, health, making his community seem fairer – not much is really moving.

I went for a haircut and afterwards popped into the Chamber where Geoff Hoon was doing a statement on allowing gay personnel in the armed services. There wasn't really much of a fight on this. Some filthy reactionary prejudiced Tories stood up and warbled away, making themselves look foolish and managing to alienate every single gay person in the country. How idiotic and pathetic they are. The armed services will adjust to this as they adjust to every change of society and aim off, as it were, without losing their main *raison d'être*. In a wonderful Freudian slip, Geoff turned to Michael Lord, the Deputy Speaker, and referred to him as 'Madam Speaker', which brought the House down. He is feeling his way into his job and I think has got the respect of the Commons as a serious and effective politician.

I then waited for the committee stage of the Representation of the People Bill, which was also about the issue of British citizens living overseas being able to vote. I had caught a bit of this when the committee stage had its first day before Christmas and Gerald Kaufman had made a speech moving an amendment to remove completely the right of UK passport holders overseas to vote.

He continued his interrupted speech and I then got up to have a go at him. I had told him I was going to do this and he had actually fed me a bit of information about some salt-beef sandwich maker in St John's Wood who flew home to Israel to vote, rather proving my point that other countries allowed their overseas citizens to keep the right to vote. I had good stats and I think reasonable arguments that

made a more effective ten-minute speech than my longer one covering a bit more ground on Monday. When I sat down, the notes came
down from the Hansard office above. I had referred to Lord Palmerston's doctrine of '*civis Britannicus sum*' (I am a British citizen from
the Roman '*civis Romanus sum*') adding that when he enunciated it,
he didn't say that the *civis Britannicus* had to live at 24 Park Villas in
St John's Wood (where Kaufman lives). The Hansard query simply
asked for the full quote around the word '*Britannicus*?' That is what
has happened to our teaching of history, that the people upstairs do
not know one of the greatest bits of parliamentary speech-making
and doctrine-announcing in nineteenth-century history. Sad.

SATURDAY 15 JANUARY 2000

To the LSE for a Fabian New Year's conference. I found 600 people
listening to Oona King, Douglas Alexander and Stephen Twigg.
All sounded self-satisfied, rather right-wing, with Douglas bravely
proclaiming that the next government would be 'transformatory
and radical and deal with redistribution', but it will be the first time
in world history that the second term of social democratic government has been more left-wing than its first term.

Just as I took my seat at the edge of the lecture theatre, I heard
Will Hutton, who was chairing the meeting and acting as the question master, announce:

I heard one of our best pro-European MPs on the *Today* programme
utterly unwilling to talk or defend the euro. All he had was the Millbank line. He didn't have the guts to talk honestly about the euro. It
was really shaming. Who is this man? It was Denis MacShane.

Douglas Alexander pointed to me sitting in the audience and said, 'There he is.'

Will gulped a bit and went on with his question-master duties. Afterwards, he came up half apologetically. 'You are one of the best people on Europe we've got. You have been an absolute rock. This is how bad it's become,' he spluttered. I said that there was no point being boxed into a row over the euro at the moment. This was like the calls to open a second front in 1943. I also attacked him, saying that he had left behind on *The Guardian* a whole gang of economics writers who were anti the euro. On *The Observer*, of which he was nominally editor-in-chief, Bill Keegan was hostile to the euro. Ditto on *The Independent*, where the chief columnists were anti the euro. 'We can't make any headway as long as all we get from the left liberal press are diatribes against the euro,' I snarled at him.

'Larry Elliott is a real problem,' he said sheepishly and we left it at that. But I am fed up and the whole European debate is becoming dangerously Majoresque. It was made worse walking to my workshop on foreign policy with Ed Balls. We had the usual friendly chat in which he was contemptuous of Charles Moore and then added, 'Why was Robin Cook giving that stupid interview to *The Spectator*?' Robin is in *The Spectator* saying silly things, but Ed, acting on behalf of Gordon, spends his whole time rubbishing the euro in a naive and juvenile way. I can't be bothered to argue with these kids any more.

WEDNESDAY 19 JANUARY 2000

Down to the Commons where I spot that there is a question to the Prime Minister this afternoon from Julian Lewis on funding for referendum campaigns. I phone up Bruce Grocott in No. 10 and ask him if I can put a counter-question outlining the huge amount of moneys that Paul Sykes and the other anti-Europeans are putting into the 'No' campaign already. He is very cheerful and supportive, slightly to my surprise as I would have thought that Blair perhaps didn't want any mention of Europe at all from his own side.

It's really odd standing up in that bear pit. You don't know quite where your hands are. I noticed yesterday at Foreign Office questions, as Cook turned on Portillo, that his hand was kept rigid along his trouser seams but his fingers were moving furiously, drumming and flicking against themselves as the tension of performing and the terror of making a mistake consumes you.

Yet you have to do it spontaneously, without a note and without it having been an ultra-scripted question, because if you are reading or seem to have over-prepared it loses spontaneity. My final roar about being pro-European and against the isolationist Tories who wanted Britain isolated from Europe got a great shout of approval from behind me and I sat down to cheers all round. It's childish, but it's still a terrific parliamentary thrill to make that kind of impression in the Chamber, and as I left and thereafter, people were patting me on the back.

THURSDAY 20 JANUARY 2000

A beautiful, cold, frosty day. I went out early for a good Battersea Park run. The tide is out and the Thames runs as a thin stream in the middle of the mud banks which catch the boats. The sun coming up over the east of London down river is just like Monet's paintings from a hundred years ago. There are times when London is very beautiful.

At midday I have lunch with a rising Australian MP called Kevin Rudd. He is nice, a Christian, which he proudly confesses, and a former diplomat specialising in China. Obviously very competent and reform orientated. He is part of the team that helped win and then hold Queensland for Labor, so he can't be bad. We have a pretty good talk. He is all for constructive engagement with China and no grandstanding on human rights.

Gordon Brown has pulled out from speaking at a conference on employee share ownership. He is going cool on the whole idea. Damn. The Treasury maggots who hate workers have got to him. All that's left is just managing things to please the City and the M25 region which is powering ahead as a kind of a mini Luxembourg within the whole of the UK while the rest of the nation rots.

TUESDAY 25 JANUARY 2000

A meeting in Keith Vaz's office bringing together all the different ministries on Europe.

As I arrive, Alastair Campbell is waiting in his private secretary's office. He is friendly. We go into Vaz's room and there is a circle of chairs with a large armchair that is clearly reserved for the minister. Alastair plonks himself in it. Keith comes in and finds a hard stool to sit on. It is clear who is boss.

Alastair's line is simple:

Europe is all about positioning ourselves. A debate on the single currency is not very helpful. We have to get out the message that we want Europe to reform itself. We need to stop this domestic media row of Brown v. Cook v. Tony Blair spilling into the foreign media. They mustn't get hold of this.

Robin's aide, David Clark, told me he and Andy Hood were called in to see Alastair and told firmly 'to get all that European crap out of Robin's speeches'. Alastair has a house in France, has some German and to hear of him ranting away like a little Europhobe is sad.

THURSDAY 27 JANUARY 2000

I bumped into Dennis Skinner walking rather stiffly across the Members' Lobby and asked him how he was.

He replied in a subdued voice:

I'm OK. They took a tumour out, but they say there's nothing else linked to it. The surgeon said he had a good look at my prostate and there was nothing on it. I had been passing blood, so I was very worried. But I think it'll be OK. I have to go back for tests in five weeks and we'll see.

I really like him. When he goes, the loudmouths who want to take over his mantle as the conscience of the left – like Andrew MacKinlay and one or two others – won't in any way be able to replace his working-class authenticity and his deep education and sense of what's right and what's wrong. Damn. Why do the best people get taken out?

TUESDAY 1 FEBRUARY 2000

Portillo is back on the Tory front bench. He replaces Francis Maude who becomes shadow Foreign Secretary. And the biggest bombshell of all – John Redwood is dismissed to the back benches.

Getting rid of Redwood, or 'Deadwood' as Nick Soames calls him, is odd. He is one of their hardest-working parliamentarians. He has got the scalp of Geoffrey Robinson and Lord Sainsbury on his belt and has caused trouble over punches. I can only assume that Hague wants to create a hard-right, anti-European wing which will be headed by Redwood, and so he can say that he has a right wing and a Europhile left wing grouped around Ken Clarke and David Curry and he is firmly in the middle with Portillo and Maude. At any event, it opens up politics in an exciting way.

THURSDAY 3 FEBRUARY 2000

To the Commons for the first outing by Michael Portillo as shadow Chancellor. It is electric. This is parliamentary passion at a very high-octane rating. Brown and Portillo clash in a way that Hague and Blair can't manage. Portillo announces that the Tories will drop their opposition to the minimum wage and independence for the Bank of England's Monetary Policy Committee. We wave our order papers and cheer. Brown has dug up horrible things that Portillo did as Chief Secretary – putting VAT on fuel, raising taxes and all the other sins that we like to accuse him of.

Brown is magnificent and I think outpoints Portillo, but Portillo is a star as well. I got up on the second question and asked about Objective One, EU funding for South Yorkshire, saying that there shouldn't be any 'departmentalitis'. I got in good digs at Portillo, but Andrew Smith got very shirty, saying that there was no 'departmentalitis'. It was great to be there on such a stunning occasion. There was an electric current between Brown and Portillo. They are made for each other. They are wedded to high politics, they are natural plotters, they are good speakers, though Brown is much wittier and technically a better orator, they love power and they love playing with power.

SATURDAY 5 FEBRUARY 2000

An ISTC steel union meeting at 6 p.m. John Healey turned up and I left it to him to make the MP's report. Afterwards we had a pint. He is Gordon's PPS and I told him how good I thought the clash between Brown and Portillo had been on Thursday.

John said:

> Yes, it was absolutely amazing. The moment Portillo was announced as shadow Chancellor, Gordon dropped everything and spent every waking hour going through everything he had said. He assembled everything. He got it all into order and then threw away what wasn't necessary. He spent forty-eight hours preparing for question time.

I told him the effort had been worth it because Brown had raised his game faced with real challenge, and his mastery of Parliament was central to his mastery of both the Treasury and the party and the country.

John agreed: 'Especially if you compare him with Alistair Darling, who spends about half an hour getting ready for his questions and it really shows.'

SATURDAY 12 FEBRUARY 2000

A long day preparing for our party and then a sleep from 4 p.m. to 5 left me in a good mood for the whole of the evening. It was a joy to see lots and lots of friends. The chief of staff of the Prime Minister and the private secretary to the Queen as well as Patricia Hewitt and one or two other ministers were there. When Roger Alton came in, having just published my article on the marathon in *The Observer*, I felt pleased with myself even though I had hardly a chance to talk as I was opening the door endlessly or rushing around pouring drinks. Well, I like being a host and it was just good to repay a lot of hospitality and maintain a network of friends, which, whatever happens, is still very important to have.

SUNDAY 20 FEBRUARY 2000

Ken Livingstone has been defeated as Labour candidate to be Mayor of London. It was a fix for Frank Dobson, but Frank is a wounded bird and won't win the mayoralty. It all seems to have been handled incredibly badly. We have got the administrative set-up for devolution right but nobody thought about the politics of it. Livingstone actually hates social democracy, but he is a primal force in politics and one of the best communicators in the land. We are right to stop him running, but surely a better way could have been found. Blair actually doesn't like the mess of politics. Someone has always done his dirty work for him as he has risen effortlessly up to the top spot. But politics is a continual process of selecting, selecting, selecting and getting your people into the right place at the right time, and they certainly haven't done this in London.

FRIDAY 25 FEBRUARY 2000

Just after 9 a.m. a BBC Radio Sheffield discussion, with Tony Benn before me. He is appalling. He denounces the Labour Party as 'the New Labour Party which Tony Blair has created' and is distinct from the Labour Party to which he belongs. It is smug, ahistorical, complacent and full of an upper-class arrogance which I find despicable. I have quite a sharp go after him, pointing out that he had served *in* a government which had arrested journalists for telling the truth, allowed the IMF to run our economy, seen unemployment double and inequalities increase. I really was quite angry and I don't know if it sounded that good.

FRIDAY 3 MARCH 2000

At lunchtime I sit with Jeremy Corbyn, who is nice about a short intervention I made on Chile yesterday. When he is proved right, he deserves great honour and he has been resolute on the evil of Pinochet all his life. I admire his inflexibility and wish at times I might take up unpopular causes the way he does. Yet he is my age and has broken up from his wife and I really couldn't bear that at all. A life without family is no life.

TUESDAY 7 MARCH 2000

To Robin Janvrin's for a little dinner party with Jim Naughtie and the new German ambassador. Staff from the palace were there to act as butler and cook and the dinner was based on each course being served on a plate and that was all you got.

The main course was a heap of mashed potato with a bit of veal in a mushroom sauce. Although I thought for Lent I would give up drinking, the palace champagne and the claret were too tempting.

Robin talked a lot about the Commonwealth and clearly that plays large in their thinking.

'Our problem is it's now becoming an old monarchy. But if William grows into a nice young man, he will provide a new continuation,' he said.

Interesting that he simply didn't mention Charles, who doesn't feature, at least in this conversation. William is the key to it all, but how on earth do they stop him being a normal young man, keen on sex, drugs and rock 'n' roll?

WEDNESDAY 22 MARCH 2000

In the afternoon I drove up to Oxford to go to Keble College for the Königswinter conference. I don't think I had ever set foot in Keble during my three years at Oxford. It was a lost red-brick nineteenth-century Anglican monstrosity and I can't actually think of anybody I know now or knew then who was at the college. But as usual I was wrong. Once inside, it was the most beautiful red-brick Gothic architecture with large quads and a stunning chapel and a sense of space and calm which I found more pleasing than the rather more miniature quads and greens of the Oxford colleges I know better. My room had a shower in it, which was a revolution for an English university, and we had jolly good drinks and dinner before going off to sleep.

FRIDAY 24 MARCH 2000

Up early and I bought all the papers and saw *The Times*' business section had run my article on flexible labour markets, which will promote the Fabian pamphlet I have written. It actually reads quite well, though I don't know who gets as far as *The Times'* business news to read comment pieces.

Breakfast was in the hall. A great plate of thick bacon and eggs. A real throwback to thirty-odd years ago. Nothing has changed in the great greasy British breakfast served to students everywhere. We met in a nice seminar room under the chairmanship of a retired German diplomat, who had to add a speech to everybody else's contribution. The discussion was on the enlargement of the EU. Everybody had a word but nobody had an idea except that it was a good thing but nothing might change though nothing could stay the same.

Ken Clarke was there in a kind of Tory dress-down weekend gear of sports jacket and red woollen shirt. He is very fat close up. He waffled about the World Trade Organization and complained about Blair's lack of leadership on the euro. He really has a bloody cheek as his economic stewardship and failure to stand up to the anti-Europeans has left us with a pound in particular and an economy in general that is diverging all the time from Europe and a culture of such relentless hostility on European issues that is difficult to move.

At lunch George Weidenfeld grabbed me and said, 'Denis, I want you to come to Istanbul for my next "Club of Three" meeting.'

I didn't know what he was talking about, but he was very insistent and he is the world's greatest networker so I said yes.

MONDAY 3 APRIL 2000

John Healey and I had had a friendly talk on the train down to London from Doncaster. Jackie, his wife, has been fired by the Labour Party. Out of sight, out of mind. 'They are in real financial trouble,' he said. I guess she will become an MP's professional wife assistant now.

They are a lovely couple. As always, we skirt round the big issues. He won't say anything about Brown and I don't want to say anything to him and he in turn feigns or appears to feign ignorance on European and international matters, so I say as little as possible about Robin and the FCO. So much for joined-up PPS work.

TUESDAY 4 APRIL 2000

To the Swiss Embassy for a lunch for the President of Switzerland, Adolf Ogi, who I made friends with in Davos at the UK–Swiss MPs' ski week. I arrived just as everybody was sitting down and found myself next to a vice admiral who was the chief of naval intelligence and next to him, Prince Andrew. He came over as a perfectly reasonable and friendly sort with beautifully manicured nails. He and I were the only ones at the lunch table who drank water. He said that Prince Charles was flying to Switzerland tomorrow with his two boys. 'It's only the second time he has taken a commercial flight and he phoned me up to ask how you do it. The last time he flew with BA, he took so many pieces of luggage there wasn't room for them all in the hold.'

According to Andrew, this turn to using the same aeroplanes as everyone else has been forced on the royal family by new accounting rules brought in by the Ministry of Defence acting on behalf of the Treasury.

He continued:

We now have to pay full fixed costs, like a share of the cost of running the airfield, and it's all become very expensive. I took a plane the other month to the West Indies. I needed it, as I had to do a number of islands in a week or so. But there were nine members of crew on the plane. I could have leased one far more cheaply. The Queen has gone and bought her own helicopter and she likes it so much that she goes everywhere in it and she wants now to buy a second one.

WEDNESDAY 5 APRIL 2000

Jonathan Powell told me that Blair had been full of praise saying, 'Denis knows everybody in our sister parties. He has to be put in charge of contacts. He's the only one.' I also got a nice letter from Blair after I had written congratulating him on his performance with Schröder at Oxford. In his reply, he wrote:

Thank you for your very kind letter; but more, thank you once again for all the great work you do in Europe. Everywhere I go, people tell me how impressed they are with you, it really is a great help to the government and the party.

Yours ever,

Tony.

We'll see where all that leads.

At 5.30 p.m. I go up to hear John Lloyd talking about his new pamphlet on Russia. The star turn was a great brute of a man who is the new Russian ambassador who listened patiently to Keith Vaz's finger-wagging homily and then got up to say, 'As far as Chechnya is concerned, the new President has made clear that he will annihilate these bandits!' So that's that. Annihilate. A good Russian word. Oddly enough, he described Putin as a 'workaholic'. That's an unusual description by an ambassador for his new President and I think a rather frightening one. The last workaholic leader of Russia was Stalin.

SUNDAY 16 APRIL 2000

Marathon day today. I have a column in *The Observer* about it. Out of bed at 6.30 a.m., a taxi to pick up my brother Martin's friend in Sloane Square and on to Charing Cross. We arrive at Blackheath and there is just such a crowd that already you know it's going to carry you along. I want to pee, two, three, four times before the race starts. Although the starting gun goes at 9.30, I am at the back of the 30,000 runners so I don't cross the starting line until about 9.50. And then it's on and on and on. Everywhere there are crowds who cheer you and clap you. There are bands left and right. Every mile or so or even less, there are great trestle tables full of mineral water or the kind of orange drinks that are meant to give you extra energy.

I pace myself, very quietly, just focusing on a pretty woman in front of me and running gently behind until the time comes to overtake and I find another one. I do a mile every ten minutes. The worse moment is going over Tower Bridge and turning right and you realise you've only done halfway. The marathon winds endlessly through Canary Wharf. But already the people who are running fast are coming back on the other side. You have done thirteen miles when the sign shows they have done twenty-two. Your heart sinks, but you just keep plodding forwards. The crowds see your name on the T-shirt and shout 'Come on, Denis!' and that is enough to keep you going until the next cheer of encouragement. I just kept padding forward doing a pretty steady mile in ten minutes so it was six miles an hour, twelve miles in two hours, eighteen miles in three hours and so on.

The crowds get bigger and bigger as you run through the City and along the Victoria Embankment. There were three shower tents you could go through which I ran through just for the sake of the change. Finally, you're on Victoria Embankment and never was I so happy to see the Houses of Parliament, which meant I was nearly there. Up Birdcage Walk and I tried to run a bit faster to show off to the crowds. I was in the middle of a big gang so I didn't feel in any way like a straggler, and then the final shove to get across the line in four hours twenty-nine minutes? I had done it. Never, I think, again. And yet, Martin and Linda were full of praise, full of flattery about how I'd lost weight and was looking younger and fitter. Is this the price you must pay to edge into your older years?

WEDNESDAY 26 APRIL 2000

I meet two gentlemen from the Heritage Foundation in Washington.

Their thesis is that the European defence initiative should be supported in exchange for Europe spending more on defence in order to lift some of the burden from the United States. They go through the arguments which are well known and which revolve principally around the fact that Germany only spends 1.5 per cent of its GDP on defence compared to just under 3 per cent by France and Britain. 'We are not isolationist. We do not want to withdraw from Europe. But it will become increasingly difficult to justify in Congress the American commitment to Europe if the Europeans don't do anything to help themselves,' says Dr Kim Holmes, the director of the Heritage Foundation.

I point out that while the theory is good there were problems in seeing Germany become again a massive military power on the

Continent. If Germany spent 3 per cent of its GDP on defence, it could double the size of its army, get a real blue-water fleet and then if you are a real military power why on earth do you not have nuclear weapons which are the badge of global political puissance?

A very odd business today. Someone from the Rotherham Council Housing Department phoned up about a man who claimed to be called Gabriel Attila saying he was a Romanian refugee. He had turned pretty violent and had withdrawn his application for asylum saying that he was an EU citizen – which he clearly isn't and he has absolutely no papers to prove it. He had told this woman when she had seen him to say that he was losing his right to free housing and that 'the only way I can get anyone to take any notice of me and stop me from being homeless is if I go and do something drastic, so I will go to MacShane's surgery this week and slit his throat'.

I wouldn't really have bothered about the threat except having seen him he looked quite capable of a dirty deed and there had been that awful tragedy of the Lib Dem MP in Gloucester, Nigel Jones, who had been attacked and his assistant killed by someone with a big knife or sword.

So I phoned up both the police and the Home Office, the latter to ask how on earth could he be properly interrogated and deported if he had no right to stay here. The answer is, they don't know, because if you have no papers where on earth can you be deported to? I suppose in honesty the real answer is to give him a National Insurance number and let him wend his energetic way into the British economy and society, save that I just had incredible doubts about who he really represented or was connected to. I assume I shall still be alive tomorrow.

WEDNESDAY 3 MAY 2000

Prime Minister's Questions was notable for the strength of the attack by Charlie Kennedy on Hague. He called him a bigot more or less to his face. I wish to God Blair had had the same courage. But the focus groups sit on his shoulder like a raven telling him not to join in this condemnation. Instead, he and Hague swap insults over asylum seekers, each trying to prove he is tougher than the other.

TUESDAY 9 MAY 2000

I dash off a quick article called 'The Twelve Labours of Tony' to be translated into French to go into a French paper. There may just be a window of opportunity to get something in based on the third anniversary of the government's election, his own birthday and the arrival of the new baby Blair. Later in the lobby I see him and say I am working on a piece called '*Les Douze Travaux de Tony*' and he gives me a good smile. Peter Mandelson, who is walking with him and whom I didn't notice, said, 'What does that mean?'

I translate and Peter says, 'Yes, somehow we've got it wrong with France. It was all going so well until I went to Northern Ireland and we've really lost touch since then.' I said that the Blair–Schröder paper had been received very negatively in France.

'No, no, that wasn't the problem, we just weren't maintaining the contacts.' I mumbled something about not really being in the loop on that, but I suppose my face must have given away the sheer amazement at Peter's ego and effrontery. Just because he occasionally did a *pas de deux* with Pierre Moscovici, he assumes that once

that stopped happening, everything had to go wrong. Or perhaps
he is right. Perhaps he is the indispensable cog that allows good relations with all the European governments. But for sheer chutzpah
and self-absorption, he takes some beating.

WEDNESDAY 10 MAY 2000

David Mathieson called me up for lunch. We talked in Bellamy's.
Emma, his wife in Spain, has had their daughter. She had the birth
au naturel with ten hours of labour. But now David is a proud papa.
We talked a little of that, but as usual it was about Cook.

'Anji Hunter was in to ask that Robin makes some bigger speeches supporting Tony's line in a domestic context. She said that Blair
made his speech on "Britishness", but there was no follow-up.
Robin is keen to re-enter domestic politics. He needs to make an
impact.'

I said to him, 'OK, we can fix something up easily and get a platform for Robin whenever he wants, but what is he going to say?'

'That's the problem. Tony wants Robin back and Robin wants to
come back, but what are the key themes?'

I said that Robin was soon to become chairman of the Party of
European Socialists. Whatever happened to him in terms of his
Cabinet portfolio, he would have a big European role on that. He
needed to build those networks now. There was a good story on
Europe to be told. David half agreed, but no one quite knows what
the political possibilities are.

He said that the problem remained of Robin finding time to do
things. Gaynor still was important in keeping him at home. 'They
went to the Azores last weekend for a break. She thought it was

going to be some kind of tropical paradise. When she found it was cloudy and Spanish, she lost all interest.'

Once again, a go-nowhere, what-do-we-do kind of conversation.

I slumped back upstairs to do some work and then went over to question time. Blair crushed Hague. The master of the despatch box was left wordless as if he was a novice backbencher. What was also interesting was Blair's admission that the overvalued sterling was a problem. The Tories kept chanting that it was 'the weak euro', but Blair would have nothing of this. Just briefly this week, we are seeing the admission that our policy on the currency is badly wrong. But overall, the strongest impression is of an infinitely weak Hague.

I had tea in the Pugin Room with Peter Oborne and gave him my line on how the Tories were seeking inspiration from the right-wing in Europe on their anti-foreigner discourse, which he got interested in. Oborne represents the Tory class interest in the media. They cannot believe that they will not come back. But as I told him, the Labour Party represents the material interests of Britain and the Lib Dems represent the moral interests of Britain. Who needs the Conservatives? We may be witnessing the strange death of Tory England. The wish is father to the analysis, but my God, what a bit of history now looms before us?

SUNDAY 14 MAY 2000

Andy Marr is to be the new BBC political editor. I am delighted for him. But it is a loss to political journalism. He is a writer, an analyst, a collector of metaphor and image. The two or three hundred words he will be allowed for his nightly BBC reports allow no room for other than fairly factual reporting. At least he isn't hostile to Europe.

There is a story in the *Sunday Times*, 'Atticus', about me talking about Frank Bruno, saying that I had raced past him in the marathon and his reply, 'But I was walking.'

Again, a do-nothing day. I went for a run around Hyde Park and bumped into Winston Churchill, grandson of the famous Prime Minister, who looked trim and fit for his years. As we talked, the band of the Household Division walked past us playing. It was a kind of memorial day for the cavalry divisions and regiments. Winston snorted, 'Why are they walking? You see, you have taken away their horses!'

The band did look a bit pathetic and very undominant. There were lots of men there in bowler hats and furled umbrellas. This was once the pride of the British Army, but it all looked a bit second division now.

MONDAY 15 MAY 2000

I work on a paper about Joschka Fischer's speech on the European Federation. As I suspected when I read the full German, it is a much more complex and nuanced speech than the crude British press reports, which talks of a German–French drive to a single federal Europe. The idea that either Jospin or Chirac will go into the next French elections proclaiming that France is to be dissolved into a federal Europe is simply laughable. But we have no political project on offer, having spent three years nagging on economic reform. Until we find something political to say, we will always be lagging behind.

At 11.45 a.m. an interview with Anne Perkins for *The House* magazine. It is one of their profile pages. I actually wrote it out myself and gave it to her. She looked at it. 'Well, how do I earn my fee if I can't interview you?'

So she asked half an hour's worth of questions and the top of them was 'Why aren't you a minister?'

TUESDAY 16 MAY 2000

A quick run round Battersea Park and then to the Foreign Office to prepare for questions. Robin has put up a ghastly John Bratby painting over his main desk. It used to be occupied by a giant portrait of a fighting rajah, which was utterly appropriate for the monumental dimensions of the Foreign Secretary's office. This is just a tacky provincial Bolton art gallery type of painting in a very thin poor white frame. There is another picture of Newmarket hung beside his big glass-fronted library, to the right of the door, which you don't even notice. Robin has many strengths, but an eye for art clearly isn't one of them. I whispered to Sherard, his private secretary, that I wanted to be on the hanging committee for any future choice. Sherard giggled back: 'Oh, you want Palmerston or one of the imperial reminders, don't you, Denis?' Too damn right I do.

Robin is also sitting at the other end of the long conference table with the light streaming behind him, which actually makes him look a bit stronger. He seemed reasonably in command. The worry was where would the Tories be coming from? As usual, we get it half right and half wrong. I said that I thought Fischer's speech would be raised.

Robin said:

Actually, if you read the speech and take out the word 'federation', there's not a lot in it that we would disagree with. His ideas on having a different type of European Parliament with a big role for national parliaments are absolutely fine and he clearly doesn't like the commission much.

I wondered if he had thought of this himself or if this was what the embassy in Bonn had sent over. As usual, the meeting rambles on and only the first two questions out of twenty are properly looked at before suddenly it is 10.30 a.m. and Robin shoos us all out. He will spend the rest of the day with officials, getting right on top of every question he has to answer. It means that when he gets up at 2.30 p.m., he is completely prepared and trained and thus will dominate at the despatch box. It is a huge investment for a brief hour, but it means that he remains unrivalled – except possibly for Gordon Brown, who spends as much time himself getting ready for his parliamentary performances – in terms of mastery of the Chamber. It is still an important asset.

After Prime Minister's Question Time, there was a meeting in Blair's office for the so-called 'shadow MPs' who are meant to be looking after relations with all the European countries.

With the new countries from east Europe included, there were about twenty around the table. Blair was very positive. He lolls back in his chair, looking at the ceiling and says:

Look, well it's been very difficult to get this going – our relations with Europe. We came in and thought we could just turn things round, but after a year or so we realised it just wasn't working. I told civil servants that they have to build good relations with their individual opposite numbers in the capital cities. I have told ministers the same thing. The parties are important. That's what I want you to do. To get over there and build contacts.

Then he suddenly started to praise me, which was rather embarrassing. 'Look at what Denis does in the French media. It's absolutely fantastic, explaining our position. It really is a very big help.'

I needed that in front of my peers like a hole in the head, but luckily attention was distracted by Andrew MacKinlay who started ranting at the Prime Minister from a long list he had in front of him:

Look, Prime Minister, what you have to do is to get the Secretary of State for Trade over to east Europe. He goes all over Asia and elsewhere, but he hasn't been once to east Europe. Other ministers aren't coming as well. It really isn't good enough. We don't get taken seriously if we don't send over our top people. Can you talk to Steve Byers and make sure he gets to east Europe as soon as possible, especially to Poland?

His list of complaints went on and on and Keith Vaz just shut him up as Tony apologised about having had to have cancelled yet another trip to Poland a few months ago. Tony McNulty grinned at me and whispered, 'I was overruled on MacKinlay. The decision to include him came from on high!'

I finish the book by Edward Pearce called *Lines of Most Resistance*. He has trawled through the parliamentary debates and the newspaper libraries to examine how the Conservatives handled home rule in the 1880s and 1890s or the reform of the House of Lords twenty years later. The pleasure of the book is the most wonderful quotes from the foul reactionaries. Here, for example, is Lord Salisbury in 1886 explaining why the Irish cannot have home rule:

When you narrow it down, you will find that this which is called self-government but which is really government by the majority, works admirably well when it is confided to people who are of Teutonic race. But that it does not work so well when people of other races are called upon to join in it.

You couldn't have made it up and it is just so redolent of the approach to Europe from today's successors to Lord Salisbury who run the Conservative Party.

MONDAY 5 JUNE 2000

Up to Groucho's for a *Critical Quarterly* dinner. I tell Brian Cox that he should do a memoir on Kingsley Amis and Philip Larkin, and of course he knew Larkin when both of them taught at Hull University:

> I only met Kingsley Amis a couple of times, but Larkin was a funny man. He was always chasing women at Hull. But he made them miserable because he refused to take them to London to meet Amis and his other smart literary friends. He had one open affair with his secretary, but he always used to tell me that he simply couldn't bear the thought of taking her down to London as she wasn't smart enough to be shown around.

I had been reading some Larkin on Sunday night, his pathetic poems about wanking at 3.10 a.m. and although his power of language and many of his images are still incredibly gripping, there was just a second-rate seediness and sense of provincial dowdy despair that comes off the poems, but then I suppose if you live and work in Hull it's what comes with the territory.

Back to the Commons for an 11 p.m. vote on Northern Ireland. Peter Mandelson seems more in command than ever and really is making the transition from being spin doctor to being a serious politician. Surely the foreign secretaryship is his for the asking, though I wonder how Robin will react.

TUESDAY 6 JUNE 2000

The House magazine has published the profile of me with a rather fetching cartoon of me as a kind of wasp stinging a rotten anti-European apple. It reads OK, if a bit overcolourful. I wish I could get rid of the impression I give of being a mischief-maker and get taken more seriously, but then you are what you are what you are.

Sarah phones up to say, 'Daddy, you never told us you had been arrested,' because there was a reference to my brief imprisonment in Poland running money to the underground Solidarity union. She sounds really hurt, as if there is a whole story of her father's life about which she knows nothing. One day I will try to write some of it down, because I wish to God my own father had done that for me.

WEDNESDAY 7 JUNE 2000

Blair has been booed and slow handclapped by members of the Women's Institute at their annual event at Wembley Stadium. It looks ghastly on television. First the boos, then more hisses, then a speech almost brought to an end by slow handclapping and then some of these grisly Tory ladies of the Shires getting up and walking out. Christ! This will not do at all. Blair is hated by the left, not admired by the trade unions, but now the ladies of middle England are deserting him. I don't like the smell of this at all.

THURSDAY 8 JUNE 2000

Wake up to a horrible assassination story. Some left terrorist group has killed our military attaché in Athens. Last night he was having dinner with Liz Symons. It sounds all too ghastly.

Into the Commons for a debate in Westminster Hall on Gibraltar. Keith Vaz whispers to me, 'You see. We got the WI speech off the front pages. The business in Athens. Good work, eh?'

Even given my love for gallows humour, I am not sure Keith should be thus indulging himself.

The debate is tedious beyond belief. There is a long whining Foreign Affairs Select Committee report on Gibraltar. This wretched place has twice as many offshore banks as it does citizens and has been used as a haven for smuggling for years. Its tobacco prices are half that of neighbouring Spain and I wonder how we would react if the Isle of Wight, say, was a haven for low-tax goods. The Gibraltar authorities pay a fortune to fly people backwards and forwards there and have a little lobby going in the Commons which is very effective. It is run by Lindsay Hoyle, the Lancashire MP who is son of my old trade union friend, Doug Hoyle, who was president of ASTMS, the industrial white-collar union. The Tories love it as Gibraltar is redolent of empire, and Labour loves it because this little

enclave on Spanish soil with about half the population of my constituency is usually run by the local Labour Party.

It is helped, of course, by the unbelievable stupidity of Madrid,
which continues to harass and make life impossible for the people
who live there, so instead of blending quietly into neighbouring
Spain so it all becomes one single territory of prosperity and exchange, there are the hideous border controls of half a century ago.
To while away my time, I read the 'Treaty of Peace and Friendship
between Great Britain and Spain signed at Utrecht 2 July 1713'. A
key phrase reads 'and her Britannic Majesty, at the request of the
Catholic King, does consent and agree, that no leave shall be given
under any pretence whatsoever, either to Jews or Maws [Moors],
to reside or have their dwellings in the said town of Gibraltar'. So
that's what it's all about. A nice little racist, anti-Muslim and antisemitic treaty which we expend mounds of energy in defending.

MONDAY 12 JUNE 2000

The newspapers are full of huge briefings by Gordon Brown in
which he is slapping down Stephen Byers for making a strong
speech in favour of the euro. The news agenda is running very
positively for us on this and I really don't understand Brown's determination to expose rather fake divisions in the Cabinet. The
Tories are a thousand times more divided and yet somehow we are
creating an impression of division for no obvious reason.

On my way to the House, I pop into the *New Statesman* at
Victoria to deliver an article to its editor, Peter Wilby, about how
the Conservatives are now becoming much more like a standard

right-wing European party. Wilby has made the *Staggers* almost unreadable and has no interest in the politics of Europe, so I don't know why I bother.

Dinner with Charlie Falconer in the Barry Room, which is a kind of Strangers' Dining Room for peers. Charlie has a friendly word for everyone. Ann Mallalieu, the fox-hunting Labour peeress, is there. 'Have you had a really ghastly day, Ann?' he says in the most unctuous way, as if this wretched reactionary was someone who had to be cosseted and loved at all costs. But it is his style. Tories pass by threatening to wreck government bills and Charlie just smiles and wishes them well, as if it was all a little club of no importance to the world outside.

For the rest of the meal, he quizzes me and I notice that he orders a carafe of wine, fills a glass but drinks nothing from it, watching me take two or three. He wants to know all about my background and my life, which I fill him in on, so he has some idea of my character. He doesn't really know when I became an MP or actually very much about me at all, so I am quite happy to tell him what I think.

Again I make the big complaint about the lack of a party project. I finish by inviting him to Rotherham to speak at a GC and he is very, very keen. A desperate need to be in touch with the outside world. We have a bit of a chat about the Speaker of Parliament and to his surprise, I tell him that the custom in the past was that the Speaker announces his or her retirement before the election, so it is the existing parliament that selects the Speaker and it's not something that can be easily manipulated by the government. I say that Patrick Cormack is interested in it and he just snorts in derision. He, in turn, floats the name of Jack Cunningham, and I think there may be something in that but not much.

TUESDAY 13 JUNE 2000

My oral question is today on bicycle lanes in London. I bumped into Nick Raynsford walking across the plaza from Victoria Station and said I was going to make a joke about Ken Livingstone to the effect that if the new Mayor of London could bring in a bicycle lane, then he might get my second vote at the next election. Nick exploded.

'Look, I'm walking around, Denis. I don't use a car,' he said, with his private secretary nodding beside him, 'but you can't mention Livingstone. He is a bad man. He is going to implode before long. We can't give him any credibility.'

How out of touch they all are.

Patrice Claude, the *Le Monde* correspondent, comes for dinner, along with Jonathan Powell and Sarah Helm. It is a balmy night and Patrice can't believe how beautiful the Terrace is as we sit out watching the rather high Thames flow gently by, drinking our Pimm's.

When Jonathan arrives, he says that Blair is always telling him to spend more time mixing with MPs in Strangers' Bar or on the Terrace. But in fact it's rather a small self-serving and inward-looking group that congregate in Strangers'. Phil Woolas, Fraser Kemp and Peter Kilfoyle breeze up for a word with Jonathan.

Jonathan was surprised that I hadn't been in Berlin at the Third Way or progressive governance conference. I said I hadn't been invited and that no MPs went as it was just for academics. 'Well, you're an intellectual as well as a politician, so you should have gone,' said Jonathan nicely.

He continued with a disgust that I fully share: 'Jospin loved the fact that Blair wasn't there as it made him king of the show. There were

leaders representing 600 million people discussing centre-left political ideas and of course it got absolutely no coverage here in England.'

SUNDAY 25 JUNE 2000

Bad political news. Lord Levy, Tony's super-rich crony and money
raiser, turns out to have paid only £5,000 tax last year. Given he is
worth millions and zillions, this is just an absolute insult. I think of all
the money I have paid as a taxpayer and for this guy to arrange his tax
affairs not to pay anything makes me sick. Why are the greedy always
let off from their social responsibility? I listen to him on the *World at
One* talking about growing up without a bathroom in his flat and it is
just humiliating to think of the Labour Party being in hock to these
people. God, it's disgusting and I feel very bitter and angry.

Colin MacCabe phones up to say that an attack on Chris Smith
in *Critical Quarterly* has been received very badly in the Department for Culture. According to Colin, his private secretary called
up the vice chancellor at Exeter University to put pressure on
Colin. 'I called up this man and told him I was going to raise a
stink in *The Guardian*, and he got really frightened and said it was
all a matter for the Secretary of State,' said Colin. God knows why
the pair of them have fallen out, but it's symptomatic of how this
Labour government only seems to know how to lose friends rather
than convince people or make new supporters.

MONDAY 26 JUNE 2000

This was a wonderful, easy day. I had been asked to go to an official lunch with Keith Vaz for the president of the European

Parliament and then a dinner with the German ambassador at the Foreign Office. Or was it the other way round? No matter. Both were cancelled. I was superfluous to requirements. Hooray, David Marquand once told me that the key ingredient for any successful politician was stamina. I don't have it.

And then I bumped into Don Macintyre and we went off for a curry. He told an interesting story about Ivor Roberts, our friend from Oxford who is now Sir Ivor. Because of his knowledge of Serbia, Robin Cook had sent him off on a little mission to write a report on what might be done about Milošević. Ivor came back. Sent the report in. But Robin never bothered to call him to see him.

By contrast, Peter Mandelson had breakfast with him and showed enormous interest in the report and in Ivor's diplomatic activity. Of course, Peter has a stake as Northern Ireland Secretary and Ivor is now the ambassador in Dublin. But the crucial point is that Peter knows how to make friends and influence people. I wish Robin did.

FRIDAY 30 JUNE 2000

At King's Cross I saw Ed Balls and we decided to share dinner up to Doncaster.

He ordered a bottle of the most expensive wine on the menu, a delicious Chateau Musar, a Lebanese red. But the main point of his conversation was to assure me that he and the Treasury were not hostile to Europe.

'You don't think we're anti-European, do you, Denis?'

I said nothing. Or rather I made soothing noises. But I did protest about the briefing I had read in the papers clearly coming from

Treasury sources attacking Robin Cook and Tony Blair over the withholding tax and generally over Europe.

'Yes, but we had to hold the line,' replied Ed.

This is complete bullshit. He knows it and I know it. It is a dirty little gang around Brown and a lot of their politics are coming unstuck. The low pension rise is a disaster and the tilt of all economic policies against manufacturing has cost 200,000 jobs and destroyed morale in working-class industrial heartlands. But I don't say all this. What's the point? Ed's a very bright young journalist who has moved far and fast and is very nice with all, but like all arrogant young journalists, he can never ever admit he has got anything wrong, whereas at my age I find it a miracle if I get anything right.

SUNDAY 2 JULY 2000

More rubbishing in the newspapers with a sensational article by Ken Follett attacking the 'rent boys' who do spinning on behalf of Blair. He says that Blair is 'unmanly' and has no inner core principles to help him take tough decisions. I talk briefly to Michael White of *The Guardian* about it, who is very scornful of Follett, but the point is that a bit, indeed a lot, of what Ken has to say is true. But why say it now? What is wrong with old-fashioned loyalty? I know he is frustrated to be cut out of the inner circle. But so what? That's politics. You either believe in your party and believe in some of what it tries to do in government, or you don't. But if you don't want to get out, then for God's sake shut up.

At home Colin MacCabe phones me up to say he is going to have a big row with Chris Smith, the Culture Secretary. One of his clever young men wrote a very cocky article in *CQ* saying that Labour's cultural policy was the same as Stalin's and digging up lots of quotes from Russia in the 1930s which sound eerily like utterances from Smith or Blair. It's complete crap, of course, and from just a clever-dick undergraduate, but Colin has circulated the article and asked Smith for comments.

Chris wrote a pompous ministerial reply back and when Colin replied to that and said he was going to publish it, his private office got very niggly and faxed copies of letters to the vice chancellor at Exeter University – the clear implication being that this Professor MacCabe of theirs is wicked. It's a foolish way of behaving. But now Smith has made it worse by writing an even more pompous letter to Colin, and Colin has been talking to Simon Heffer at the *Mail* about doing a big article trashing Labour over the issue.

I tell him to take it easy. I love Simon's company, but there is not a nonreactionary thought or impulse in his nature and for the fleeting privilege of an article in the *Daily Mail* it's hardly worth Colin unleashing this kind of all-out war. But it's his affair, not mine, and I am fed up with being endlessly defensive about this sodding government stuff.

THURSDAY 6 JULY 2000

Oh, God, another 5.30 a.m. start. The 7 a.m. plane to Poland gets me to Warsaw at 10.30. The residence is a nice late nineteenth-century villa on one of the main roads into Warsaw, but the embassy is the most ghastly squared-off building with a giant crown on its front like some horrible decoration with all the charm of Rotherham College of Technology.

In the main dining room, which is a hideous mix of loud carpets and strident wallpaper, there is a painting by Lawrence Toynbee, Clare's father, and I phone her up to give her the news. How young we all were once, but actually I still think it was bliss.

The ambassador, John Macgregor, is a cheerful, tall, goofy-toothed, amiable professor with a lovely smile and a bit of a paunch. He has a stunningly pretty blonde wife, Judith, who is perfectly *soignée*. As we are chatting, she tells me a nice Thatcher story:

> I was just down from university and working as a desk officer on Yugoslavia in the Foreign Office when a call came saying that Mrs Thatcher, then the Leader of the Opposition, wanted someone to brief her before a visit to Yugoslavia she was about to make. She wanted a desk specialist and I was sent over to the Commons. I came with all my facts and files, but she had read everything that we had sent her and just asked me very specific questions. She was very brisk and clear and said, 'Good, now I've got what I want. I know the questions I want to ask. By the way, have you ever been round the House of Commons?' I said no and off she took me for a tour. It was amazing that she could find the time to do this and, of course, although I thought of myself as a lefty, I was completely bowled over.

God, if only Robin or even Tony could find the resources to behave like that.

I have lunch with Macgregor and a woman from the Foreign Office who is in charge of Poland. There has been some kind of Wilton Park conference here at which Joyce Quin attended. The ambassador complained that they wanted to get Keith Vaz but ended up with Joyce Quin. I gently hinted that Joyce might know an awful lot more about Europe and European politics than Keith, but the nonstop moan from the ambassador was that Blair had twice cancelled a visit to Poland and was now looking at a date early in October which would clash with the first round of Poland's presidential election. Cook had not been out there either and had snubbed a rather grand meeting put together by the Americans to issue a declaration of democracy which the French refused to sign as it was said to have been implicitly hostile to the United Nations.

I borrowed the ambassador's guide book and set off. It was a lovely walk, though thank goodness a cloudy day so it wasn't too hot. How Warsaw has changed. It now has the feel of a city in Italy in the 1970s or Spain in the 1980s. A mixture of dirty and modern, dusty and old and clean and shiny. But there is advertising everywhere. McDonald's maketh the man. The people were brightly dressed. The roads were chock-a-block with new cars. You could sense the pumping creativity and business energy in this great European capital city. I thought of my time here twenty years ago and the help I tried to give to Solidarność, how I had tried to keep the faith in supporting democracy and freedom in Poland, and felt very happy. Only the tiniest of tiny footprints in European history, but ones I could be content to have made.

Up the Nowy Świat, past all the posh new shops. I turned to look at the Victoria Hotel and the sad, much diminished Europejski. All these souvenirs but overtaken by the new Marriotts and Sheratons and the Chicago on the Vistula that is being built.

On into the old town, which is now a bustle of markets and cafes and life.

Then a taxi to see Helena Łuczywo. She is just as I remember her. A little sparrow of a woman still chain-smoking and drinking black tea with great hoods under her eyes. So smart and clever and elegant. She looked at pictures of the girls and Benjamin and said how much she envied the big family I had.

Late in 1989, she had created with Adam Michnik *Gazeta Wyborcza*, which is now Poland's biggest selling newspaper with 5 million copies sold each day.

Now she is working on some complex email project to spread the paper's wealth even further. She explained that it had been set up in the form of an employee ownership trust. A couple of weeks ago it was floated. Cleaners and cooks and lorry drivers who had shares according to length of service walked away with $100,000 while she was now a millionaire. Darling Helena. How I'll never forget those dark nights tramping around Warsaw and driving to funny places, hiring a taxi for a whole day for $20. How do I explain to my children just how dismal and grey and without the faintest sign of colour life under communism was? I felt strangely and oddly at home and these Poles have accomplished so much more in their lives than we complacent slippered Brits have in ours.

I take a taxi to Gienek Smolar's flat. It is rambling, scruffy and home to one of the great Jewish intellectual political activists of our time.

His energetic wife Nina is there and a wonderful Polish meal of sour herring and smoked eel and roast veal is prepared with vodka and lots of wine. God, it's good to be back with part of my bloodline again. Janusz Onyszkiewicz turns up. He looks as young as he did twenty years ago. The blond hair, the blond moustache, the precise dapper English he learnt while teaching mathematics at Leeds University. We go over old times. He describes how he regularly had to correct Lech Wałęsa for announcing a general strike when it wasn't going to happen. 'I would tell the press that the President had simply got it wrong and was postponing the strike for another week or two,' he said.

They are all satisfied with their Poland. The big achievement was the round-table talks of 1989.

'This allowed the transition out of communism, more than a few people wanting to get out of East Germany via Hungary into the west,' said Gienek.

He was generous in the tribute he paid to Neal Ascherson and Tim Garton Ash.

'Tim is very self-important. He thinks he made a big contribution. He was undoubtedly a great ambassador for what was happening in the west, but nobody in Poland or anywhere else knows about him outside a small circle of the intelligentsia,' said Gienek. He was nice about me.

'You brought us money when we needed it more than anything else.'

Both he and Onyszkiewicz were dismissive of the book published a couple of years ago by Carl Bernstein that Solidarity was a CIA–Vatican plot.

'That's complete and utter rubbish,' they both said.

I asked about the role of the 1968 diaspora of Jews who were forced out of Poland in the last upheaval of antisemitism.

'No, that didn't make any difference, there were only fifteen of us around the world,' said Gienek. I think he is downplaying his role.

Nina runs a publishing house in Poland and had published Garton Ash's book on Germany. I said I thought it was his professor book, to show what a good academic he was.

'Yes, an awful lot of it was boring and unreadable, but there were some really good chapters that were like elegant essays in it,' she said. Of course that's right. Tim is just such a wonderful writer with more insights in a paragraph or two than most of his fellow authors can manage in a whole book.

Jan Lityński turned up. He is Gienek's great friend. I don't really know him so well. Unlike Janusz and Gienek, his English isn't so good.

There was a lovely Jacek Kuroń story. Earlier this year, he was on holiday in Capri. As he and his Polish friends sat looking out over the blue bay, at least four coachloads of Polish tourists arrived, spilling out ordinary workers who were doing a tour of Italy, picking up Rome, Pompeii and Capri. Kuroń was a bit snooty about this commercialisation of their lives but was told: 'No, Jacek, this is wonderful to see ordinary Polish workers able to enjoy an ordinary Mediterranean holiday.'

FRIDAY 7 JULY 2000

A bacon and egg breakfast is served in my large double bedroom in the ambassador's residence. The shower is good and strong, the soap is fresh, there is fruit everywhere and all the luxury of staying in a top-class hotel.

Gienek picks me up and takes me to the Polish radio studios. He is now the boss. So many of my friends from 1980 are now big cheeses. We are there to meet Lech Wałęsa. He comes rolling into the little office. There is still the same pugnacious and self-confident gait that I remember from twenty years ago. His suit is cheap and it still has the Black Virgin of Częstochowa on its lapel. The shirt stretches across his paunchy chest and a cheap polyester tie is the reminder that we are talking with an authentic robotnik.

There is a kind of gush of words that never stop. The main story is that what happened in 1980 was 'a gift of God'. It is all about the Pope and how his election was a signal for Poland to throw off its chains.

He rambled on and on. I asked him how many grandchildren he had and he said, 'I am not a grandfather. Danuta [his wife] is a grandmother and she looks after the children.'

We took pictures and I got him to sign a copy of my book and then he swaggered off for the next round of his election campaigning.

Later when I had dinner with Chris Bobinski, he said that Wałęsa in his radio interview just before meeting me had said that the presence of the Polish President, Aleksander Kwaśniewski, in the big Polish millennium pilgrimage to Rome had triggered off anti-semitic reactions. Unbelievable. There are barely 2,000 Jews left in Poland and still Wałęsa is trying to drum up antisemitic nonsense.

I walk round the Jewish ghetto, which now is a kind of shabby empty park with plain paving stones, a few trees and shrubs – that's all that's left of what was the ghetto. I just tried to put myself back and feel what it must have been like in those days, but of course, how can one possibly imagine it. Predictably, there was a big notice announcing the arrival of a new Holocaust museum built with American money.

Lunch was with a couple of functionaries and diplomats and the rather nice American boy who is the *Financial Times*' new correspondent in Warsaw. He had just come from Vienna and was very contemptuous of the European line on Haider. I took no notice of this *bien pensant* rambling. Again Warsaw struck me as being full of life and colour and a successful European city. I wish I knew more about it, but how many bits of Europe can you digest in a lifetime?

A final dinner with Gienek Smolar and Chris Bobinski and then back to bed in the residence.

SATURDAY 8 JULY 2000

Up early and a cup of tea with John Macgregor, the ambassador, in his pyjamas and dressing gown. He is off to spend the weekend with Anne Applebaum and her Polish husband, Radek Sikorski, who had been a member of the Bullingdon Club in Oxford in the 1980s with posh-boy Tories like Boris Johnson and David Cameron.

An easy flight home and I arrive to the news that Mother has had a stroke in Glasgow. She has gone into hospital and is seriously unwell.

I phone all over the place and can only find out that she was with the woman who comes to see her every day, Jean McCallum, when she just collapsed. Tomorrow I'll go up and see what's going on.

SUNDAY 9 JULY 2000

On to the plane and a taxi to the Victoria Infirmary in Glasgow. It is a pathetic sight. Mother lies shrivelled and small, unable to open her eyes and barely able to talk. What comes out is partly lucid, partly gibberish. There is a sign over her bed saying 'nil by mouth' and she has drips going into her as she cannot swallow at all. She is in a general medical ward, transferred there from the A&E ward. But everyone else there seems to be very old and frail women. The nurses bustle around, kind and sympathetic, but there are so few of them and so many of these old ladies parked there waiting to die. The hospital, of course, is shabby and grubby and has had no real spending on it for years. How miserable our NHS can be, though its treatment of people I'm sure is good. She falls asleep while I am talking and then wakes up with a start, but the crunched-up eyes and crunched-up mouth make her look like almost a little rodent.

Gone, gone, is the woman I saw not two weeks ago full of enthusiasm about buying the bungalow in Harthill, near Rotherham.

I leave in some misery and get a plane back to London. When I arrive, I find I have lost my keys in the rush of getting onto the aircraft. Blast.

MONDAY 10 JULY 2000

Off in the rain to Buckingham Palace. The Queen has offered a reception to backbenchers and we drive right past the guards into an inner courtyard to park the car. Then up to the Royal Gallery with fabulous paintings. The wine served is excellent. It's nice to talk to the wives of Labour and Conservative colleagues. I saw a number with the word 'Lady' in front of their name and thought they were ladies-in-waiting but, of course, one forgets all the knighthoods distributed by Thatcher and Major and the number of Tory MPs who are Sir-this and Sir-that.

We chat a bit to Robin Janvrin and then it's our turn to be presented to the Queen. There isn't much of a queue and she stands there, a very small and upright elderly woman with Philip beside her, not appearing much taller. I had always had the impression that he was a tall commanding naval officer, but he seems shorter than my 5ft 9ins – perhaps it is old age and he is bent over slightly.

The Queen wears a white glove, which one shakes gently, and I said, just to make conversation, 'Thank you for having us.'

She smiles benignly but obviously isn't going to get into conversation mode and then I shake hands with Philip and he leans forward and says, 'Harrogate?'

I looked at him and said, 'What?'

'From Harrogate, did you say?'

The Queen turned and said, 'No, Philip, he said, "Thank you for having us."' The duke grunted and we passed on.

We finished the drinks and drove down to Dulwich for Harriet Harman's fiftieth birthday party. It was a much quieter affair with no big-gun Cabinet ministers but good to salute a good friend.

As we were leaving, Anne Campbell chimed and asked if anyone was going back to Westminster. I offered her a lift and then Julie Morgan, the wife of Rhodri Morgan, came along as well. In fact, it wasn't a lift back to Westminster but a huge drive all over bloody south London to deposit these people. We spent an hour in that ghastly part of London looking for the places where they stayed with barely a thank you when they got out. Never again.

TUESDAY 11 JULY 2000

At lunchtime, to Chatham House where I joined Martin Walker and John Lloyd in giving a talk on Europe. I thought I was chairing the meeting but instead I was one of the speakers. Thank God I had my paper on 'Ten Theses on Democracy in Europe' to hand. It went down pretty well. John was very competent, but Martin was just a bit too much of an anti-American, saying that the United States was now a great military imperial power and had nothing but contempt for Europe and just expected Europe to pay the bills for the Middle East peace process and be completely subordinate to Americans in any military operations. There was just too much exaggeration and broad colour in his remarks for them to be accepted. We had no time to talk as he rushed off, so I had a friendly coffee with just John afterwards.

WEDNESDAY 12 JULY 2000

A great Prime Minister's Questions today. Blair really creamed Hague. The interesting aspect is that Portillo simply cannot control his face. He smirks and grimaces and then breaks into an uncontrollable grin whenever Hague suffers. Portillo has got style, but he needs some deadpan seriousness somewhere in his character. I don't think he is that big a player.

MONDAY 17 JULY 2000

I dash off to the Commons to meet Kevin Rudd, the rising star of Australian Labor politics. He gets in to see David Miliband and all the smart people and we have a discussion on how to make the party work. The party, the party, the party – the unthought-through aspect of Blair's policies. Kevin is neat, precise and thoughtful. 'The important thing is to pick up change and deal with it before it overwhelms you. In Australia, we had stopped listening to the base and they simply walked away from us. That's why we lost.' I hope he passes the message on.

TUESDAY 18 JULY 2000

Question time was fairly boring. In the briefing that had been prepared for our backbenchers, I had slipped in a reference to the horrible Tory MP, John Bercow, who had a question on Africa referring to his past service as the secretary of the Monday Club's Immigration and Repatriation Committee. Duly one of our backbenchers got up and started to make the point. Bercow began squeaking in protest, flapping his hands in upset anger. 'I was only seventeen, I was only seventeen, I was only seventeen at the time...'

The guy is odiously unpleasant about Labour ministers and others and this barb will prick his pomposity. It's a dirty game, but the Tories play it in a much more dirty way than we have yet learnt to do.

But the big show of the day wasn't Cook but Gordon Brown, who was going to announce his comprehensive spending review. John Healey gave me the two big books that Brown uses to place on the despatch box to place his speech on. He has sight of only one eye and isn't sure of the other and everything has to be prepared for him in enormous for-the-almost-blind script. But on the PPS bench behind the front bench, it was already occupied by Joe Ashton, Helen Jones and Piara Khabra who were sitting from the gangway inwards. On the other side were lots of pushy women like Shona McIsaac and others who weren't going to budge. So we were squeezed like sardines and in the end Ken Purchase got up and left to allow John Healey and Bruce Grocott in to sit behind their masters.

As usual it was a tour de force by Brown. He rattled out statistics and described how debt had shrunk massively. What that meant in real terms was that he had raised lots more tax than he was giving out in public spending. I don't think many of our backbenchers realise the implications of that. We are now a government that looks after the rentiers more than the voters who elected us. There was one glorious Freudian slip when he came to a sentence saying that 'our policy will underpin long-term growth' but what he said was 'underspin', which produced a huge laugh.

But he was saved by the incompetence of Portillo. He was incredibly nervous, shaking at the despatch box and his voice

becoming squeakier and squeakier. At one stage, the Speaker Betty
Boothroyd rose to say gravely that she wanted silence in order to
be able to hear 'the Leader of the Opposition' and it was our turn to
have fits of laughter. In fact, Hague looked surprisingly cheerful as
Portillo made a bigger and bigger hash of it. Both of them obviously loathe each other and their faces can't quite control the rivalry
and *schadenfreude* that overwhelms them.

THURSDAY 20 JULY 2000

Down to the Commonwealth Society to speak at a session on conflict prevention and the role of the Commonwealth. The Foreign
Office had provided me with a script, but it was completely useless,
so I chatted to a few people over coffee and made my own comments. It went down quite well in the sense that I got my laughs
and people were happy with what I had to say.

Then a bike down to Chatham House to chair a speech made by
Imran Khan, the Pakistani cricketer, would-be politician and husband of Miss Goldsmith. He burbled away about the poverty and
depression in the country and how people had no faith in justice,
in the civil service or in politicians. As a result, they were turning
to Islam. His own programme, he said, was based on an employment programme which involved widening and making a proper
navigable canal of the Indus River.

'This is a bit like what Hitler did in the 1930s when he built all the
autobahns and got Germans back to work,' he said.

I gasped a little and said to him afterwards that perhaps the
Hitler comparison wasn't the most advisable one if he wanted to get
good publicity in the press over here.

MONDAY 24 JULY 2000

Lunch with Andrew Gimson. He was the *Daily Telegraph*'s correspondent in Berlin and is now back freelancing as foreign editor for *The Spectator*, leader writer for the *Evening Standard* and doing other bits and pieces. He wants to pump me on Europe. I am happy to make the connection, but I feel I spill over with enthusiasm. He is hostile to the currency and basically to the idea of greater partnership, power sharing and participating in the European Union. He is friendly and open, but I wish I hadn't given him the time. Trying to get a Tory Europhobe to let go of this article of faith is like hoping to convert a Wee Free to Catholicism.

At 4.30 p.m., across to Downing Street for one of Blair's regular meetings with PPSs. We all sit in the Cabinet Room. I make sure I sit as far away at the end of the Cabinet table, almost behind one of the pillars. Blair repeats the usual messages. The most interesting thing is his denunciation of reference to the word 'heartlands'.

He doesn't like it at all:

This is a Tory trap. If I simply do what voters want in my constituency of Sedgefield, then I'll be back where I was in the 1980s. If we allow ourselves to be pushed into ignoring the south of England and the broad mass of voters and just buy this Tory line that we are not doing enough for the heartlands, we'll lose the support that helped us win the election.

Ultimately, he doesn't believe any more in the need for an effective party organisation and wants an ever-shifting coalition of associates to deliver both a strong economy and the social issues which are of concern to him. He repeats endlessly the mantra about a clear divid-ing line with the Tories on their tax cuts, a promise which means cuts in public spending and thus we can say in each constituency which are the improvements in schools or hospitals that the Tories will axe. It's a convincing dialogue by planners in the political general staff in Downing Street, but it doesn't really cut an awful lot on the ground.

Was I impressed? Not really. I think we are incredibly lucky with a fatuous stupid opposition, but I don't think that we are changing the country in a sufficiently interesting and commanding way that is impressive either in terms of a new political project or narrative or impressive in terms of delivery. The jobs that are being created are being created all over the western world as growth is back. But our education is still in a dire, dire way.

THURSDAY 3 AUGUST 2000

A good quote from the dust cover of a book by Alan Moorehead, published in 1960, which I picked up but couldn't be bothered to read. How could I fail to do so after this recommendation: 'The White Nile is an enthralling reconstruction of half a century of Brit-ish achievement, which makes us proud of our Victorian ancestors.' And still in 1960 they were writing that.

SUNDAY 13 AUGUST 2000

The Observer carries my article on the twentieth anniversary of the arrival of the union Solidarity in Poland, which signalled the end of communist rule in Europe. I have a whole page in the foreign section. It reads quite well, though I guess readers may ask why on earth is this opinionated MP waffling on about Poland when there are bigger bits of *actualité*? Well, who cares, Roger Alton is a great friend and he's done me proud.

SATURDAY 26 AUGUST 2000

After seeing Granny in Glasgow, I dash over to Edinburgh to see Wagner's *Das Rheingold*. John Tusa, the former boss of the BBC World Service, spots me in the theatre entrance. 'Escaped from the TV festival have you, Denis?' asks Tusa.

I shake my head. I cannot imagine anything more loathsome than the sheer provinciality of English TV executives. Greg Dyke, the odd new BBC boss, made a speech yesterday announcing that the 9 p.m. news would be moved to 10 p.m. and the BBC would now have thematic channels – lots of pop stuff on BBC One, a bit of information on BBC Two and two new digital channels, Three and Four, where the news and serious programmes would go. It's the end of the BBC as a public service and I see little reason to think that the licence fee will survive.

I share some of these thoughts with Tusa, who is both a great public service broadcasting upholder and a real tough political operator who loathes the meretricious Dyke gang.

FRIDAY 1 SEPTEMBER 2000

Up early in the morning and I rewrite an article for *The Observer* about *métissage*. This argues that Britain is a country where peoples and races and faiths all co-mingle and we are much better and stronger as a result. It's a classic liberal statement and I am glad to have it off my chest. But the old Powellite racism based on colour is morphing into a xenophobic dislike of Europeans. When the Berlin Wall fell down, we dropped all visa requirements on east Europeans. Rotherham is full of Poles and Lithuanians. And since we don't have ID cards, we don't know who is in Britain. As the son of a Pole, I can't object, but the Tories and the xenophobic parties like UKIP are making latter-day anti-European racism into a big political theme you pick up all the day on radio phone-ins and on the doorstep.

SUNDAY 3 SEPTEMBER 2000

The sixty-first anniversary of the outbreak of the war. But really it was in the previous century, and apart from the Conservatives, who have launched some kind of anti-European policy project, there is nothing to remind us of the grisly politics of mid-century Europe. *The Observer* has carried my article but badly cut down and shunted away as a subsidiary of the op-ed column. I wonder why Roger wasn't prepared to take a punt. I had put in some strong anti-Tory stuff and also a crack about Rupert Murdoch marrying a Chinese woman, with the argument that if he now had children they would be of mixed race and so perhaps he would tell his editors in England to go easy on their xenophobia and their anti-foreigner and racist attacks. I suppose it was just too crude for *The Observer* and on the whole, Sunday newspaper dog doesn't eat Sunday newspaper dog.

WEDNESDAY 6 SEPTEMBER 2000

Our beloved Prime Minister has written an absolutely first-rate article jointly with German Chancellor Gerhard Schröder and the

Dutch and Swedish social democratic PMs, Wim Kok and Göran Persson, offering a left view of global economics. There are references in it to employee rights. Otherwise it is just a first-rate wish list, but at least they are nailing their colours to the mast and defining their world view as being of the left. Good for them.

MONDAY 11 SEPTEMBER 2000

The fuel blockade is getting bad. You can't get petrol in Glasgow. At the TUC, there are very few MPs around. I enjoy myself talking and gossiping and seeing old friends. But it is nostalgia, not as it once was building a network for tomorrow. I need to get on top of my life in a way I haven't done for some time.

TUESDAY 12 SEPTEMBER 2000

A rainy morning. The fuel crisis has now fully set in. I go for a bit of a run in a rain-sodden Rutherglen. Endless ministers pop up on radio. David Blunkett, Jack Straw, Stephen Byers, but none of them seem to have a line. There simply is no grip. I now feel embarrassed that last week I was on the BBC and on French radio declaring pompously that 'we British didn't do things like the French'. On the contrary, we are out-Frenching the French and the sense of panic is palpable. Where is Brown as this is about fuel duty? Where is the Prime Minister? Why has no one got a grip on this?

I have a speech to do at midday on trade unions and globalisation. I list twelve points which would allow trade unions to grapple effectively with the issue of globalisation.

I print it out and dash into the TUC. There is a debate on the euro. Bill Morris and a woman from Unison and some weird person from an outfit called the Unity Youth Workers, which I have never heard of, make very anti-euro speeches. I am dismayed.

Will Hutton and Rodney Bickerstaffe come up to me and I express that dismay.

'For God's sake, Rodney, the eurozone countries protect the public sector and pay public service employees a lot more than we do in England. Of all the unions, Unison should be the most supportive of Europe and the euro!'

'Look, Denis,' he says rather sharply but as always in a friendly way, 'have you ever heard me criticise the euro? Look who spoke on behalf of Unison? Has anyone ever heard of her?'

Of course the answer is no, and Rodney has to deal with a hardcore of either Trots or CPers in Unison who dominate the conference. But it is a pathetic inability of a major union to get to grips with real economics and to defend its members' interests rather than promote the ideology of a small group. And yet, as I make these points, do I remember what I was like in the 1970s on the hard left of the NUJ?!

FRIDAY 15 SEPTEMBER 2000

I go to 10 Downing Street. When I arrive, my name isn't or doesn't appear to be on the policeman's list. It is pelting monsoon rain and there is a small figure, Tim Garton Ash, who finds my name tucked on to his for a meeting with the Prime Minister. We arrive together and get rid of our wet coats. Then the usual Foreign Office gang arrives. Kim Darroch and the man he has just taken over from, Nigel Sheinwald. The fuel blockade is the only story and the Foreign Office wallahs are contemptuous of Gordon Brown.

'Where is the Chancellor?' asks Darroch.

I know Gordon always absents himself from any difficult scene, but it's really no business of these so-called neutral civil servants to wallow in the government's discomfiture.

In the Cabinet Room, the meeting is brisk and purposelike. Blair is in a dark blue shirt and badly tied tie, actually looking quite relaxed given the state of national emergency and crisis there is around the place.

'What is the structure of what I have to say in Poland and where do we want Europe to go? Let's decide that and then the words will fall into place,' he said.

Tim Garton Ash is there and the only other outsider is Charles Grant. Tim, as usual, is extremely self-assured and goes on and on about making a commitment by the year 2003 to get Poland into the EU. The debate goes backwards and forwards, all of it highly critical of the proposals either of Chirac or Fischer. The key word is 'intergovernmentability' as opposed to Europe being more *communitaire*.

The big story to emerge is that of a second chamber for the European Parliament consisting of delegations from the national parliaments. It is an old idea, but it was endorsed by Fischer and I think has more and more sense. I am convinced that connecting the national parliaments to the European process is the right way forward. Blair nods approvingly.

At one stage, one of the Foreign Office mandarins – Stephen Wall, I think – says of a point that has been made: 'I don't know, Prime Minister, but surely that's rather Gaullist?'

Blair looks at him, sticks up his right thumb and says, 'De Gaulle, top man!'

Stephen Wall blinks nervously and quickly replies, 'Yes, indeed, Prime Minister. The general was a great man!'

Oh boy. This is the real Tony: 100 per cent European and 100 per cent for the nation state. He goes on and on about 'the nation state' and I gently suggest that Europe consists of states which aren't nations and which are sharing state power, but he doesn't really understand the point I am making. Nevertheless, he is very flattering and insists that the paper I wrote on speeding up decision-making be circulated along with Charles Grant's paper on Europe in 2010, so at least I am in the loop. At the end, he coyly says to Tim, 'Tim, could I ask you to write something for me along the lines we have been discussing?'

Tim looks equally modest and shy and says, 'I am honoured, Prime Minister.'

Actually, I am delighted because Garton Ash is one of our great intellectuals and he uses words in a way that very few other people who currently write in the English language are capable of. But he writes to be read, not to be spoken. He may produce a very good text. But will it be a speech for a Prime Minister who has to use words in a different way from the intellectual writing for other clever clogs? Tim's obsession is enlargement to include his beloved Poland. He quotes George Bush, the President, not the son, in saying that after 1989 it was important that Europe became 'whole and free'. Basically, Tim is a Conservative. As we were waiting to go into the Cabinet Room, I made some remark about Mrs Thatcher and he rebuked me, saying she had been the only politician who had fully celebrated the twentieth anniversary of Solidarity by going to Gdańsk last month. In the end, although he will do the business for Blair, his heart lies with the liberal right rather than the liberal social left.

I urge the importance of cities and the need to find new language to describe the new Europe. At the end of the meeting, which went on for two hours, I called Blair to one side. I swapped the language of 'Prime Minister' and called him Tony again. All I said to him was that the weekend before, the Rotherham Labour Party had had such a successful two days at the Rotherham Show that although this week in terms of loss of public support was devastating and horrible, he shouldn't read total meltdown into it. He smiled but rather wanly. 'So it's not so bad at the base, is it,' he said. I hope I'm right. In the end, I cannot bear the thought of those racist, intolerant, isolationist, homophobic thugs coming back from the Conservative Party and running Britain again.

MONDAY 18 SEPTEMBER 2000

To Tate Modern where at a little art gallery there is the wedding party for Gordon Brown and Sarah Macaulay. I walk in with Neil Kinnock and the photographers all shout, 'Neil! Neil! This way, Neil!' And then beside us up glides Diane Abbott and the photographers start to focus on her.

'Diane, could we have a picture with you and Neil?' they say, quite sensibly ignoring my existence.

Neil giggles, loving to be in the limelight again and says, 'Diane, I don't mind, if it won't cause you any trouble?' She, of course, giggles, and I leave the pair of them for their fifteen nanoseconds of flash bulbs.

Inside there was a long queue which I thought was to salute Gordon, but as I waited in it, I realised it was actually for the cloakroom. Everyone seemed to be there. Eddie George glided by with his wife, Will Hutton was in conversation with Melvyn Bragg, Anna Ford was there and suddenly the Archbishop of Canterbury was gliding by in a wholly unimpressive way. Dominic Lawson of the *Sunday Telegraph* was there, Charlie Whelan who greeted me warmly, lots of other MPs and journalists and a great crowd.

Sarah was dressed in a white linen or chiffon dress, which somehow made her look a little insecure, unlike Gordon who was as always in a very dark blue, masculine, power-broking suit. Sarah had a nice mother, a small, lively-faced woman with whom I chatted briefly and who obviously was exceptionally intelligent and pleasant. I just wish to God that this marriage works out. I wish to God all marriages do.

I gave Steve Pound, the funny, waspish Ealing MP, a lift back to the Commons. He also was in despair at the handling of the fuel protest. As usual he was flattering. 'You would have been very good, Denis, on television or radio. Charles Clarke is as well. I think he is excellent.' Charles is obviously a rising figure. Well, good luck to him. His father was a top mandarin so maybe he will know how to make the civil service work for the country as well as for itself.

WEDNESDAY 20 SEPTEMBER 2000

I write a message for Tony Blair to be read out at the unveiling of the statue to General Sikorski in London on Sunday morning. It is a strong emotional message of friendship between Poland and Britain and about the blood shed at Monte Cassino and Arnhem. It also says he looks forward to the Prime Minister of Poland sitting alongside him at the Council of Ministers. I wonder if it will be used.

SUNDAY 24 SEPTEMBER 2000

I drive up to Portland Place, already late for the ceremony of the Sikorski statue. As I thread my way to the front of the crowd, Keith Vaz reads out his message. The first bit is Foreign Office waffle and then he says he has a message from Blair which he stutters out. It consists of my words and I see the Polish journalists scribbling them down furiously. I look at the Polish Guards of Honour with their funny square top hats and tears well into my eyes as I think of my father. How proud he must be, if somewhere up in heaven he can look down on his son writing words of friendship and solidarity between Britain and Poland to be spoken by the Prime Minister at the unveiling of a statue of his wartime chief. Or is this sheer romanticism?

I walk into the embassy for a drink. Tim Garton Ash is there and tells me about a piece of self-promotion by Charles Grant in the *Financial Times* which is very shocking. The article suggested that Blair was going to follow an ultra-nation-first line, as dictated by Charles in his speech in Poland in a fortnight's time, which Tim is writing a text for.

'Don't they realise the impact of that in Berlin or Paris? People just assume that Britain is going to do the usual "no, no, no" line on Europe and Charles's article will only have confirmed those fears before Blair even speaks.'

I demur slightly, since Charles actually is a very good European but is finding it hard to square the circle of being pro-Europe and pro-the-nation-state. It is a hard task for Tim to write a text that will really resonate. I will have to send something in as well.

Down to Brighton for the party conference. One of the first

people I see is Don Macintyre. He says that Treasury officials are phoning political editors to draw their attention to certain pages in Macintyre's biography of Mandelson which suggest that Mandy also lied over the Ecclestone affair. This is sheer self-indulgent and mutually destructive tit-for-tat briefing and I am frankly ashamed that Gordon – a man who I admire and respect in so many ways – still hasn't learnt the lesson of just how destructive this is.

I bump into John Healey and tell him the story, which is probably a big mistake as it will go straight back to Gordon, but he insists the Treasury isn't doing any briefing.

'All that stopped when Charlie Whelan left,' he says.

Who on earth is he kidding? I hope to God not himself. *Tribune* had a long editorial saying that Brown was the new leader of the left and left wingers should all rally around him against the Blair camp. It's untrue, as Brown is a classic right-wing social democrat who has certainly reversed the normal Labour priorities of spend first and pay in pain later, but the Treasury remains one of the most reactionary financial ministries in Europe. But the invitation to Labour to *split* into two camps, which this war of briefers is encouraging, is a recipe for utter disaster. Brown must know that surely.

MONDAY 25 SEPTEMBER 2000

The *International Herald Tribune* has run an article I wrote on Poland linked to the Sikorski statue unveiling yesterday. I feel as usual pleased at seeing my ideas in print. It is still a buzz.

At the Labour conference, a virtuoso performance by Gordon Brown. I lean against a wall and in front of me is Douglas Alexander and some other little Scottish acolyte who had worked on the words. They were reading out some of Brown's riffs as if they were proprietors of the words themselves. Brown makes no concessions but manages to exude support for a better deal for pensioners and other poor people at some stage in the future. It's not quite 'pie in the sky' or 'jam tomorrow' and is all mixed up with an earnest moralising about purpose and socialism. At the end, he quotes the John Smith line, 'we simply asked for a chance to serve', which has everybody on board.

The standing ovation is genuine but is as much a signal of the party to the public that the attempts to divide us via the Andrew Rawnsley book on the making of New Labour alleging that No. 10 thinks Gordon Brown has 'psychological flaws' or the attacks on the Dome or the fuel protests won't work. Brown is one of our own, and in clapping him, we are putting up two fingers to the press and the public. But as I look at the delegates as they stand up to clap, having heard a very rigorous and in economic terms a rather right-wing Labourist speech, I see no real ecstasy or enjoyment on their faces. This is the standing ovation that a leader gets from the led, not a real engagement with the ideas. I lean forward to Douglas Alexander and point out, 'There's no ecstasy on their faces' and he turns to snap at me, 'It is not that kind of speech.'

Why do I even bother to engage with these aides-de-camp? They have to obey orders and to query the general is an act little short of treason. What we need is a new discourse of explaining ideas and policies and discussing choice rationally. Brown belts out slogans and a 'accept this or drop dead' mode of delivery. He leaves no arguments in people's minds that they can mull over and use themselves as they make the case for a Labour government and its policies.

It is raining hard and I get soaked as I run to something called the Brighton Sea Life Centre. It is a funny kind of old municipal aquarium and I chair a Fabian meeting on Europe. In fact, there are more meetings on Europe organised by different organisations than on any other theme this week.

And yet I sense the European discussion is on a plateau. Nothing new to say. No new passion to engage with. The young but very sharp Scottish MEP Catherine Stihler points out that 7.5 million people voted for Craig Phillips in *Big Brother*, far outstripping participation in the European elections. Now that's what I call a fact.

Afterwards, the Fabian reception with the fish tanks and sea creatures swimming around. I swill white wine and then go back to one of the posh hotels where there is a huge crowd of people for the 'Key Britain in Europe' meeting. Robin Cook is doing the speech and says he will accept 'Tory asylum seekers who want to come over to Labour on account of the Conservatives' anti-European position'. It is triumphalist and cocky and somehow Robin, although a major political bit of geology on the landscape, hasn't quite got it any more.

I was attacked by Joyce Quin over the proposal for a second chamber for the European Parliament. 'Oh God, not that old idea. I hope Tony isn't going to propose it. It won't work. It's what we had in the 1970s. It's just another layer and will be seen as more and more junketeering.'

I was taken aback by her aggression and tried to argue that the whole politics of Europe had moved on dramatically in the past ten years, with more and more sense of alienation from decisions taken in Europe's name. The European Parliament had no legitimacy. We had to do something to reconnect people with Europe and what might have been inappropriate twenty years ago could be made relevant now. But she wasn't having any of it.

On the train home, I chatted with David Clark, the veteran north-east Labour MP, who was Chancellor of the Duchy of Lancaster for a year after the 1997 victory. He is running for Speaker but I don't think has any chance. He said that Cabinet meetings in his time never lasted more than fifteen minutes. The longest indeed was over the issue of the Dome. 'I was sent into No. 10 with an impressive red leather folder embossed in gold with my title "Chancellor of the Duchy of Lancaster". It looked good on TV, but there was not a single piece of paper in it.' Cabinet government is all but dead. Thank God Doug Henderson was on the train with a bottle of whisky and so we could have a slug or two before getting back to London.

TUESDAY 26 SEPTEMBER 2000

On the train down to Brighton, I sit beside Michael Wills who reveals that his parents were Austrian Jews. That may explain his intellectualism and analytical ability. He thinks the fuel protests are only a wobble and is full of confidence that investment and business in Swindon, his constituency, will be rewarded by voters, keeping him as an MP. He agrees, however, that the briefing by the two camps has to stop.

The metaphor I have been using for some time is that the Brown and Blair gang are like the scorpion in the fable who stings the frog taking him across the river and when the dying frog complains, the scorpion says, 'Sorry, it's in my nature.' The mention of scorpions, however, was a mistake, as in Don Macintyre's biography of Mandelson, Wills is quoted to the effect of saying, Mandelson and Brown are like 'scorpions in a bottle' and only one will crawl out alive. I have to listen to a five-minute tirade from Michael about how

Macintyre is a liar and he never said that, but methinks he protests too much. He also agrees with me that we are seen as being too close to big business. In America, Al Gore is bashing 'the powerful' and in Germany Schröder has attacked 'big oil'. But Blair never breathed a criticism of the oil companies despite their disgraceful behaviour in the fuel crisis and he has been very careful never to suggest anything is wrong with multinational business in the UK.

'It's easy to deal with thirty or forty big companies, but Blair doesn't realise that all the small companies are there and are quite fed up with the big ones. Yup, we need to find some new words on this,' says Michael.

Into the conference room for Robin Cook's speech. It was one of his worst conference efforts. He at times almost parodies his very slow delivery, leaning back and rocking as he searches for a laugh, which comes, but not that natural spontaneous laugh that he used to enjoy. In the middle of it, Keith Vaz's beeper goes off and we all snigger on the ministerial team dais as Keith desperately searches in a bag to switch off the offending noise.

The only new line in Robin's speech was one I had put up a few months ago, saying that we should run a campaign against the death penalty. He announces that in the second term, we will appoint a special envoy to campaign against the death penalty. Afterwards, he said that No. 10 were very hostile to the idea and wanted it taken out but Robin insisted. I can imagine that, and it's a tribute to the radical and moralistic genes that haven't been cloned out of him that he put the idea into his main conference speech.

Into the crowded hall before the Blair speech and Tracey Allen, Phil Woolas's lovely wife, pulls me into a reserved seat. Blair actually makes an unusually good speech which has a lot of joined-up arguments. It really is Mendès France stuff, 'to govern is to choose', and Blair does it well. He has a bit in the middle where he clearly is not reading off the text and talks about 'an irreducible core'. One of the lines is that if people wanted to vote for racist language on asylum seekers, they could go and vote for Hague. He throws his hand over his shoulder with contempt and the place just erupts in cheering. My generation and a younger generation are absolutely passionate on the question of race and community relations. It's not just a moral engagement. It's a response to the fundamental miscegenation of British society and a desire to see it made to work. The Tories have got this desperately wrong and Blair has it absolutely right.

Dinner with Simon Heffer, Tom Baldwin and Matthew d'Ancona. Heffer is very cross at any suggestion from Blair that the Tories are racist, but I tell him they are and he'll just have to live with the political consequences. To win power again there will have to be more black and Asian faces on Tory benches in the Commons. Heffer goes on and on about how the Tory high command is gay, including the leader himself. Heffer's homophobia begins to irritate Tom Baldwin and they are tetchy and snappy with each other. I wonder if Simon's star is fading. I hope not. He is actually a serious intellectual historian on aspects of England's political history, past and present. And he remains extremely good company.

WEDNESDAY 27 SEPTEMBER 2000

Down to Robin Cook's suite in the Metropole Hotel. He is on the third floor. Blair is on the first. I wonder if they even *talk* during the conference week.

As usual, Robin can barely control his scorn for Brown. 'On Monday, he called for a great national debate on tax and spend. I look forward to it actually taking place,' he says sarcastically.

Doing a bit of crawling, I say, 'It already took place on Monday, Robin, for half an hour in Gordon's speech.'

I said that the announcement about a special envoy to campaign against the death penalty had gone down well and he said it 'was extremely hard to get by No. 10'.

Always a storyteller, I recount the tale of my time in Florence, of Jospin calling for an end to the death penalty and Blair and Schröder looking in terror at this direct assault on the United States and how Clinton burst out clapping, saying, 'Yeah, yeah, yeah...' and the others, having got their cue, joined in supporting Jospin's call for an end to capital punishment.

Robin laughs out loud at this confirmation of the absurd pusillanimity of Blair on these big issues.

I tell Robin that we are running rather on empty and now have a simple economistic programme of managing the economy well and trying to keep revenue and expenditure in balance with the social edge:

But there is no politics of process. What is going to deliver better health and better schools? Nobody trusts councils or a highly centralised NHS administration. If we are to have effective government below Whitehall, they cannot be elected on first-past-the-post. We have to keep electoral reform alive. But please, Robin, don't call it PR but ER.

At the end of the hour, I shove him across my text, which he hasn't seen, and I'll see if any of it appears in his speech tonight.

Along to the Ship Hotel, where Robin does his speech. It is preceded by Polly Toynbee. She demands a newspaper ownership law in the vain hope that our right-wing papers would suddenly become rational and sensible. She says the British press has made the British people 'inward-looking, isolationist, grumpy, bitter, uncertain of anything...' and I call out, '*Guardian* readers' and everybody laughs.

Back to the Metropole Hotel, where I have to pick up the speech drafted by Tim Garton Ash for Poland. As I go up to Blair's suite to fetch it, I cross him and Cherie coming down the stairs. He thanks me again for my work on the speech and Cherie gives me a kind of friendly pat on the head as I bow in her direction. They do seem genuinely quite friendly, but what can one read into all of this?

Upstairs there is just a messy hotel room turned into an office with a nanny walking up and down with Leo, who has a big dummy stuck in his mouth. He has a round face and rather blondish-orangey hair and just seems a bit unhappy. She clings on to him fiercely, frightened in case anyone robs her of her charge. There are a couple of women and a man there who say, 'Where's the speech for Denis? Where have we put the thing for Denis?' As if I was a familiar part of the establishment.

When I get Tim's speech, it's actually rather disappointing. The words are good but there is an awful lot of waffle on globalisation, which we all know and don't need, and a really rather pathetic set of paragraphs on reforming the European institutions. Instead of speaking clearly in English and calling for a 'constitution', Tim suggests a 'Catalogue of Competences' setting out what is done at the national or European or regional level. The other stuff about having a presidency that runs for a year just is boring, and if Blair doesn't go to Warsaw with a big picture speech, it's hardly worth going beyond the stuff on enlargement which we can all agree on.

I go back on the train. I went into one first-class carriage for the journey back only to find somebody had vomited on the floor. The only effort the train staff had made to clean it up was to cover the foul, stinking mess with a sheet of toilet paper. What a disgusting country.

THURSDAY 28 SEPTEMBER 2000

Back down to Brighton for the last day. In the conference hall for an absolutely magic moment – the speech by Nelson Mandela. I do a short TV interview beforehand, poking fun at the Conservatives for being so opposed to Mandela in the 1980s and their support of the apartheid regime. It is cheap point-scoring, but what fun it is to score cheap points.

Inside, Mandela walks in on Blair's arm to a delirious ovation. The man is pure charisma. It is a much better feeling than when he addressed us all in Westminster Hall five or six years ago. Now he is with his political own, and at the end of a very clever speech, he waves his arm partly open-palmed and then in the clenched fist salute of African communism. The speech itself was beautiful, making a joke about being a 'pensioner' – a sensitive subject for the platform. It is the only platform speech which offers a critique of globalisation. 'No country can avoid it, but we must not hesitate to condemn those aspects of globalisation which lead to more poverty in the world.'

It is necessary 'to become once more the keeper of our brothers and sisters'.

The African National Congress and the Labour Party must 'represent a voice for those exiled from power and privilege'.

This is all marvellous stuff and I wallow in it and feel privileged just to be there for a great public speech in my own country.

Mandela mentions Aristotle and Plato, saying that as we inter people in the earth, we are all of the same value whether we are unknown or a great Greek philosopher. Again the references belong to another age. The spin doctors and speechwriters would never let Blair mention Aristotle or Plato and I doubt if half the Cabinet know who these two gentlemen are.

A profound moment of joy and standing ovation he gets and I scud out to go to a hotel for an interview which doesn't actually materialise, but then Mandela is coming through the entrance and I join the greeting line and get a handshake and a smile. Just a simple handshake, nothing to report in this old man with his grey and silver African shirt with such a serene smile. We are all so small in his shadow.

MONDAY 2 OCTOBER 2000

I write a piece on Paul Sykes, the South Yorkshire property developer who is in the news because he claims that the money he gave to the anti-euro campaigners in Denmark to pay for big adverts in the papers there helped swing the vote. Now he is offering £20 million to the Conservative Party if they will come out against Europe. I am trying to stir the shit a little but as usual get the snobby, frosty indifference from *The Guardian*. The only thing worth reading on their over-wordy comment pages now is the diary. The letters column is intellectually more lively and politically more engaging.

TUESDAY 3 OCTOBER 2000

The Polish speech problem won't go away. Julian Braithwaite, who is coordinating Blair's speech, says it is hopeless:

> We have got too many ideas and versions. I pulled them all together and sent them to him, but he will have to decide exactly what he wants to say. He doesn't know yet. Alastair [Campbell] is meant to go tomorrow to brief the Brussels correspondents and we haven't got anything like the final version yet.

I am reading a book on how to save a relationship by a man called John Gray called *Men Are from Mars, Women Are from Venus*. I go round telling everybody that 'voters are from Venus, politicians are from Mars'. Anji Hunter bursts out laughing and says, 'Don't I know it!' I have a word with Sally Morgan about the speakership. She says that Blair is keeping right out of it and No. 10 is giving no instructions to anybody on how to vote.

'Tony has written a nice letter to Michael Martin, wishing him well and making clear there will be no Downing Street interference.' But she then goes on to say that she is very unhappy at the thought of Labour tribalism winning out and I get the definite steer that they would like George Young to have it. I talked about it briefly with John Healey on the phone earlier, suggesting we might write a joint article calling for a non-tribal approach to the speakership, but he fled from the idea, saying it would be seen as a message from Gordon. I suppose he's right, but the response is just a little pusillanimous and disappointing since he is a very clear person on other issues.

THURSDAY 5 OCTOBER 2000

I go up to the Polish Embassy and look at the lovely statue of Sikorski which was unveiled the other week. It really is a fine bronze sculpture with nice plaques around it and will always be there for the generation of Poles who can come and wonder what their ancestors did in Britain in the Second World War.

In the embassy, the acting ambassador says that the Chinese Embassy next door objected to the statue going up and tried to put pressure on Westminster City Council to stop it. Dear oh dear, I really am a bit old to be feeling anti-communist, but the Chinese are close to top in today's running order of foul regimes, with their stinking little embassies up whose fundaments we have to crawl.

I am in the Polish Embassy to have a lunch with Tadeusz Mazowiecki, the first Polish Prime Minister of democratic Poland after 1989 and since then a great UN and EU figure.

Tadeusz is delighted with Blair's endorsement of EU accession for Poland and the warm words he will say tomorrow in Warsaw on this topic.

'If I hurry back to Warsaw tomorrow, I might just catch Mr Blair at the cocktail party. But I believe that if I haven't heard a speech, I shouldn't go to enjoy a drink with the man who has made it.'

'God,' I say, 'this is a new theory, that you have to hear the speech in order to enjoy the *après-discours!*'

'Don't put it in a new diplomatic handbook,' says the former Prime Minister.

SUNDAY 8 OCTOBER 2000

The news is just too funny. A few weeks ago, we were all laughing at William Hague because he claimed he used to drink fourteen pints when he was a boy in Rotherham. Now we have a gaggle of shadow ministers explaining how they all smoked joints of cannabis as younger people. Of course they did. I did. Everybody did. Big deal. But it is not just a clean breast of things event. No. This is a statement by part of the Conservative Party trashing and seeking to bury the ludicrous Ann Widdecombe. At their conference, she had called for punishment and fines for anyone caught with any tiny amount of cannabis, a policy which if applied would place more than half the young population of Britain in the criminal category. She is a deeply silly woman, but Hague has to support her and so all the Oxford-educated joint-smoking Tories have come out to reveal their useful inhaling practices and made her look thoroughly stupid.

Actually, if it starts a debate on what we should do about cannabis, so much the better, but I'm afraid there is just a pure reaction of political pleasure at the Conservatives' discomfort. Shameful, but there it goes.

I checked the Web and found lots of positive coverage of Blair's speech in Warsaw. There was a nice story in *Le Monde* and *El País* has reprinted the entire speech.

The British press has been pretty fair as well. Hugo Young in *The Guardian* was ecstatic and even *The Times* gave it a good report in the news section and a very fair editorial.

I was pleased that Blair had all the references to de Gaulle in the speech which I pushed him to make. Jonathan Powell and Sarah Helm and their two little daughters came round for lunch and Jonathan said he was sorry that in the press discussion of the speech I hadn't got credit for my input. I shrugged with false modesty, saying you can get anything done providing you don't mind who gets the credit. We'll see.

He said that Chirac had spoken to Tony about the speech and said, 'It is a very good speech, I am very impressed with it and I shall certainly read it.' Otherwise there was little that was strong or new.

The big fears at No. 10 are Geoffrey Robinson's memoirs and Paddy Ashdown's diaries, both of which are scheduled for publication later this autumn.

'The *Daily Mail* wouldn't be paying out big money for Geoffrey's book if they didn't think it was going to damage us,' said Jonathan. Well, they should have thought of all of that and managed Geoffrey a bit better. Either he shouldn't have had the ludicrous job he did or else he should have been let down far more gently. In the end, it was Brown's promotion, but it is Blair who will pay the price. The Ashdown stuff will just irritate all the Liberal haters in Labour, but otherwise it isn't important. I asked about the speakership and Jonathan turned up his nose at the idea of Michael Martin. 'But Tony says things will change before the election and although Martin has the support now, it could all start to unravel. He has a good feeling for how parliamentary things develop.' But he confirmed what everybody else in the government machine says and that is that No. 10 isn't remotely getting involved in the fight. Quite right too.

MONDAY 9 OCTOBER 2000

I bump into Andy Marr on the Tube who says that Hague is much more fanatically right wing – anti-abortion, pro-capital punishment and even pro-birching – than people realise. Hague is completely with Widdecombe in her ludicrous lurch to the right. I got called up by the *Daily Mirror* asking if I had smoked dope and just cut off the interview while I was talking, which makes it look as if the phone had gone wrong at the other end, and then disappeared when the man called back. What a coward! But if I want to do this story, I want to control it on my terms and at the moment I see no reason to throw out any planks of wood to Tories sinking in their own quicksand of bad news.

FRIDAY 13 OCTOBER 2000

The British Embassy in Athens helps put together a British–Greek annual event along the lines of Königswinter. They asked me to come in the summer, but in the letter it seemed clear that unless I was a minister or a civil servant, I would have to pay my way. So I said no. But in the last two or three weeks, they have been most importunate, begging me to come and saying my fare will be paid.

An early morning flight from Gatwick. Roger Liddle and others are there, but I sit on the plane reading all the papers.

Athens is two hours ahead of London, plus the three-hour flight, so it is mid-afternoon when we arrive. We take a catamaran from Piraeus out to a little island called Hydra, which has no cars on it, just off the southern Peloponnese.

The hotel is charming with a cluster of rooms on two floors and a water heater you have to switch on yourself. I go off to find some rocks to dive off into the Aegean. The water is translucent and without goggles I open my eyes to see the fishes and the rocks and the sand below. It is warm, much warmer than the Atlantic off La Baule ever is. I splash left and right and for a minute think I am again on holiday from Oxford or just afterwards with all of my life in front of me. Bliss.

Then to drinks at a house owned by Loukas Tsoukalis, a handsome Greek professor who is an economist at the LSE. He is one of that generation that under the colonels went abroad for their education and was perhaps the last generation to come to England rather than America. He is well off. When asked if he was renting a flat in London for his job at the LSE, he said, 'No, no. I bought a house in Chelsea.'

Helen Liddell is there and in a tizzy. It is the Scottish school half-term and so she is also going on holiday with her sons to Cyprus. But Donald Dewar's death means she has to go home for the funeral next Wednesday. I talk to her about the election for the Speaker and she says that Frank Roy, the Motherwell MP, had come up to her and said, 'You're a Catholic, you're a Scot, you're Labour, you vote for Michael Martin.'

Helen said, 'Look, with the number of Catholics in my constituency it's not worth going against them.'

Andrew Dismore, the Hendon MP, is here as well. He speaks some Greek and has been holidaying in Greece for twenty years and so is the Step Change MP responsible for Labour contacts with Greece. He says he is actively campaigning for Michael Martin:

He was the only one of [the Speakers] who took any interest or helped the 1997 intake. The two Tories and Betty were very rude and unpleasant, but Michael allowed us to make mistakes and was encouraging. So I am campaigning for him. We have done all sorts of flow charts to show what happens depending on when Ted Heath accepts certain names for nomination. The crucial thing is that Michael isn't called too early and then he will not only be in with a chance but probably get it.

SATURDAY 14 OCTOBER 2000

Helen Liddell and I talk about the succession in Scotland after the sudden death a couple of days ago Donald Dewar, who has been the First Minister in Scotland and by far the sharpest Scottish Labour brain after the death of John Smith. The real problem is that all of Scotland's reservoir of first-class political talent in Labour came down to London in the 1980s and 1990s and left no one behind to run Scotland once it got its own Parliament. Labour under Dewar could not get a majority of seats in the first elections for the new Scottish Parliament last year. He had to form an uneasy coalition with a few Scottish Lib Dem MSPs. This left the field open for the nationalist demagogy of Alex Salmond, hostile to anything and everything that Blair, Brown, Cook, John Reid, Helen Liddell and all the Scottish Cabinet ministers are doing in London. Dewar was politically astute enough to keep Salmond's catch-all left-right nationalism at bay, but there is no successor of his stature in the rather low-grade pool of Scottish political talent amongst MSPs in Holyrood. Might Robin or anyone else give up Westminster and go back to Edinburgh? I doubt it. Alex Salmond will soon enough be in charge.

SUNDAY 15 OCTOBER 2000

The conference finishes with a presentation by Roger Liddle. He and the other official speakers from the government are extremely economistic. It is all about making Europe more of a capitalist paradise and very little about the other democratic or social values that count. There is some correction here from Mary Honeyball, a hard-working MEP from London, who is very quietly spoken and goes to bed early but is a true believer on Europe. I prod the Greeks on Turkey a bit as the Greek speaker said that they were opening up a good relationship with the Turks. But when I suggested they followed the example of the South Koreans and went for a real opening of dialogue and dropping of barriers, they all quickly hurried back into their shells saying that it was the Turks that had to move first and it was the Turks that presented all the problems, not the friendly democratic Greeks. Greece spends 6 per cent of its GDP on maintaining a huge conscript army with lots of tanks and aeroplanes in order to fend off the perceived Turkish threat. It is a huge dislocation of resources and matched by equally wasteful expenditure on the Turkish side.

The sea was too choppy to allow a hydrofoil to leave and so I couldn't get my planned early afternoon flight home. Instead, after a final nasty lunch, I went for another swim, though it was distinctly cooler than the first balmy day. But three days of swimming in the sea is a rare treat at this time of the year.

The smartest guy there was Sir Nigel Wicks, who has recently retired as number two at the Treasury. He said that one of the surprising things about Gordon Brown and other ministers is how shy they were. 'Nigel Lawson could hardly bear to speak to anyone and

I have noticed that Treasury ministers in particular are very shy beings. I wonder if that's why people become politicians, because then they are obliged to break out of their shyness?' I wasn't too sure about this thesis given the raging vanities and egos of most of our top ministers, but there is something in the thesis that the people who get to the top of politics are socially dysfunctional. He said that while the royal family were relaxed about not having the Queen's head on euro banknotes, they had fought very hard to keep her head on the euro coins if they come into circulation in the UK. Banknotes are issued by the European Central Bank, but coins are still minted by the individual national mints so can put whatever national symbols they like on them.

I read most of the Sunday papers on the way home and the big story is Geoffrey Robinson's attack on Mandelson. His book will be serialised in the *Daily Mail* and will say that Mandelson has told less than the truth on the loan he got for his house. My reaction is so what? But we are in for a bit of trouble.

MONDAY 16 OCTOBER 2000

A meeting in Keith Vaz's office, but as usual, it is simply a list of meetings with nothing concrete decided. Keith complains about going to a dinner of the leaders of the Party of European Socialists in Biarritz. 'I didn't know what I was doing there, I didn't know anybody else at the meeting and I didn't know what to say to them,' he complained. I just sat dumbfounded. What is the point of having a Minister for Europe who doesn't know anything about European politics and politicians?

WEDNESDAY 18 OCTOBER 2000

I started reading again Lewis Namier's book *The Structure of Politics at the Accession of George III*. Reading it now as an MP, it is a completely different work from when I looked at it as a student all those years ago. His first chapter is called 'Why men went into Parliament' and he argues:

> Men went there 'to make a figure', and no more dreamt of a seat in the House in order to benefit humanity than a child dreams of a birthday cake that others may eat it; which is perfectly normal and in no way reprehensible. The figure of their daydreams differed with their rank and profession, with age, temperament, and circumstances; so much, however, was common to practically all: the seat in the House was not their ultimate goal but a means to ulterior aims.

A shiver went down my spine as I read those words. Nothing but nothing ever changes.

MONDAY 23 OCTOBER 2000

It is Speaker election today. And what a British comedy it turned out to be. We all trooped into the Chamber, but by 2.15 p.m. all the seats on the benches were taken and I sat under the gallery with Doug Henderson and Ian Pearson laughing at the whole farce. Sir Edward Heath sits very old and shaky at the clerks' table. First off is Tony Benn, who makes a long rambling speech about the war in Iraq, unelected people in Europe, multinational capitalism and every other bee in his bonnet. This, I guess, is his last major parliamentary outing. Yes, he dominates because he is fluent and speaks extremely well. But no sense comes from his mouth. Fifty years of being obsessed with Westminster has left him unable to propose the necessary reforms to make our country a fairer or more efficient place.

Tony thus pressed a button that allowed ninety minutes of increasingly irritable waffle from people. Ted sensibly read out the list of the names in the order that he proposed to call them and with Michael Martin's name at the top, it meant that everybody had to combine around one candidate to defeat him. Over the weekend, the papers had been full of Margaret Beckett and Clive Soley, saying that they wanted support for George Young. This, as I told George later, was his kiss of death. The PLP will not be told by the executive who to vote for and the rumblings about class solidarity were strong.

I just sat back, hunched in dismay at people making a spectacle of themselves and realised that the headlines tomorrow would be all about how Parliament looked foolish and stupid, as indeed it did.

We came to the first vote, that of the other Deputy Speaker, Alan Haselhurst. That was easily defeated. The rigmarole demands that a person moves and seconds one of the candidates and then he or she gets a chance to make a little speech saying why he or she is so honoured and humble to be proposed for Speaker. After the Haselhurst vote, I went out for a cup of tea with Doug. We were both pretty cheesed off. Just before I left, Keith Vaz sidled in and I told him he had to vote for George Young. He said 'why?' I said that's what No. 10 wanted and he grinned cheekily. I shall check to see how he voted if he even bothers to do so, as I expect he has got Foreign Office events to go to.

Out on the Terrace to get a breath of fresh air and we were joined by Shaun Woodward. As always, he was dressed in a 2,000 guinea suit with a crisp white shirt and a cigarette in his hand. He has curious rheumy, milky eyes but is very easy to talk to.

'I shall be voting for Michael. When I was opposing the Conservatives on Section 28 – and it was quite a hard thing to do – he was very kind and supportive.'

Yeah, yeah. But the plain fact is Martin is an absolutely smashing person and when we went back in I regretted going into the lobby for George Young, but I still genuinely believe that the Labour Party should not collar everything. Whoever is chosen as Speaker, the House will not change because of that one individual and all the rubbish in the press about how important he or she is is just that – the press jacking off without any real understanding of how the Commons functions.

WEDNESDAY 25 OCTOBER 2000

I voted twice at 10 a.m., having a quick word with Douglas Alexander who was critical about Blair's over-focus on the economy in his PLP speech this morning. I wish I could get on better with Douglas as he is extremely bright and interesting. But like all Brownites, he is ruthlessly focused on the domestic agenda and extremely tactical rather than strategic. I gave him a memo I have circulated about why George W. Bush may become President, but he will achieve that by espousing all the new Third Way and Clintonite social agenda. I have listed ten things that William Hague has to do to become more like George W. Bush, including appointing black members in his Cabinet, supporting gay themes, allowing more immigrants into the country and not being perceived as isolation-ist. I still hope Al Gore wins, but if Bush does this at least will be a marker.

WEDNESDAY 1 NOVEMBER 2000

I stayed in my office to work on a speech I am to give at York University on Friday. I had decided to make a public call for tactical voting – Lib Dems voting for Labour to keep the Tory MP or candidate out and vice versa. It will cause trouble, especially amongst the tribal wing of the party, but if we retreat into tribalism and fail to attract the much broader coalition of voters that supported us in 1997, and in particular fail to persuade Liberal Democrats that it's better to have a Labour MP than to allow the Conservatives to win seats, then we will be thrust back on the defensive and Hague, while not winning power, could make a serious breakthrough and the show would be over.

Afterwards I go round to Blair's office in the Commons and ask to see Sally Morgan. She comes out and I tell her what I am going to say on Friday in York and say would there be any problems with it. 'No, I think that's exactly where Tony is. I don't think there'll be any problems with that at all. Tony will be quite relaxed.' Good. Now if any hacks ask me, I can say it has been cleared with Downing Street.

TUESDAY 7 NOVEMBER 2000

To the Foreign Office and I arrive a minute after 10 a.m. to find to my surprise that Cookie has already started his meeting. Cook is obsessed with Europe as the only issue. I tell him to focus on the Treaty of Nice as being essential for the enlargement of the European Union and the Tories shouldn't oppose that. I also tell him about US Defense Secretary William Cohen's speech praising the European Defence Initiative. To my amazement, he hadn't heard about it and didn't know of Cohen's strong endorsement of the European Defence Initiative which the Tories are busy trashing all the time. At the end of the meeting, I also said I saw one of Francis Maude's researchers making a photocopy of an article in that morning's *Daily Telegraph* about Zimbabwe. Robin chuckles. 'Who do you really work for, Denis, the SIS?' I feel embarrassed though because his own staff and aides ought to be pumping all of this in and they are not awake on so many political issues that matter to Robin and to a Labour government.

FRIDAY 10 NOVEMBER 2000

Up to Oxford this afternoon to talk at Nuffield College.

At Nuffield I am greeted by Godfrey Hodgson and the legendary David Butler. I am there to speak to a seminar they run for international journalists. Butler says that he did tutorials in PPE with Tony Benn in Oxford in the 1940s and once again the tiny enclosed circles of the British elite leave me gaping with wonder. It is so hermetic and incestuous. The seminar is fairly ordinary. I waffled away a bit about politics and the media, arguing that all politicians wanted to be journalists and all journalists wanted to be politicians and that there was simply no reporting of facts any more, merely endless comments. I also had a go at the coverage in the liberal press of Europe and will see if any of it gets picked up.

Then dinner, which was really very, very good on the high table. The master of Nuffield is some top economist who was very doubtful about Brown's policy of massively reducing public debt: 'If the government doesn't borrow, what happens to the gilt market and all those savers who want to place their money with the government? Where do they go? The equities market is offering poorer returns day by day.'

Afterwards, port and cheese and I was sitting beside Gillian Shephard's son. He is now an economist at Nuffield. I made nice noises about his mother and he said she really only enjoyed politics when she was a county councillor and thought she was achieving something. I don't know whether he was being discreet, but I can't for the life of me think of a single thing she did as a minister that I now remember.

To the Fabian annual general meeting. I have to debate with Janet Bush, the director of Lord Owen's anti-euro organisation. I arrive a bit late, about halfway through her speech. She reads the text out. I instead play about with lots of nasty remarks attacking the anti-Europeans as isolationist and generally being hectoring and negative, which when the questions arrive I realise was exactly the wrong tactic. This is a Fabian audience that wants calm, reasoned analysis, not knock-abouts. Janet gets very upset and I don't think she has been exposed to the kind of rhetoric that all of us who are pro-European have to put up with from the Trevor Kavanagh gang. They love dishing it out and then get very prickly and sensitive when the balls are sent back across the court.

We agree to have lunch. I really like her and just don't understand what the hell she is doing mixed up with some of those evil bastards.

MONDAY 13 NOVEMBER 2000

I dine at a table full of Blair's Babes: Siobhain McDonagh, Caroline Flint, Laura Moffatt and we are joined by Beverley Hughes, who eats one dish and a glass of water, says nothing and goes back to her boxes. There is absolutely no decent gossip or ideas from any of them. And I really wish I'd sat down with the chaps, except all the chaps' tables were full of club bores as well.

WEDNESDAY 15 NOVEMBER 2000

As usual, the question time was just a slugfest between Blair and Hague.

To my right, Caroline Flint also kept popping up and down. She was dressed in bright red to catch Speaker Martin's eye. I could see him leering at her. She was very much one of his campaign managers, so I expected she would get called. But he kept calling people to witter on about floods. Prime Minister's Question Time has now become incredibly hermetic, inward-looking, only fretting over English domestic headlines. So I didn't get called, but Caroline did and she popped up and said, 'My question has already been asked' and sat down again. Claire Ward, the MP from Watford, had asked a greaser's question about the minimum income guarantee and that apparently was what Caroline intended to ask. Unbelievably, she didn't have a second question in reserve. Chris Mullin once told me that in opposition, you must always have two questions in your pocket whenever you get up at Prime Minister's Question Time.

I had dinner with Ruth Kelly and Harriet Harman in the Members'

Dining Room. Ruth was interesting, saying that after the next election all sorts of divisions and tendencies would erupt in the PLP.

'There's all sorts of stuff simmering just below the surface. It's going to be quite a bitter and fractious Labour Party after the election,' she said.

Absolutely right. Blair's basis of appointing just cronies is driving everybody mad and there is real anger over Brown's incessant refusal to say anything positive about Europe. I don't like the smell of future politics.

Behind the Speaker's chair, I bumped into Peter Mandelson who said, 'What news have you for me, Denis?' He has this very Hogwarts's schoolmasterly way of talking at times and I'm not surprised he doesn't have a single friend in the PLP. I told him my concerns about the two MPs last week, Ian Davidson and David Taylor who had asked questions at foreign and Treasury questions saying, 'Who needs the euro?' and that if we started to push away the decision to join the euro to a third term, then there was absolutely no difference between us and the Conservative Party and in consequence the pro-European business community would simply transfer their support.

'They were put up to it by Gordon. He is behind all of this,' Peter snarled, turning on his heel and walking away. For him, it all comes down to personality. He looked very strained and unrelaxed.

THURSDAY 16 NOVEMBER 2000

Mandelson is on the front page of the *Financial Times* saying that the government's strategy on Europe is wrong and we have to make a political and constitutional case for going into the euro. He is right, but why say it and stir all the shit now? In any event, I have to go on to the *World at One* to talk about it, not so much defending him but just trying to attack the Tories and fill in space that otherwise might be occupied by a more awkward person. At least Andrew Marr is there, who points out that the French and Germans have equal difficulties and divisions as we do and demand vetoes and their domestic audiences are also surly and not sure about the whole European project. But Andrew's remark was right at the end and the main line was how divided and unsure the government is. Well, it's true, you can't have a Chancellor taking a fundamentally hostile position on this great issue and not expect there to be awesome repercussions.

Up to Russell Square for the ISTC annual dinner dance. I just stayed for some food and had my picture taken with John Prescott, who mentioned me nicely in his remarks before the dinner. John Monks was there, pretty much in misery on Europe. It's not moving forward.

TUESDAY 21 NOVEMBER 2000

Dinner in the House with Uncle Joe and my brother, Ed. In the Strangers' Bar, John Hume came up to talk and, of course, I had forgotten that Uncle Joe's uncle, Monsignor Doherty, had been headmaster of the school in Derry that both Hume and another Nobel Prize winner, Seamus Heaney, had attended. So there was the old Donegal connection flashing away. Hume said he was unwell and that he couldn't find a hotel to stay in in London so was flying back home. I still don't know how he does it. A member of the European

Parliament, the British Parliament, a Nobel Prize winner – what drives him on and on? But in that Strangers' Bar full of nothing, we were close to greatness for a moment.

THURSDAY 23 NOVEMBER 2000

The day was devoted to the six-monthly debate on Europe before the EU Council meeting. It was a collector's item. The first point to note: there were only about eight Labour MPs present. Europe has no political salience. Robin no longer attracts a crowd. Admittedly, there were three by-elections today and it is a one-line-whip but it should be a warning signal. And of those who were there, Denzil Davies and Austin Mitchell were just present to make their usual hostile speech against Europe.

That being said, Robin turned in a sparkling performance. He, as usual, had taken time off to craft his own speech and it was full of wit and scorn for the Tories.

Menzies Campbell said something to the effect that Margaret Thatcher had opposed German reunification, and Francis Maude jumped up to say that she had been in favour of German reunification and he should know because he was her Europe Minister. I raced out to check her autobiography and sure enough in the section headed 'German Unification', she said again and again that she had sought to slow it down, felt it was a threat and opposed it. I slipped all this to Alan Whitehead, who jumped up and accused Maude of misleading the House. But there was even more to come.

Andrew Robathan, the Blaby MP, jumped up and said that the Tory MEP Bill Newton Dunn, who had just announced his defection to the Lib Dems because of the Conservatives' hostility to Europe, had been 'a liar' at his selection conference for the MEP job. Immediately, Ken Clarke got up and contradicted Robathan. Clarke said that he had respect and regard for Newton Dunn and did not feel that he had misled people at the selection meeting which he, Clarke, had attended. It was a wonderful Commons moment to see two Tory MPs at such loggerheads.

It got better as Clarke himself made a speech comprehensively trashing the hysterical opposition of the Conservatives to the European Rapid Reaction Force. This is in real terms quite a modest military proposal which leaves NATO firmly in the driving seat. But the anti-European Tory press has gone bananas on it, saying that it is a European army which will undermine NATO and destroy the Atlantic alliance. Complete tosh and Clarke showed how the lineage of this proposal was directly traceable to Conservative policy and thinking. Without being insulting or being aggressive, he completely demolished the position of William Hague and Francis Maude. A parliamentary tour de force.

Then it was the turn of Sir Peter Emery. He has been an MP for forty-one years. A knight of the Devon shires, he lamented that the Conservative Party of Churchill and Harold Macmillan, whom he quoted effectively about the need to pool sovereignty, had disappeared to be replaced by the present anti-European mob. It was a long lament delivered in his plummy right-wing voice. Nothing aggressive. All sorrowful complaints asking, 'What has happened to the Conservative Party?' in terribly sad and plaintive terms.

Speeches from our side were virtually irrelevant. This was the Conservative Party going through the most extraordinary agony over Europe. How stupid they are.

FRIDAY 24 NOVEMBER 2000

Up to Rotherham on this incredibly long, slow train. I met Yvette Cooper and her little baby girl, Eleanor. We chatted and I played with the baby as much as possible. Like all one-year-olds, she is a handful, but Yvette seems a strong, clear, competent mother. She has one great policy idea, which is to give a piece of fruit to every English schoolchild. An apple a day keeps the Tories at bay. Otherwise, we just skirt round issues. Her husband is Ed Balls and anything that I really want to say about economic policy or the management of social policy which Gordon also runs, let alone Europe, will go straight back to Ed and Gordon, so I keep my counsel to myself.

MONDAY 27 NOVEMBER 2000

I go into defence questions and there is a silly Tory question about combined cadet forces. This allows me to get up and announce I was a company sergeant major in the Combined Cadet Force (CCF) and its training of discipline and team work was jolly good for me as an MP in contrast to the lack of team work and discipline on the Tory side, so I suggested that they set up a parliamentary branch of the CCF for the Tories in order to inculcate basic training and the values of loyalty. It got shamelessly a huge laugh from all over the place and once again my little star rose as a parliamentary performer. But, oh God, I wish it didn't really have to be on this basis.

TUESDAY 28 NOVEMBER 2000

I saw Robin Cook and said that he should leak into the papers the fact that he and Gordon had dinner together with their wives to re-build relationships. But what Robin wanted to know was who was briefing against him.

'I know Ian Austin [Gordon's replacement for Charlie Whelan] is involved, but I need details, chapter and verse, so I can nail him.'

I shrugged my shoulders and said, 'Sorry, Robin, the bits and pieces I hear are on a very confidential basis, but nobody will give me that kind of direct evidence with the detail you need.'

SATURDAY 2 DECEMBER 2000

A surgery followed by handing out mince pies in the town centre. There was a good crowd of Labour people. The reception wasn't bad either. People were happy to participate and take a mince pie from their MP or a councillor. There wasn't much politics about, but it reminds everyone of my presence. It's now become almost a Rotherham tradition.

Afterwards, I go over and see Mother and then drive back down to London.

In the evening to Harriet Harman and Jack Dromey for dinner. A very fun evening. Andrew Marr and Jackie Ashley were there. She is going off to interview Gus Macdonald. He is another one of Tony's peer cronies. Because he is rich and successful, he gets a big government job. I just think he lucked out with his ex-Trot or hard-left credentials. Like all transport ministers, he is a complete disaster. There is some Soviet ten-year plan to spend lots of money, but that is little different from any plan to spend lots of money over ten years. Transport is still in complete chaos. Oona King is there with a lawyer friend. She says it is disgraceful that so many unelected people like Macdonald are in charge of big government departments. She delivers her message with real venom and I expect Jackie will put it in her profile.

Margaret Prosser, the lovely T&G deputy general secretary, is there. We reminisce about the 1992 Clinton economics conference that I helped set up and the T&G organised.

I had mentioned this to Margaret McDonagh in Berlin. She thought it had all been done by Philip Gould, but he belongs to the falsification school of history at which he is the central object around which everything else revolves. Bill Morris is soon to retire and Jack Dromey, of course, would love to get the succession but like me he is just slightly out of tune with the new rising wave of appointments. I hope Oona King gets a job soon, as she has all the capacity of being a star, but she is also her own woman and that Blair can't stand.

TUESDAY 5 DECEMBER 2000

Into the Foreign Office to see Jeremy Cresswell, who is off to Germany to be deputy ambassador. In the next room, I see Colin Budd who is off to be ambassador in the Netherlands. He shows me a twelve-page vindicatory memo he has sent to Robin Cook about what we are doing in Europe. I don't have the heart to tell him that there isn't the faintest chance that Robin will read all of this worthy stuff. Why on earth can't these people boil it down to one or two sentences? They are highly paid and have been highly trained to make words serve the interests of the nation. So why can't they find words that will actually get read by their political masters?

I had lunch with Tom Baldwin and Patrick Wintour at a nice

restaurant called the Zander at the St James's Hotel, where I ate oysters and a *confit d'oie*. We had two bottles of decent Puligny Montrachet and, as it was close to Christmas and I have started going to the Commons gym again, I let myself go. We were joined by Bob Seely, who is the media and special adviser to Francis Maude. He scuttles up and down the press corridor of the Commons making sure Francis is in the newspapers every ten seconds. I ask him if he is going to go to Nice for the EU Council and he shakes his head. I tell him he should because he will have great fun, though, of course, my real motive is to encourage the incredibly manic air there is now about all of Maude's pronouncements on Europe.

Seely and he are making the same error made by Gordon Brown before Charlie Whelan arrived as his press officer, namely to mistake a quantity of appearances in the form of quotes in newspapers for a quality of political intervention. Maude is becoming a chirping cricket on Europe and as a result is taken less and less seriously, even if he automatically gets his paragraph or two of quotes in the *Daily Mail* and *Daily Telegraph*. The bottom line is that their position of saying 'No' to everything from Europe is faintly ridiculous.

Seely is really nice and good and intelligent to talk to. I expect I would like Maude too. He seems decent, thoughtful and with a great political pedigree. Why on earth are they in such a cul-de-sac of politics? William Hague's decision to turn the Tories into an anti-European party, as he has no idea otherwise how to lay a finger on Blair, will damage UK politics.

SUNDAY 10 DECEMBER 2000

In the morning out for a run and I go to Victoria Station where

The Observer on sale there has an article I have written attacking Tory isolationism. Yesterday, *Die Welt* published a long piece I wrote called 'The Five Europes' and gave it a big space. All of this is happening while the Nice European summit takes place. It seems we are doing very well. On Friday, there was a ludicrous row about the European Rapid Reaction Force, but Blair slapped down Chirac making clear it was not going to be divorced from NATO.

Yesterday, the main television news on the BBC said Blair had won his campaign on keeping the veto on tax rates. It's a false victory but will play well with the electorate. Today, we see that the idea of Europe as a steamroller super-state is nonsense as the fifteen nation states fight it out with each other to get the best they can for each individual nation. It is unseemly, but it shows the public that Europe is not moving to a homogenised single political entity. Nor should it.

MONDAY 11 DECEMBER 2000

A great success from Nice. Blair and Cook return triumphantly. It is a long Commons day as not only is there Blair's statement but it is the Foreign Office speech on the Queen's Speech afterwards.

As Blair gets up to speak, Cook is at his side constantly chirping. He never stops chattering into Blair's ear as Hague makes a bigger and bigger hash of his reply. Were I Blair, I would be irritated. But Cook is too good and professional to be disposed of. Hague is, well, there is only one word – pathetic. On his best terrain – in front of the despatch box – and on his best issue, Europe, he should have at least landed a blow. But he is shrill, he makes no jokes, he goes on and on about qualified majority voting, which means nothing to anybody, and he has no positive image to offer.

Blair, by contrast, is passionate. He lays into Hague. He asks him if he wants a referendum on whether the pensions of the officials of the Court of Auditors should be decided by qualified majority voting or not. It is a debating point but then the House of Commons is about debates, and Hague shrinks into a horrible hole as if he wished he could go away. It is not a nice sight to see such a ruthless crushing of an opposition. But Hague and the anti-Europeans he now allows to run the Conservative Party deserve everything but everything they get. Will it make them think again? I doubt it.

On to the BBC Two despatch box programme at midnight. I am there with John Redwood and Shirley Williams. Steve Richards kindly introduces me as the 'influential backbencher' and buoyed up by that and the wine I had taken in the dining room, I had a good go at Redwood. He simply didn't have a leg to stand on. They don't know what to argue on the Nice Treaty. The fact that the east Europeans all want it ratified as quickly as possible removes their best argument and makes them look isolationist and hostile to the Poles or the Czechs. I kept an eye on the studio manager and ended up with the last word. I felt pretty good as I cycled home.

MONDAY 18 DECEMBER 2000

An odd little conversation with Ann Taylor, who called me into her room at half-past four after I had gone to the gym.

'Denis, I've called you in for a little chat, I suppose acting as an auntie,' she opened. 'I know you want to be a minister and you're probably very pissed off that you're not one already,' at which point I nodded, and all I want to say to you, in as friendly a way as possible, is that you should try and show some more gravitas in the next few months. You're very good, you have lots of talent, you speak foreign languages, but sometimes you just say things that might lead Cabinet ministers to ask whether they really want you in their team. There was something you said last week and I heard you and I thought to myself I will call Denis in for a conversation that has never taken place and just tell him to try and be serious over the next few months while Tony and other people decide on who the ministers will be in the government after the election.

I couldn't see any special angle she was coming from and it seemed to be genuine and friendly enough. I told her that I liked making jokes at the Tories and I liked being very present on my feet in the House of Commons and sometimes that meant taking a risk with something that didn't come off and could be seen as being just a bit extravagant. But that's what I have been all my life. Since I was in short pants, my mouth got me into trouble because it said things that a wise head would have left unsaid. I told her what David Butler, the Nuffield don, had said last week, that I sounded very ministerial on television but came over as a human being not as a minister.

'Look Ann, that's what I am. I am not a grey "speak your weight" machine. I know most Cabinet ministers just want young say-nothings in their team and although I hope I'm a loyal player, I can't take my personality out of myself.'

She replied:

No, no, Denis, I know that. It's just a question in the next few months of trying to say things in a more serious way. At the end of the day,

Blair will decide but he will ask Cabinet ministers if they want you in their team and if they think that you're going to say something that might get into trouble then that's something against you.

I know all this, I said to her, and said more strongly to myself, but actually I was very grateful for the reminder and will try to be on best behaviour from now on.

TUESDAY 19 DECEMBER 2000

Into 10 Downing Street for a meeting with representatives of the PSOE, the Spanish Socialist Workers' Party. They want to know how they can win back power in Spain.

On the way into No. 10, I cross Jack Straw and behind him Charles Clarke coming out of the front door. I tell Jack, sincerely, that he was very good on *Any Questions*. Mind you, he was with John Redwood and that is taking political candy from a wounded baby. Jack beams. Behind him, Charles Clarke just looks dour.

In the evening, briefly to the Foreign Office for the annual media party. Kim Darroch, one of the European desk chieftains, asks how I am able to get so many articles into the media. I tell him because I don't allow the Foreign Office to write them for me and he recoils, hurt. He is a former head of the news department so thinks that everything the FCO writes is golden prose. The FCO simply doesn't understand that people want to read what an author really believes in. They want honesty. Of course, the papers will take an article in the name of Blair or Cook written by some hired pen, but everybody knows it's not the real thing, and I simply can write as if I believe in what I am saying.

2001

The BBC call me up because Lord Sainsbury, who is a DTI minister, and other rich business people have made huge million-pound donations to the Labour Party. I feel deeply uncomfortable about a serving minister of the Crown giving £2 million to the party that will appoint him to his post. It's not corruption because Sainsbury will get no financial benefit from his donation and yet it doesn't feel right. The BBC seem to think that I have a strong line on state funding, but as I am in Davos skiing, I am no good for *Newsnight*, nor when the call comes in a bit later, for breakfast television. Hooray.

At dinner, I sit beside Adolf Ogi, who has just retired as president of the Swiss confederation. He shows me a book of pictures about his political life, which has a quote from me in the foreword, and asks me to tell Blair that he, Ogi, was available for any international jobs that might be coming up. He also says that he can arrange for Blair to come on a winter's holiday and learn to ski completely protected from the press. I might pass the information on, for what it's

worth. He gives me a little red Swiss Army penknife with the words
stamped on it – 'Adolf Ogi, President of Switzerland'.

WEDNESDAY 10 JANUARY 2001

Upstairs to hear Tony Blair speak at the PLP. He started by telling us
not to ask him about the date of the general election, but the message was clear, we are in general election mode. I was struck by his
self-assurance. He's still very much managerial, in a crisp white shirt
and red tie and with his funny hand movements of holding up first a
hand then pushing it palm forward and then putting up one, two or
three of his long strong fingers. The argument was pretty much the
same about campaigning on our achievements rather than offering
anything new to the electorate, save that we are not the Conservatives. On Europe, he said, 'It may not be a vote winner for us, but I
believe it could be a vote loser for the Conservatives.' So Labour is
simply the non-Conservative Party. I wonder if that is enough.

Blair was good against Hague. But the pair of them took until
3.20 p.m. with their exchange, which really is unacceptable. There
is some poor Conservative candidate in Edgbaston who has put on
his website all sorts of rude things about Hague and how useless
the Tories are, and Blair seized on this to make this man an instant
hero to Hague's great discomfiture. Good dirty electoral politics
but very little to do with governing the country.

SUNDAY 14 JANUARY 2001

An odd article by Steve Richards in the *Independent on Sunday*. I
had sent him a memo I had circulated about regional government,

pointing out to Ed Balls that regional government could not be a set of cheques sent out by the Treasury to regional development agencies for specific projects which the Treasury would monitor, control and decide whether or not they had been successful. There had to be an elected element in it.

'What governments can create. Governments can uncreate. What voters create tends to last,' I had written.

Steve, however, wrote that I had a fatal flaw, which was to tell bad jokes in the Commons and treat the whole business as a bit of a laugh. He also then wrote that I ranged more widely than any other MP, which was nice, but I was a bit shocked to have that impression of my style in the House actually written down black on white. It is, of course, similar to what Ann Taylor, the Chief Whip, told me before Christmas, so I suppose it's just how others see you. Damn. How else does one get attention there without making people laugh now and then? But to be dismissed as a jokester, no thanks.

THURSDAY 18 JANUARY 2001

Up early to get the Eurostar to Paris for the British–French *colloque* and it's the usual gang with some new faces like Evan Davis, the open, friendly but very know-all BBC economics chap, and Diane Coyle from *The Independent*. The speaker at the dinner is Peter Mandelson, who comes in with a very odd speech which he reads carefully. I couldn't see if it had been typed or if he had written it himself, but it was a disconnected and disjointed speech making the case that Europe needs to develop what he called a '*Westpolitik*'. By this he meant that Europe should go to Washington, ask the new Republican administration what they wanted and give it to them. It was a weird *plaidoyer* for acceptance of American hegemony and the American world view on trade, defence and other issues.

All the Frenchmen there are pretty ruthless bosses of big multi-nationals and are in no way anti-American but they were all shaking their heads in puzzlement at Mandelson's message. I murmured to one of them that surely the Americans need to develop an '*Ost-politik*' and meet Europeans halfway over the Atlantic, instead of insisting on the supremacy of their national economic interests and their world ideological perspective. My remark was greeted with warm nods and for the first time I had the feeling that Peter was losing it in terms of being a big European player.

As I went out to bed, I put my arm around him and gave him a friendly squeeze but found that the very trim Mandelson waist had become rather fleshy with a spare tyre. I think he is under very great strain at the moment and knows that after the next election, which will be won on the government's record rather than on Mandelson's spin, Blair may no longer need to rely on him as greatly as he has in the past.

FRIDAY 19 JANUARY 2001

It's a lovely hotel, this Trianon where the Treaty of Versailles was signed. The French politicians and commentators are divided into those still living somewhere in the late years of the twentieth century and those trying to make a breakthrough into the next hundred years. What was odd, however, was a sense of political morosity amongst the French. They all see the Treaty of Nice as an absolute disaster. They see Chirac and Jospin locked like Sherlock Holmes and Moriarty on the Reichenbach Falls in Switzerland wrestling with each other and both about to plunge over the edge. There are horrible corruption cases involving top French politicians or their offspring and no sense of political confidence in a country which economically is doing very well. French job creation and growth is better than that of the United States at the moment and, by gosh, I would love to have a bit of French wealth and public services spread around my own country.

The star turn was Gordon Brown. He had come down in a train from Brussels to Paris with Laurent Fabius, the French Finance Minister. There had been an Ecofin meeting and clearly during the train journey, Fabius had worked as much charm as possible. He spoke first before the dinner. His speech was full of praise at what Brown had accomplished in turning round the UK economy and offering leadership in Europe. He flicked into English at the end and with a charming French accent said, 'Dear Gordon, we want Britain and we want you to be at the heart of Europe. Please, that means that Britain will have to join the euro.' It went on and on with lots of oily Gallic, unctuous flattery, but the message was clear. He would be an ally with Gordon in a great process of liberalising and reforming Europe along social democratic lines, but Gordon couldn't keep out of the euro and play that game.

But the surprise of the evening was Gordon's warm response to Fabius. Unfortunately, he couldn't pronounce his name. He kept referring to 'Law-renn' as if the former French Prime Minister, now Finance Minister, had the same first name as the American film star Lauren Bacall. But he was warm in his enthusiasm for the single currency. 'We want to see the single currency succeed. We think it makes sense. We see no constitutional or political reasons not to join. The economic tests remain, but we expect to succeed and we want to be in it.'

Written down like that his remarks are no different from the formal ordering of words that one gets from any government minister talking about Europe. But it was the warmth and the repetition and the body language that left myself and I think everybody in the room who looked at each other in surprise with the clear impression that Brown was warming to both Europe and the euro.

He is actually on safe ground. Blair has made clear there will be no possibility of replacing the pound with the euro without that being approved by a referendum. That was also John Major's line and William Hague hasn't changed it. I have spent four years at the FCO and never once heard Robin, any minister or official, or anyone in Downing Street who shapes EU policy ever mention holding a referendum. Making the pro-EU case has been sub-contracted to Britain in Europe, set up in 1999 on an all-party basis. Robin Cook made sure he was on the launch platform along with Tony, Gordon, Ken Clarke, Michael Heseltine and Charlie Kennedy. Like the European Movement, it is a worthy outfit, but William Hague with the backing of most of the press has turned the Tories into a full-on anti-European party.

Gordon knows as we all do that Blair is not going to call a referendum on joining the euro and allows his epigones to fan out to spread anti-euro briefing. So he can tell Laurent Fabius what he wants to hear, knowing that with the euro-entry referendum pledge in his pocket, nothing will happen.

Gordon does however also set out an ambitious programme of reform for Europe. Energy market liberalisation in 2003, capital market liberalisation in 2004, recognition of professional qualifications and then 'on to aviation and postal services'. By 2010, 'Europe should have improved its productivity by 40 per cent to match that of the United States'.

It was a typical Brownian discourse, full of sweep and ambition, but it set the evening on fire. Curiously, he repeated word for word one of the jokes that Fabius had made – to the effect that people take the TGV from Paris to the Channel Tunnel and 'then have time to explore the English countryside at leisure'. It is an old Mitterrand joke, but Gordon obviously hadn't bothered to listen to Fabius as he repeated it word for word. That is Gordon's problem. Always getting ready for his next speech and never listening to what people are saying around him.

Ed Balls gave me a wink and a smile as if to say, 'Hey, don't brand us as anti-European' and David Miliband was there, quite cheerful at the idea that the Chancellor and the Prime Minister might be working off the same script in the future. That is probably an over-optimistic gloss and we'll see, but it's certainly the warmest endorsement of Europe and the euro that we have seen from Brown. Of course, when I changed some pounds into French francs yesterday, the rate had fallen below 10 francs for the first time in a long while. Good news for exporters, but for tourists and the ordinary British punter?

TUESDAY 23 JANUARY 2001

In the Commons, I tell Robin Cook that I was surprised at Gordon Brown's support for the euro at the *colloque* in Versailles, and he asked me to do a quick memo on it. I have already written one note on the new triangulation between France, Germany and Britain and sometimes ask myself if this endless trying to analyse and assess what is going on is worth it.

WEDNESDAY 24 JANUARY 2001

Crumbs, where has all this come from? Mandelson is in unbelievable trouble. Apparently, he spoke to Mike O'Brien, the Home Office Minister, about a passport for one of these wretched Hinduja brothers but he claimed he didn't and Alastair Campbell briefed the press and Chris Smith gave a reply in the Commons, which in effect denied Mandelson's personal involvement. Now it turns out that he had made the phone call.

I bumped into Mike O'Brien who said it had been a quite innocuous two-minute phone call and really something that anyone might get up to on behalf of a powerful person. Yet Mandelson has tripped over the magic barrier in parliamentary life of misleading the Commons. The papers are gunning for him. I bumped into Tom Baldwin who says that he will have to go and then around midday out comes the news that Blair has fired Mandelson. Christ, this is amazing stuff. Peter seems now well and truly finished. You can rise again after three days, but you can't rise again for the third time in British politics. And yet, having a piss in a bathroom near the dining room at the top of the stairs above the members' cloakroom is Keith Bradley, the deputy chief whip, and I ask him if Mandelson is now finished. 'Yes, for about a week,' comes the cynical reply as he shakes his willy. And that is the mood everywhere. Nobody knows quite how to take it.

There is no sorrow, of course. Mandelson is the most hated man in the Parliamentary Labour Party. Actually, many of those who dislike him have no personal reason so to do, but he has come to symbolise all that is manipulative and coterie about the government.

I slip into the bench just to the right just behind the front bench and to the immediate right of the Speaker's chair at 2.30 p.m. and give Peter a little cheer as he rises. It's partly personal solidarity but more I don't want those Tories to make hay out of it. He actually looks OK and answers one question well. Then in comes Blair and there is an immense shuffling of Brown and Blunkett and Straw, but Blair insists on sitting beside Mandelson and side by side, like two lovers who now have to part for ever, they face their foes for the last time.

Hague is useless with a stupid sub *Daily Mail* rant about him. There is no cutting phrase or wounding jibe that lasts in the memory. Just bar-room bluster. But Blair is shaken and the whole House can feel it. It is the most monumental drama. Mandelson has resigned and yet still takes questions. He remains a Cabinet minister until 3.30 p.m. No one can quite believe it. Here is the man who helped invent New Labour. Here is the man upon whom Blair utterly depends. Here is the man who represents both the government and the party and huge sections of business and the glittering salon classes and the European bigwigs in a way that no one else can remotely manage. He is better known in Europe than Cook or Brown. And now it's all finished? No more Mandy? Does he stay as an MP? And all of it played out in that most awesome bullring of the House of Commons.

I think there is some admiration on the Tories' side for his sheer bravura in sitting on the front bench, but it is quickly all over. I go out behind the Speaker's chair and turn right to head for the tea room and there he is just in front of me, turning left into the room that leads either up to the press gallery, long his favourite hunting ground, or down to the car park for ministers and oblivion. I lean over and give his arm a little pat and squeeze and he turns and gives me a rueful smile. Poor Peter.

THURSDAY 25 JANUARY 2001

I do a TV interview, a kind of *Meet the Press* thing for Sky with Adam Boulton, Paul Routledge, who has been campaigning for Mandelson's dismissal non-stop now almost since the government was formed and is in seventh heaven, and Michael Cockerell, the clever BBC maker of TV political biographies. He says that he couldn't be bothered to do one on Mandelson because you just wouldn't get proper cooperation and 'you simply could never trust anything he was telling you'.

I defended Mandelson as a contributor to the New Labour project but said his career was over so I am part of the burial squad. All the people whose careers he advanced, like Geoff Hoon and Steve Byers, are now hastening to bury their former mentor and spend as little time as possible praising him. It's a shabby business. The papers have huge pictures of Vaz asking all sorts of questions he has to answer and which frankly he won't be able to. There's a real whiff of fear and worry about the place. Neither Mandelson nor Keith Vaz represent anything important, though in a funny way I think Keith is more significant as he's Asian and if he goes it will be seen as removing a non-white face from front-line politics, but he doesn't have many friends in town, though I am sure Downing Street will now have to rally round and try to protect him as much as possible.

FRIDAY 26 JANUARY 2001

The media frenzy now fully turned on Vaz, and Mandelson has simply disappeared from view. Journalists are excited about Keith's links to the Hindujas, the property he owns, the political machine he runs in Leicester. There are explanations but taken together it is a feeding frenzy on Vaz. The night before, I had gone out to Hounslow to stand in at a Labour Party meeting for Peter Hain, who has been abruptly moved to the DTI. This follows Helen Liddell's promotion to be Secretary of State for Scotland. My goodness, she entered Parliament the same year as me and is now in the Cabinet. And her move is because John Reid becomes Ulster Secretary. I wish I could be as much in favour of Reid as everyone else. I like him well enough because he is a serious hard political intellectual, but he seems a real Vicar of Bray who has shifted and trimmed to every move in the Labour leadership, from being a Scottish communist in the heyday of 1970s workerism to being more Blairite than Blair in the past two or three years. Anyway, good luck to him as he is a decent enough man, though he smokes far too much and I find his style on radio far too hard, like a company sergeant major barking orders, not the politician that you could have any rational dialogue with.

His number two was Brian Wilson, who is the hammer of Holyrood and the Scots Nats – the most publicly identified of the antidevolutionists amongst all the Scottish Labour MPs. In consequence, the Holyrood government, or administration as we are meant to call it, won't have him as Secretary of State, so Helen is promoted over the top of his head. To try to soothe the humiliation, he has to move and I suppose a Foreign Office ministerial slot can be described as a promotion or at least not a demotion. Poor Brian, whose family home is out in the Hebrides, whose constituency is south-west of Glasgow and who has a young boy with Down's syndrome, what kind of life is it rushing around the world doing these tedious embassy visits? At any rate, it will be a friend at the Foreign Office for the few weeks that remain.

So, as I type away, I reflect on the number of ministers who have come and gone since I have been a PPS at the Foreign Office. Nobody has stayed more than a year or fifteen months and it will be interesting to see the pecking order when this is formally published to find out whether John Battle, who was also booted out of the DTI and dumped in the Foreign Office, is over or under Brian Wilson.

SATURDAY 27 JANUARY 2001

The broadsheets are full of Vaz, Vaz, Vaz, but curiously not the tabloids, who relegate it to a couple of pages on the inside. So he may yet survive. I don't care because there is just something deeply unhealthy about all of this and he is going to be such a wounded animal for ever more. I wish to God Blair had never appointed him to be Minister of Europe. It was a gimmick appointment and it's turned into degrading the whole nature of our European political engagement. Keith gave an aggressive interview press conference outside the Indian High Commission yesterday, but when I phoned up John Williams, he complained that Keith had done this all by himself and had refused to listen to advice from either himself or Alastair Campbell.

John complained:

He has even taken to ringing journalists in the *Daily Mail* straight back. He won't listen to advice. We told him not to attack the press. We wanted him to make a statement in a controlled situation, but he went into all that rigmarole outside the Indian High Commission. He is now just out of control.

Yet with luck it may die down.

SUNDAY 28 JANUARY 2001

It's getting worse, far worse. Mandelson has gone insane with a front-page *Sunday Times* attack claiming he was forced to resign and that the crime he committed didn't justify his dismissal and in any case, he didn't actually make the famous phone call to the Home Office Minister, Mike O'Brien. All this following a press briefing by Alastair Campbell on Friday in which he implied that Mandelson had lost his marbles, had become 'detached' and was in the same league as Ron Davies, the Welsh Cabinet Secretary who was fired after being caught on Clapham Common in some kind of gay pick-up event.

Obviously, all of this was relayed pronto to Peter and he has exploded and decided to try to play at Samson and bring the whole temple crashing down with him.

It's been made worse by lots of Cabinet ministers like Geoff Hoon who said that Peter should go back to knocking on doors and delivering election leaflets or Clare Short who was on one of the *Question Time* programmes and could barely contain her glee at his dismissal. Mandy is now raging around wanting revenge or at least, I expect, wanting the offer of again some return to power.

This could all go hideously badly wrong. The *Mail on Sunday* has a story of Vaz acting directly as the representative for the Hindujas. One side aspect is the claim that Anji Hunter was given a pashmina scarf by the Hindujas and yet Nathalie has had two from Keith each Christmas since he was Europe Minister. It's just the way they operate to wrap up and keep warm.

WEDNESDAY 31 JANUARY 2001

Up horribly early to go, however, to a really interesting event in 11 Downing Street. This is Gordon Brown showing he is master of the political universe. It is a seminar on moral values or social responsibility and he has a very right-wing professor called James P. Wilson from America. This man is keen on taking young single mothers and locking them away in hostels where they will be taught to be good citizens. It was a deeply conservative right-wing presentation and the room at No. 11 was full of right wingers like Melanie Phillips. Only dear old Polly Toynbee stood up with a pure bit of Pangloss saying that women and everyone were living in a much better world with more opportunities and a more decent life than ever before in history and we shouldn't work ourselves up into a lather. But Professor Wilson and our good Scotch Calvinist Chancellor have hit a point about moral emptiness and a value-free existence that we're all concerned about.

Gordon told a good joke about Gladstone and Disraeli, whose portraits hang downstairs as you come in to No. 11. 'When you met Gladstone, you left thinking he was the wisest man in the world. When you met Disraeli, you left thinking that you were the wisest man in the world.'

Wilson, the white-haired American conservative, was followed by Jonathan Sacks, the Chief Rabbi. He was in cracking parable form. Everything was told as a story. He quoted Abba Eban at the LSE. 'Here I learnt a passion for truth, justice and fair play, but these have been such a disadvantage in my political career.'

Sacks went on to talk about the importance of values. 'If I share power with nine other people, I have one tenth of my power. If I share £1,000 with nine other people, I have £100 left. If I share love or tolerance with nine other people, I keep the whole of what I had.'

He argued that people believed all problems would be solved by either the state or the market. The left liked the state and the right liked the market, 'but what we need is society based on covenanted relationships. Not a contract but a covenant that links us all together. We need above all to learn moral literacy.' It was beautiful language, spoken so clearly that one could easily see why this man became Chief Rabbi at an early age. Yet, afterwards, Samuel Brittan said that he wanted to ask Sacks to confirm that he had issued some kind of statement in Israel asserting the Jewish supremacy over all of the holy places in Israel. Not much tolerance or moral literacy there.

It was a rich couple of hours and showed as ever the conquest of thinking in government that one associates with Brown.

At noon, over to the Foreign Office to meet Keith Vaz and go with him to the Polish Embassy, where there was a BBC crew waiting for Vaz, but he swept by without a word. He had been given a lecture to read out, but he ignored it completely and just spoke off the cuff in a rather incoherent way.

At one stage, he referred to all the jobs being created in America and urged Europe to follow suit. But, of course, the boot is on the other foot now, with Europe being the job creator and American unemployment looking very dodgy. But his mind was so obviously on so many other things. He referred to people who had Polish connections like Alan Whitehead who was in the audience and 'our friend Denis at the Foreign Office', without giving me the benefit of a second name. In the car on the way back, he said he had been taken to hospital last night for a couple of hours and it was already in the local papers. Apparently, he had shooting pains in his head and heart and had a little panic but was given an all clear at St Thomas's. He wondered how the story had got out and I said that hospital staff will phone up anybody for £50 if a famous person comes in. Just like the police who talk to journalists every day. He seemed surprised at the workings of it all.

At Prime Minister's Questions, Blair had a good bash at Hague and more than held his own. It's all pre-election stuff now. Hague didn't seek to exploit the Mandelson and Vaz problems. The trouble is that the Hindujas have spent as much on entertaining the Conservatives or allowing Conservative fundraising to revolve around them as they have on schmoozing Labour or paying for pet Labour projects. It's an all-round loser in which all MPs emerge as sleazy. Thanks Mandy, thanks Hague.

SATURDAY 3 FEBRUARY 2001

A lovely dinner at John Lloyd's Hampstead flat with his new wife, Ilaria, David Goodhart, the editor of *Prospect*, and Lucy Kellaway, his extraordinarily pretty fluttering birdlike wife. An easy conversation between friends. They want all the gossip on Mandelson and

Vaz and I don't really have anything to add other than what can be read in the papers. David, as always, slightly contrarian, says he thinks that Vaz is getting a raw deal.

'He hasn't done anything that can be proved against him. So if he is not guilty, he should not be made to resign.'

I, of course, have a slightly more political turn on the story. Blair cannot fire Vaz without turning what is a very seriously political management problem – Mandelson's departure – into a governmental crisis. In addition, the newspapers will simply move down their food chain to destroy the next weakest link minister. They won't even bother to feast on Vaz's remains if he is thrown to them. The latest story is about all his properties. He has a house in Leicester, a family house in Stanmore and a flat in Pimlico, so together those properties amount to several hundred thousand pounds without anything improper in their accumulation. Unless, unless, unless. Even as I defend the man, my mind keeps asking what if, what if there is something more, something distinctly naughty that will emerge and then I will look a fool for having put so much energy into defending the indefensible. John was rather quiet, suffering from a bad cold. Both he and David agreed I should be a minister, and I told them to write it up and tell as many people as possible. If you don't campaign for your own promotion no one else will.

The evening finished with Goodhart telling us about an essay he was trying to write or edit on Jürgen Habermas. And then all three of us spilled the beans as we confessed that reading the great German political philosopher left us more perplexed rather than more clear in our thinking or the instruction on what we should do.

MONDAY 12 FEBRUARY 2001

I spot a little opening in defence questions on European defence and get the French Embassy to send me over the text of what Chirac had said at the Cahors Franco–British summit last Friday. Excellent. He said in French that European defence, contrary to what people said, could only be made in complete harmony with NATO. I drafted a letter to Iain Duncan Smith, the extremely nice but fanatically Europe-hating shadow defence spokesman, in which I said that he should not go to Washington as he plans to this week to use domestic political differences to try to carry our party fight onto foreign soil.

I had said to Crispin Blunt just outside the members' entrance that it was a pretty bad show for Duncan Smith to try to go abroad to try to stir up trouble against the UK's defence policy. Crispin said, 'But we have no choice, Denis, Iain's got to go to Washington to get them to try and make you people see sense.'

The Tories really are quite shameless in seeing their party advantage, their anti-European ideology and their desire to pray in aid a foreign power all jumbled together. I showed the letter to Geoff Hoon behind the Speaker's chair as he was waiting to go into questions before 2.30 p.m. and he was quite happy with it. I don't really care, but it's courtesy and it covers my back.

In the Chamber itself, I read out a bit of a sentence in French quoting Chirac and then went into an attack on Duncan Smith, saying it was a disgrace he was going to Washington in order to tell 'lies…'. At the mention of the word 'lies', the Tories started screaming and shouting at me. The Speaker, who now looks with intense suspicion whenever I get up to speak – especially as I was wearing my light camel-coloured mohair jacket from Paris which is really rather loud – got up as soon as he heard the word 'lies' and said the minister didn't have to answer the question. It was a brutal put-down, though I had made my point.

I glowered and glared at him and when Duncan Smith talked about Labour 'spinning', which of course is parliamentary speak for lies, I just said loudly in the direction of the Speaker, 'Why one rule for them and one for us?' In effect, he has enshrined in a short time a remarkable new doctrine. The Tories can tell lies about us, but we can't tell the truth about them. I take his point that ministers have to answer for their own actions across the despatch box, but my constituents, if I can put it so pompously, send me not just to hold the executive to account but also to test the future executive-in-waiting. If there is a chance to vote against him, I shall most certainly take it after the election.

Robin Cook at the PLP had spoken on foreign affairs and had done so very effectively. When he finished, John Healey, who was sitting beside me slipped out saying, 'He's still got it, hasn't he?' and other MPs murmured in approval. I passed the message on to David Clark so he could tell Cook. I can hardly be bothered to talk to him since rational exchange seems so impossible.

On to a dinner at Claridge's for Joschka Fischer, the German Foreign Minister. I got a prize from one of the committees that David Marsh runs and all the Anglo-German bigwigs were there. James Naughtie was dancing in attendance, completely hysterical about Mandelson. Fischer made a brilliant speech, essentially pleading for more integration while accepting the centrality of the nation state as a source of democratic legitimacy and attachment of peoples in Europe. It was beautifully done. I slipped a note to Nick

Butler, who was sitting beside David Miliband, saying 'who on earth could do this in our political system and in a foreign language' and Nick scribbled back that he had made exactly the same point to Miliband. We have great power as a rich leading country, but we have no politicians who are fully capable of shaping the European argument other than Blair himself and he doesn't want to get engaged.

WEDNESDAY 14 FEBRUARY 2001

Lunch is at *Private Eye* with Francis Wheen and Jonathan Green to talk to. There isn't much quality political gossip. There are no real good scandals around. The *Private Eye* gang are serious scandalmongers and they know that the Vaz story is a bit of a fake. He is naughty but nice, wanton but not wicked. And they all have a sneaking admiration for Peter Mandelson, who has brought so much colour to the political landscape, and they want him back badly.

In the Commons, an indifferent Prime Minister's Question Time where Hague again completely fails to bite. He surely has to go now. Unlike, say, José María Aznar in Spain or Kohl in Germany, where a Conservative leader could stay as party leader over two or three losing elections because there was no alternative, our parliamentary system demands that you produce the goods every week and if you don't, people find you wanting. The Tories surely are too ruthless not to get rid of Hague as soon as they decently can after the election.

A drink with Derek Wyatt. He has a nice little flat in Marsham Street but is completely fed up now at the thought of losing his seat.

He'll make money. He's an ex-rugby international and those contacts last a lifetime. I shall miss him badly.

SATURDAY 17 FEBRUARY 2001

Inside the Scottish Exhibition Centre in Glasgow. It's a rather dull
and dismal Labour Party event. The usual gang are there, but there
is no excitement. British and American war planes have bombed
Baghdad. It's front page on all the newspapers and Bill Rammell,
the nice sensible MP who heads the Labour Movement for Europe,
is having a piss with me in one of the toilets and muttering, 'Why
on earth do we have to do it, Denis? Why do we endlessly have to
run after the Americans?' His views are shared by Robin Cook, who
I see just before he is due to speak and I say to him, 'The timing of
this isn't great, is it?' and he replies, 'I just don't know what they're
up to.'

Cook makes a good speech but not to the main conference. There
is a kind of side or parallel conference for European issues and local
government issues and he has been relegated to that. Nonetheless,
it is a vintage Cook performance with good Tory-bashing lines and
a coherent thesis about Britain being a proper player in Europe and
being in Europe delivering good important advances in the social
and environmental field for the British people. He dodges the euro
question, of course, but we all have to.

Afterwards, he asks me to come and interpret for him in a meeting with Henri Nallet, who is the international secretary for the
Socialist Party in France. Nallet is a former minister and a fairly
high-profile figure in French left politics, though his government
days are over, but he still has an important function within the

party set-up. He says that Jospin has yet to develop the European parts of his programme before the presidential election next year. 'We are not very keen on all this talk about a constitution for Europe,' he says, and Robin nods in agreement.

'We would all find it a lot easier if Lionel becomes President. We find it quite difficult working with Chirac,' says Robin. Not wisely, as there was some woman there and it's the kind of throwaway remark which could appear in one of the French newspaper columns of little political gossip bits and pieces.

But the real point of the interview isn't this chit-chat on French politics but Robin's request to Nallet that he confirms the support of the Socialist Party for Robin's candidature to be president of the Party of European Socialists. 'No problem. We agreed that last year and once we give our word we expect to honour it,' says Nallet, while a look of reassurance bursts out on Robin's face.

Cook and Nallet promise to work together, but, of course, once the meeting is over there will be no follow-up, as Cook simply has no secretariat support for any kind of political operation and he is so immensely busy just meeting the Foreign Secretary obligations that the office lays on him.

TUESDAY 20 FEBRUARY 2001

Half term for the children and they are all around the house. I do very little. At 2 p.m. I go to a special meeting of the council of the Royal Institute of International Affairs. The executive committee has chosen a man called Victor Bulmer-Thomas to be the next director. He is exactly my age. He is an academic specialising in Latin America who has worked in the University of London all his life, latterly setting up and running a Latin American institute. Nobody knew who he was and one of the council members started spluttering about interviewing him. But I said that we would have to support the recommendation.

'You don't keep a chicken and lay eggs yourself,' I said, coining, I think, a new metaphor. Poor Colin Marshall, the lord of British Airways, was grateful for the support. It looks like a pretty uninspiring choice to me. A safe academic with a safe background. I find it surprising that we are appointing someone I have literally never heard of, but I suppose London is a big enough place. Here's hoping.

I walk with Michael Williams down to the Foreign Office and he keeps shaking his head and muttering that Bulmer-Thomas is just an average academic with absolutely no experience in all the foreign affairs problems that Chatham House has to deal with. But Michael is more concerned about Robin Cook's future.

'You know Robin wasn't even told about the Baghdad bombing before it happened. And what's worrying, nor was Colin Powell [the US Secretary of State].' It's frightening how even the Foreign Secretaries of Britain and America are so completely out of the decision-making loop on these issues.

It's clear in America that while the new Bush people seem to be OK on economic and trade policy, and on foreign policy Colin Powell has shown interesting signs by going to the United Nations in a positive spirit on defence and security, it is real old-fashioned hardliners who can now at last bomb away to their hearts' content – something they could never do against the big enemies of the Cold War. They are also old men in a hurry. Damn. The Bush regime looks as if it's going to be dangerous.

WEDNESDAY 21 FEBRUARY 2001

To the Reform Club where Polly Toynbee and her boyfriend, David Walker, launched their book on the Labour government's record. I saw Philip Bassett there, who is getting married to his long-term partner Liz Symons. I tell him that far from Blair being 'Teflon Tony', it is Gordon Brown who is the Teflon member of the Cabinet as nothing sticks to him, whereas Blair has had to wade through endless buckets of shit dumped all over him on scandal after scandal which isn't even of his own making.

This was highlighted by an article in *The Sun* today which described how the national Launderette Federation was complaining about the climate change levy which they described as 'a tax on washing'. They use lots of electricity and don't have much labour so will be hard hit. It means each wash will have to go up by 20p to pay for it, so they moaned. *The Sun* continued that the climate change levy had been dreamt up by John Prescott.

Philip burst out laughing when I told him this story, just as I had when I read its absurdity. The climate change levy is a pure Gordon Brown concoction aimed at keeping his credentials high with the green lobby. It's a bad foolish tax which will have very little impact. But it's another example of how, like with the 75p rise for pensioners, or the NATS air traffic control disaster or the endless problems of London transport, the incompetencies of the Treasury somehow get transferred to other ministers who have to take the blame. I wonder how long it can last. If Blair wins with a very big majority, he can do what he likes. If he wins with a small one, then people might start asking who really is to blame. There's still no remote contender as a replacement for Blair if he decides to go other than Brown, but some of the shine will wear off.

Outside there was David Goodhart who asked me for my tie because the Reform Club has some rule about wearing ties and apparently the reception had run out of them for David. I gladly gave him one which I didn't like very much anyway.

THURSDAY 22 FEBRUARY 2001

Lunch with Stephen Wall, the nice boss of the European department of the Cabinet Office. He is really a rival Permanent Under-Secretary to the Foreign Office, without the power of patronage, which is essential, but with the power to influence policy, which is more challenging and more rewarding. We spent the first half-hour at the Atrium talking about *Harry Potter*, which he has devoured.

But as usual it was about European politics. 'The Prime Minister has given me the job of trying to bring the Germans round from their integrationist view towards our more intergovernmental position, and I wondered if you can help,' he said. Apparently, Blair had met Schröder recently and had been quite shocked how in private conversation Schröder had insisted that he supported a more integrationist view of Europe than Blair's Europe of nation states cooperating together.

'Perhaps in private I might be a bit closer to your view, Tony, but as Chancellor of Germany, it is the integrationist route that I will support and express publicly as my position,' he told Blair. Wall said that Blair was shocked by this, but I found that baffling since the absolutely central core of German policy is not for Germany to express itself aggressively and openly as a unilateral nation state with independent nationally decided economic, monetary, trade, immigration or defence policy. Surely Blair understood that core aspect of modern history?

Yet I didn't find Wall ready to bite. I wonder if Blair has got a more serious blind spot on Europe than I would have thought. Certainly, France has got a more nation-state orientation, but I expect that before long, France will do a somersault and pull itself in very tightly with Germany in order to advance the next stage of European construction. The French don't want a legally binding constitution and I am sure that part of it can be fudged but the Germans have to have something to please their own internal debate and above all the incessant clamour of their regions almost to be recognised as quasi nation states in their own right. But that's an internal German problem and Germany can't ask the whole of Europe to bend to its will and needs or at least it can't do that without a massive quid pro quo. In any case, as I told Wall, nothing will be clear until both the French and German elections have taken place. He agreed on the important role that Cook would have as president of the Party of European Socialists but there needed to be some political secretariat backup to support him.

The Labour Party couldn't do anything and the Foreign Office still had huge resistance to providing organised help if it could be seen as being party political. I also said that we needed someone at ministerial level who could cruise around Europe making contacts and doing public and party political things. Mandelson was doing some of this behind the scenes, but it could be done by either the Minister for Europe or possibly a minister in the Cabinet Office or possibly a supernumerary minister who was unpaid but detached to do all this kind of political work. Even if the minister didn't have the salary, they would have an office and the resources to carry out political networking to promote government policy. Curiously, Wall asked me to talk to Jonathan Powell about this, as if the idea is that he is at the heart of government and I am just a backbencher. I really don't know how the British government works at times. But Wall is a very agreeable, open, pleasant, smart man and it was an enjoyable hour and a half.

SUNDAY 25 FEBRUARY 2001

I check on the Web and find that the *Pittsburgh Post-Gazette* has given me a huge space for my article on EU–American–UK relations. They have printed it pretty much word for word and I am quite happy with it. Blair had a very good meeting at Camp David with President Bush. The American President signed off on a statement supporting the European defence project and that should shut up once and for all the wretched Tories who are trying to make a mountain out of this pathetic military molehill. It won't silence them, but it looked good on television and it allows the Conservatives absolutely no opening before the election.

Clearly, the Defense Department in Washington are hawks. Dick Cheney and Donald Rumsfeld, the Defense Secretary, are two old men in a hurry. They have spent too much time reading Tom Clancy and want gung-ho military adventures to end their careers in military glory. The Tories play on this by proclaiming the Europeans as being anti-American wimps. But Blair and his team seem to have sealed it off and I must call Jonathan and John Sawers tomorrow to congratulate them.

MONDAY 26 FEBRUARY 2001

Into question time for culture questions when I hoped to raise something on sport for children in primary schools. But Mick

Martin, as always glowering at me with his little sidekick, the Speaker's secretary Sir Nick Bevan, beside him, refuses to call me.

Then I spot an opening. A question on recreational shooting from Edward Leigh, the nice, eccentric, ultra-Catholic and very right-wing Tory MP. As soon as he has spoken, I pop up and say that I used to go shooting – which is just about true in that I used to go shooting in a range when I was in the cadet force and I've popped off a shotgun once or twice in my life – and that Labour was a pro-shooting party and had no problems with shooting in the countryside.

Kate Hoey, the pro-fox-hunting and anti-European Sports Minister, burbles away about how great shooting is and how many gold medals we've won in the Olympics for shooting. It's a wholly political exchange. The only purpose is to nail down the lie that Labour will glide easily from banning fox hunting to banning fishing and shooting. Dale Campbell-Savours smiles across in appreciation. 'They have just made a big mistake. Leigh should never have tabled the question. Now you have shut the whole story down. The *Shooting Times* and all the other shooting magazines will have to say that we are a pro-shooting party. Well done.' It was exactly my intention, though other softer Labour MPs mutter at me as if any support for shooting was to announce an imminent conversion to being a country Tory MP and squire.

TUESDAY 27 FEBRUARY 2001

Foreign Office questions today. A brief lunch with David Mathieson and I tell him that I want Robin to back me to get a minister's job otherwise I am quitting career-focused politics. He asked me if

I'd talked to Robin about it and I say 'no' but what in any case is the point as he never ever thinks of anyone other than himself. Really, after four years, there is about as much leadership, sense of team work and *esprit de corps* in the Foreign Office ministerial team as there would have been in a French Army platoon in June 1940.

It's not that we are retreating… On the contrary. There is a lot of good foreign policy work, but Robin has no idea how to create support and forge a team around him. Sherard Cowper-Coles calls me up and asks me to speak to Naz Ahmed because tomorrow the Home Office will announce a list of proscribed organisations including three Kashmiri militant groups. Good. I have no problems with London being the centre of political opposition around the world, but these people very often kill, maim and use the most foul and unacceptable methods.

I call Naz on his mobile and he is a bit put out, though obviously flattered that I say I am calling on behalf of Robin to give him advance notice. Apparently, he has been complaining in the House of Lords and of course Kashmiri activists around the country raise an awful lot of money for these organisations. I don't care. Whatever protests there will be in Rotherham, if any, it will be outweighed by support from other constituents.

TUESDAY 27 FEBRUARY 2001

Up to the German Embassy to celebrate the three years' operation of Charles Grant's Centre for European Reform. A lot of the great and good are there and it is a remarkable accomplishment. He has produced excellent material, commissioned very good papers from lots of people and has managed to put up interesting and challenging ideas without descending into the eccentricities of Mark Leonard's Foreign Policy Centre. Well done, Charles. His conversations are amongst the most intelligent and interesting that I have on Europe in London and I am glad to raise a glass of champagne to him.

Back to the Commons and dinner in the Members' Dining Room, where I sit with Calum MacDonald and Kate Hoey who says to me, 'I'll have dinner with you, Denis, providing we don't talk about Europe,' and I reply, 'Fine, as long as we don't talk about fox hunting.'

Brian Wilson joins us and I get him to tell the story I had heard him tell in the Foreign Office earlier in the day about his exchange with Margaret Thatcher on a plane coming back from Kuwait, where he had represented the government at the tenth anniversary celebrations of the Gulf War.

He regaled:

I am just sitting down comfortably in first class when suddenly I hear a voice which says, 'Hello, I am Margaret Thatcher, I hope you enjoyed the celebrations.' I told her yes, of course, and she says, 'You know, we should have finished the job ten years ago.' Again I agreed with her and said that's what I thought at the time. 'Of course, I was out at the time when the decision was taken not to finish off Saddam Hussein.' And then she looked over her shoulder where John Major was a seat or two behind us and said in a voice that anybody could hear, 'It's so very difficult when the country is led by weak men. There is nothing worse than a weak leader. I was very fond of George Bush. A dear man. But weak, terribly weak.'

Brian's story is quite delicious and he says that to be on the trip was like being on a VIP branch outing for Saga. What good fun he is and I'm delighted he is at the Foreign Office.

TUESDAY 6 MARCH 2001

A lovely memorial service for Caroline Benn in St Margaret's. It was a real old lefty establishment event. Michael Foot was there, as was his nephew Paul who's now walking around on two sticks and, like his uncle, an old man. The tributes were about Caroline's American background. She came from Cincinnati and arrived in post-war Britain to meet Tony at Oxford where he proposed, they got married and formed a couple for fifty years. Tony Benn breaks down at the end of his own speech. 'She taught me how to live and how to die and you can't ask for more than that.'

Outside there really was a feel of the old left. Not many young people there. Fiona Millar, who had come along with Cherie, went past saying, 'It's good to hear the old language, isn't it?' Do she and Cherie constitute a little left cell – like Eleanor Roosevelt – at the heart of our system of power?

WEDNESDAY 7 MARCH 2001

An early meeting in Robin Cook's office. I grab Cook for two minutes and we lean over the balustrade looking down on to the great staircase in the Foreign Office. I ask him to make a pitch for me with Tony to get a job. I stress to him that if he is to be effective as president of the Party of European Socialists, he will need proper political backup.

Robin was very friendly. 'I think you should be on the front bench, Denis. I know your name has been considered. I'll certainly have a word about it with Tony. But have you spoken to Anji?'

Anji Hunter is Tony's gatekeeper and diary person and very close to him. I don't really know her that well, though she has always been friendly whenever I have been around.

'No, but I have got good contacts with Jonathan and I will raise it with him.'

'Call Anji. She is more powerful than Jonathan. You should be on the front bench.'

I told him that if I didn't get anything, I was certainly pulling out of any formal involvement with the government.

'I won't be disloyal, but I'm not going to waste time as a bag-carrier if I'm not allowed to serve my country. I have a lot of experience and I can contribute to the government,' I said.

He looked at me slightly worried, though sought to reassure. 'I hope you won't do that, Denis. You're very much valued.'

I said:

I have been doing it for four years, Robin, and there's just a question of pride and belief in oneself. I've got a lot of things I can write and do outside of a ministerial framework and if I'm not good enough to be a minister, I'd rather go off and do things where I can make an impact.

I was getting dangerously pompous. I added that I had supported him privately and publicly as well as doing the same for Blair, using my network to promote them in Europe and I now wanted some recognition and a chance to prove myself. He nodded again sympathetically and said he would do what he could for me.

Early evening I had to go up to the National Gallery to be in place before the Queen arrived. A weird little invitation. It was from the German ambassador for the opening of an exhibition of late-nineteenth-century paintings from the National Gallery in Berlin. The President of Germany, Johannes Rau, an old SPD warhorse, had come along to honour the occasion, so I suppose the Queen had to appear as well. Derry Irvine was the only bigwig Labour person there. He was chatting to Anne Heseltine and made the point to me that she was Anne Heseltine. Well, yes, but so what?

'I am coming to the opinion following all the row over the Hammond report that we really have to move in the direction of state funding,' he opined rather pompously. Well, golly gosh, Derry, have you only really got that far? In fact, what he wanted to talk about was his own little story about organising a fundraising dinner for Labour-supporting lawyers in which he asked them to donate a minimum of £200 to the party election chest.

'It's absolutely ridiculous, as if I would even know who was there before deciding who would get made silk. It really is too much but, as I said, I do think it makes state funding a lot more attractive.'

So it's not a matter of principle, as it is with me, that if you want democratic politics then a democratic public has to pay for it – it is just a way to ensure that Derry doesn't get embarrassed in the press. Really, all these people are such ridiculous old drama queens. Where have they been during many years of politics when anybody elected had to put up with this kind of crap locally or regionally or nationally and just get on with life? Any pressure on them and they regard it as an intolerable assault on their self-importance.

I breezed around a bit, but you couldn't go and see the paintings until the Queen had been there and then suddenly she arrived. The chairman of the board of the National Gallery made a very odd speech:

> We are delighted with your presence here Ma'am. It reflects the nineteenth century when our two nations worked so closely together and your predecessor Queen Victoria sent her daughter to marry the man who became the kaiser. Then, of course, the first fifty years of the last century marked by all the troubles and, of course, the word we are not allowed to mention.

This reference to *Fawlty Towers* sent a frisson through the audience. A German woman was beside me and she said, 'What can't we mention?'

'*Die unervahnbar Dinge... ist der Krieg.* The unmentionable thing is...'

'It's all right. I have lived here for twenty years, you can speak to me in English,' she snapped.

'Well, if you've lived here for twenty years surely you remember seeing *Fawlty Towers*,' I said.

'Of course, I saw it on the television.'

'Well, you remember the thing that you mustn't mention?'

'I'm sorry, I don't know what you mean.'

So, so much for modern cultural references.

A few minutes later the Queen started to circulate and to my horror Sir Nigel Broomfield, ex-ambassador in Berlin and big patron of British–French friendship outfits, pulled me into a kind of waiting line. The German ambassador, Hans-Friedrich von Ploetz, introduced me as 'Dr MacShane, who speaks very good

German and acts as a contact man between British parliamentarians and German MPs, your Majesty'.

I simpered and made a little bow, shaking the hand, which is really just a tiny grasp of the fingers, and said, 'I'm one of your Majesty's legislators, as an American newspaper described me the other week, Ma'am.'

She looked completely nonplussed in her miniature, rather grannyish way and barely broke into a smile. Von Ploetz banged on, 'He speaks very good German and other European languages, your Majesty.'

Again, she looked nonplussed but then added, 'Well, I can only speak one European language, French,' and passed on to Nathalie, who made a little curtsey as she took the handshake. She was very professional and neat about it all. Poor Queen, there she was tucked up in Buckingham Palace with her feet up, slippers on, a nice cup of tea or a G&T and then suddenly she has to get into her best frock and coat and hack her way down to Trafalgar Square to have a tour of all these boring people in front of all these boring paintings.

George Weidenfeld bearded me and said I never came to any of the parties at his house and I said I was sorry but it really was that I wasn't in London on most days of his invitations. I asked him who actually was gathered here and he said, 'The interesting thing is who hasn't been invited.' Ah, the necessity of seeing and being seen.

THURSDAY 8 MARCH 2001

I got up at the end of business questions to have a pop at William Hague over his disgusting speech in Harrogate last Sunday in which he said that if Labour won the election, Britain would become a 'foreign land' because we would become closer to Europe. I called it a crass example of xenophobia and got a mini cheer from our side, though the Chamber was pretty much empty, with catcalls from the Tories and incessant cries from John Bercow, 'make him a minister, make him a minister'. If only.

Then to the office to do some serious preparation for my speech tomorrow on teaching foreign languages. I'll try to get some publicity for it, but it's a well-worked theme and I haven't really got anything that strong or new to say. But the speech is fun and taking time over it is worth it, as with luck it may read well when it actually appears in Hansard.

Up to Hampstead for a *Tribune* rally to celebrate Michael Foot. All the old left were there. The event took place in the ballroom in the head office of the train drivers' union (ASLEF), which is in Arkwright Road in Hampstead. It's an incredibly elegant house and you can see why ASLEF have no desire at all to forge trade union unity with anybody else in the world as long as they can operate out of comfortable bourgeois surroundings like this. Poor Michael himself was sitting down, really a weak and old man now. I'm not sure if it was his ninetieth birthday, but it can't be far off it. I bumped into Gordon Brown and said I had given a quote to Reuters yesterday saying that the Budget was 'a recognisably European social democratic Budget' and he grinned and said, 'That's excellent, Denis, yes very good indeed. By the way, I hope you won't be bringing any more climate change levy delegations to me.' It was really a pointless comment, but it's interesting that this is the only extent to which I register on his radar screen. Either that or he has a guilty conscience about this stupid tax which has caused so much damage to manufacturing and not really one serious plaudit from the green lobby for him.

TUESDAY 13 MARCH 2001

A day trying to clear away office stuff. At 4.30 p.m. to a presentation by the Ministry of Defence on what the British Army is up to. The place is crawling with generals wearing endless gold braid. Do they realise how silly they look all done up to the nines in this flashy uniform? There are Tories everywhere. John Redwood as well as Iain Duncan Smith and several others dominate proceedings. There is hardly a Labour MP there. I ask a question about whether the army can both have a war-fighting capability and be a success- ful expeditionary force, and it clearly irritates the Chief of the Gen- eral Staff who says they should be both. God Almighty! They are still dreaming of the Second World War and the Battle of Waterloo. Geoff Hoon is there, but it's the army that runs the army and tells the state what to do and providing there is a Prime Minister who likes them – and Blair does like them – all is well and it doesn't matter who holds the political posts at the MoD.

The letter inviting me to the event had been signed by Brigadier Sebastian Roberts. He turns out to be Flavia Lambert's first cousin. I half recognised the name and he was a very tall, immensely en- thusiastic and charming man in a black pinstripe suit. We had a very nice talk about Barontoli and Flavia and her son Fergus and got on quite well, especially when I said I was interested in the army and had gone out to Bosnia to see them. He said he thought there wouldn't be any Labour MPs there at all as the MoD assumed that Labour simply wasn't interested in military affairs.

WEDNESDAY 14 MARCH 2001

John Kerr phones up and asks if I will make a speech next Thursday night in Berlin on behalf of the British government at the Königswinter conference. Apparently no minister can go, which I think is really bad. The *Liebling* of British–German politics, Gisela Stuart, has got to spend some time defending her marginal Edgbaston constituency and can't get there till Friday. I'll try to make a real effort and do a good speech. Maybe even in German.

Ken Purchase says that I won't get a minister's job after the election. 'You're not on the list, Denis. It's not that they don't like you, but you're not part of the golden crew.' Ah well. If it doesn't happen, it doesn't. Time to see if I can write a bit and have fun in other areas. But dammit, I want to do something useful on Europe and as you detach yourself from the centre of power, you have no more influence than a cricket chirping in the long grass does on the play of ball and bat in a test match.

Jonathan Powell and Sarah and their two daughters came over for lunch, as did Flavia Lambert and Finn, her youngest son, the same age as my Sarah. I made a curry and we had a good time. I pumped Jonathan a bit on a post for me, but he wasn't especially forthcoming.

'Robin Cook has taken Anji [Hunter] and even John Sawers out to lunch to try and shore up his position, for God's sake. Every Cabinet minister is trying to get in to see Tony to discuss their future, but he's not talking to anyone.'

He agrees that we have no good contact with Schröder. We simply don't know who he talks to on foreign affairs. It's very hard to make a relationship with him. I say that I am seeing Siggi

Krampitz, Schröder's PA, next week and will be making a speech in German at the Königswinter conference, but I can feel Jonathan isn't going to make any real play for me. Well, I'll just have to get used to the idea of a non-ministerial political career and see what I can make of it.

We walk around Pimlico after lunch as they are looking for a house here. I tell him that I hope all the rises for MPs and ministers that have been mentioned in the papers are pushed through and he snorts, 'If Cabinet ministers are getting a rise, then I want mine as well.' I suppose actually the Downing Street gang do see themselves as more important, with heavier responsibilities and with as big a workload as members of the Cabinet. Certainly, Jonathan has had to deliver more on Northern Ireland than any Cabinet minister has been able to do.

Flavia was a joy and we had a good talk about schooling. I value her friendship more and more.

MONDAY 19 MARCH 2001

A call from Millbank because there had been an article in *Le Monde* attacking Robin Cook as a traitor and a neo-liberal front for American capitalism. It's in response to an article he had published last month called 'Six Challenges for European Social Democracy' and is an attempt to derail his bid to become president of the Party of European Socialists. The article is very vicious in tone and written by Harlem Désir – the only major black politician on the French left – and some lefty woman who, like Désir, is a French socialist MEP. There is also a French academic based at the LSE as one of the co-authors and I think it's the same chap who attacked me when I wrote a pro-Third Way piece a couple of years ago for *Le Monde*. Overall, it's an irrelevant sting, but I quickly write out a reply to send over the name of Clive Soley. I don't really want to compromise myself.

In the tearoom, I find people almost indifferent whether the general election will be on 3 May or not.

Huw Edwards, the Monmouth MP, says he isn't that keen 'because why should I want to get my redundancy notice early' and he is certainly walking around with a long face. The opinion polls all give us as big a majority as last time but that's not the way it feels on the ground to MPs in seats that were only won in 1997. Sally Keeble tells me she is studying law in the evening, so she has something to go and do if she loses her Northampton seat.

A chat with Giles Radice who says that he did push me for a job with Blair, 'but Tony told me that you were useful flitting around Europe networking and that you should just keep doing that'. Well, I told Giles that I wasn't having any of that any more. No job and no networking. Or at least only networking for myself, not being an evangelist for a man who shows me no loyalty.

But the big event after the 10 p.m. vote and programme motion was an unbelievable spectacle when poor Keith Vaz had to take a ninety-minute debate on an order noting the defence arrangements at the EU Council of Nice. A technical issue but, of course, they were out to get Vaz. And out they came. As all the Labour MPs rumbled off quietly at around 11 after the programme motion vote, all four Tory benches started filling. Within two or three minutes, they were as full as they would be for Prime Minister's Question Time or the Budget statement. It was literally unbelievable. Keith was there with a few other Ministers of State and whips filling the front bench but not a single Cabinet minister.

Tony McNulty and I made noise on the bench behind and a few other people stayed out of curiosity. But as Keith rose to speak, there was an absolute avalanche force of noise of merry hostility against him. It wasn't hate or even contempt, just sheer collective pleasure at having someone to bully. It really was pretty foul. Keith read out his text gamely and took interventions bravely from people like Michael Howard who snarled, 'As you haven't a solicitor to speak for you here, perhaps you will…', which was just ineffective. In fact, as John Maples and then John Gummer all got up to have a go at him, the atmosphere turned slightly as the Tories realised that this was simply something out of *Tom Brown's School Days* as they sought to hold someone's backside to the burning fire. It was all the nastier as there was Keith, an Indian, facing the hate of what is still a pretty racist party, at least in their private jokes and demeanour.

Quentin Davies made the main speech attacking him and went hysterically over the top, bellowing and screeching at the top of his voice for the first few paragraphs so that when he drew breath I shouted out across the Chamber, 'Why don't you speak up, we can't hear!' which drew a laugh from the Tory side. He made no real points and the debate descended into the utterly ridiculous argument about interpreting different sub-clauses of annexes to the Nice Treaty, which can be read in so many different ways but which don't sustain the betrayal of NATO thesis beloved of the anti-European Conservatives.

After about twenty minutes, Michael Ancram got up to leave and that was the sign to the Tories that the sport was over and bit by bit they dribbled out. But it was high parliamentary drama and although I just don't know what to make of Keith and can't decide how good or bad he really is, it was brave of him to take them on and, I think, like a well-greased surfboard being propelled out through the breakers, he was able to go through each crashing wave and emerge at the other side.

TUESDAY 20 MARCH 2001

I saw Keith Vaz in in the Commons souvenir shop buying a few things. He is spending a lot of time just mooching about the Commons. Not showing his face perhaps in public but certainly not hiding from his fellow MPs. He said that Jack Straw was going to replace Cook as Foreign Secretary after the election. It would be a good way of putting Jack firmly into the pro-European camp, which might be useful come any referendum campaign. I wonder if Robin is threatened with a move whether he will have the guts to threaten to resign. I doubt it.

Up to a very nice little event which was a reception offered by Margaret Beckett in her flat in Admiralty House to all PPSs. It really is a one-bedroom flat. You go in and there's a big drawing room, in which she's got one or two souvenirs, but otherwise it's completely empty with two giant sofas and 20ft between them and a television in a corner. Then there's her bedroom, where you see the Kleenex by the bed and slippers and it's all very cosy with a nice double bed for her and the lovely Leo. Good white wine and nice food is served and I scoff a lot for my evening meal. She has a small study in there, but really it's all rather nondescript and I certainly wouldn't bother moving in if I had a decent place to live in London already.

Ivor Caplin, her PPS and surely a future minister if he can hold his Hove seat, is very bullish and confident. He is an ex-IT manager and has a can-do authority that I always enjoy, save that he never seems to have any capacity for reflection or thought, but he's been a good friend in this parliament and I hope he keeps his seat and has his wish. I keep thinking that I don't want to be a minister after all because it really is just a lot of shit work. It's the status that's important and, in the case of Europe, the chance to have the logistical support to do something useful. But so much of it is just negative.

Back in the Commons, hanging around for a vote and I bump into Keith Vaz chatting amiably to Archie Norman and Andrew Tyrie.

Vaz protested:

Look, the chap I recommended for an honour was a big Tory Asian and I simply sent his name into John Major. That's all. [Elizabeth] Filkin has made a connection between allegations that one of his staff gave me money, which isn't true, and the fact that I'm quite happy to recommend anybody for an honour if he's an Asian.

Archie and Andrew listened amiably and it was odd to think that only twenty-four hours previously they had been on the benches as part of a giant gang of bullies out to threaten and destroy the man. Now to a casual onlooker in the Members' Lobby, they would have all seemed the best of friends. It really is an odd place, the Commons.

WEDNESDAY 21 MARCH 2001

I go across to No. 10 to meet Anji Hunter. For someone so powerful, her office is a cubby hole. Barely room for her table, a big computer screen which instantly converted to Sky television on the press of a button, which she started to watch intently at 11 a.m. to catch the latest horrible foot and mouth news, and one chair for a visitor to sit on. I made my pitch for having a party chairperson who would be in the Cabinet but not running a department, plus half a dozen vice-presidents of the party to cover different policy or regional or subject areas. She asked who this might be and I said, 'Margaret Beckett.'

'Yes, she's very good, she really is first rate,' she said.

I told her that I had seen Margaret perform brilliantly at an ISTC dinner sending out very left signals and Anji popped in to say that Margaret had been very good at a business dinner sending out the opposite set of signals.

Then I moved on to the need for an effective minister in charge of networking in Europe. I said it should be the Minister for Europe, or if not, a supplementary Parliamentary Under-Secretary at the Foreign Office or the Cabinet Office. I told her cold-bloodedly that I wanted that post and that if I didn't get it, I wasn't going to carry on as a PPS. She was very friendly and said she wanted to talk more about it but she had to go on to another meeting. Well, at least I got in to see her. She said she hadn't been in Portcullis House so I said I would take her to lunch there whenever she wanted.

In the corridor outside, I bumped into Katie Kay, John Birt's old PA and a friend. She is now in No. 10 as an office manager. It's amazing how Blair only recruits his friends and only his friends to work for him. Still, she will be a useful contact and friend.

Across for Prime Minister's Questions and Richard Spring stopped me as I went into the Members' Lobby to denounce Keith as 'a complete shyster'. I just find all this embarrassing. If the Tories have real proof, let them dig it out, but why come endlessly whining to me? I don't call their shysters 'shysters' to the face of other Tory MPs. What on earth is Spring trying to do with this litany of insults against Vaz?

THURSDAY 22 MARCH 2001

Out to Berlin for the Königswinter conference. The usual gaggle of *conférenciers* wait at the airport. I am glad to see David Goodhart amongst their number. His *Prospect* magazine goes from strength to strength. I just like his tall, laidback, slightly cynical style and his refusal to accept conventional platitudes. No other Labour MPs. Gisela Stuart will arrive tomorrow briefly. She, of course, is Frau Deutschland in the government. I talked to her last night in the lobby and said I was going to make a little joke about ministers learning different European languages while she was taking lessons in English. She laughed uproariously like a hearty Bavarian farmer's wife who'd just thought of a good joke while strangling a duck for dinner and said, 'Fine, go ahead.'

In fact, her English has improved enormously since she has been in Parliament, not so much the grammar but her accent, which was distinctly Teutonic and now sounds English. I wonder if she can hold her Edgbaston seat. It's almost unbelievable to imagine it as a

Labour seat, but who knows what the electoral geography will be in a few weeks' time.

I have to make the big after-dinner speech, which leaves me pretty nervous all day long. The meeting itself is taking place in Potsdam. I have never been here before. The first impression is of a mixture of East German communist buildings with long low barracks and stable-type buildings dating from the Prussian era. The conference is held in a beautiful new conference centre built where once the zeppelins were maintained and stored in Berlin. Now it's an East German savings bank conference centre with nice small rooms all laid out in an admirable German manner.

In the evening, they take us all to a beautiful old Prussian art gallery full of Rubens and van Dycks. But there is no heating and everyone shivers and freezes as a German historian reads out a long lecture, interpreted consecutively line by line, on how Prussia was really a great centre of art, of learning, of decent liberal values with never a mention of the fact that Prussia was a state invented by an army and always at the military's service. Goodhart and I have enough of this and quit to walk over to the Mövenpick where the dinner is to be held. We start swizzling champagne as the freezing delegates arrive. Soon it's my turn to talk. I threw away pages to keep the speech down to a maximum of twelve or fifteen minutes, as I had to speak after the deputy Foreign Minister and before dinner was served. It was 9 p.m. after a long day and people were hungry. The speech, I am glad to say, was a big success. Luckily, the speaker before me mentioned Henry Kissinger and I could tell my favourite Kissinger story of the CBS documentary crew making a film about his life. They interviewed his brother and after an hour's interview was recorded, the reporter noted that the Kissinger brother spoke English like a normal American.

'How come Henry still has this Nazi accent?' he asked.

'That was always Henry's problem – always talking and never listening,' came the reply.

It got a great laugh. Earlier on, Daniel Johnson, son of Paul and culture editor of the *Daily Telegraph*, had made a tabloid speech attacking Germany and Europe – accusing Germany of neither being at our throats or our feet but rather getting into our brains. It was Vansittart stuff. I had a nice riff in my speech saying that the construction of Europe today was the battle of the eighteenth century over the nineteenth century – rational, federalist papers, Adam Smith and Goethe over the nineteenth century, and nationalist imperialist Karl Marx and splendid isolation or, as I said, as it is today known, the *Daily Telegraph*. This produced a great laugh and applause and I was away. A good joke in German about Cabinet meetings now taking place in English – one speaks, one understands and the others get their translation later – also brought the house down and let me get over some serious stuff before finishing again with the Charles V joke about speaking Latin to his confessor, Italian to his mistress, French to his men and German to his horse. Again, a great laugh to end on and it was rather uplifting the amount of congratulations and pats on the back I got. Charles Guthrie, the former field marshal who is a thoroughly good egg, grabbed me with both hands to give me a military bear hug of thanks for cheering them all up. God, it's awful, but the high of a good speech is like good sex. I know I can do it and do it on a big international stage, but my chances of being allowed to do it just are so limited. Anyone in the position to stop me getting the chance again will take it. I chatted to people about promotion. John Kerr says he has spoken to Richard Wilson, Robin and Jonathan Powell. He says that they want to make Patricia Scotland a Minister of State and I say that I'm quite happy to take an understrapper job, though John insists, 'No, no, you should have the full rank.' But, of course, as I think David Goodhart said to me, 'Your trouble is, you're always in the papers and other ministers get so jealous whenever anybody else is mentioned.' Oh well.

FRIDAY 23 MARCH 2001

At midday I get an embassy car and go to the centre of Berlin. I eat a fatty *Frikadelle* and mustard in the cold street around the East German *Kanzleramt*. This is the heart of administrative East Berlin. It's actually where Hitler governed Germany and Europe from and it's gradually being taken over by the new unified Germany administration. But Schröder actually works in Erich Honecker's office. It's a dull building like a British regional gas board office. I leave my passport at the guard box and walk down a path flanking the lawn and then into the *Bundeskanzleramt*. A receptionist waves me vaguely up some stairs and says just carry on along a corridor. There is a wonderful stained glass window which shows socialist realist art at its best. '*Trotz alledem*' – the old 1848 revolutionary song – is there in verse with the word '*mir*' ('peace' in Russian) everywhere. Flaxen-haired young peasant women hold up their children to be admired by sturdy steelworkers and coal miners while over them stands the friendly protective arm of the Soviet soldier. It's a glorious piece of twentieth-century socialist kitsch and I hope when the new federal chancellor's office building is up and running they maintain this wonderful work of art. I climb up the stairs and wander off down a corridor with absolutely no one to stop me. Suddenly on the left is the large room marked '*Kabinettsaal*' – yes, it's the Cabinet Room.

A round table for about a dozen places set in a much larger room. It all looks rather dated and shabby. On down to the main purpose of my visit, which was to meet Sigrid Krampitz, Schröder's personal assistant – a bit like the Anji Hunter of Germany. She is incredibly smiling and welcoming and we have a lovely hour together over a pot of coffee. Top of the papers for Schröder to read is Tony Blair's article in *Prospect* on how the Third Way is modernised social democracy – which the *Süddeutsche Zeitung* had published in German today. That's a good omen and she is full of praise for the work Schröder does with Blair. She is very confident that they will win the election next year. She insists that Germany and France will have to maintain a good strong relationship despite all the difficulties. But Schröder finds Jospin 'to be the most introverted man he has ever dealt with'. They are establishing good relationships with Putin, and Putin and Schröder have spent two holiday weekends together. I had talked to John Kerr about what I should ask of her and he suggested that while there wouldn't be any more joint Blair–Schröder papers after the disaster of the last one written by Mandelson and Hombach, they should talk to each other to try to say the same thing in both Washington and Moscow when they met the respective leaders of the two countries. If Blair and Schröder could agree to say the same things in the same way to the two leaders, then they would, in effect, construct a European foreign policy rather than dancing to a French anti-American tune. She agreed that this was a good idea but, of course, whether it will be transmitted on and up I don't really know. She's a handsome, pretty, slight woman and said she was enjoying life in Berlin enormously. I guess she must be one of the most in-demand people imaginable and she was very warm in accepting an invitation to come to London and have a good look round the House of Commons. It's a great contact to have.

Back for the end of conference session and then out again to the centre of Berlin to the new British Embassy. It is absolutely foul: a ghastly sub-provincial multicoloured office block with a glitzy entrance like a further education college or hospital trust, and long sweeping stairs that are cold and icy and just a sub-modern pastiche that is utterly depressing. I picked up *The Guardian*'s John Hooper, who was at St Benedict's, and we went off to have dinner with his wife in the Grunewald. I wanted a simple *Eisbein* – that wonderful ham knuckle and sauerkraut Berlin dish – but instead there was all much more elegant stuff. His wife, Lucinda, was there. She is still working for the Food and Agriculture Organization in Rome so they have a commuting marriage. Somehow the evening dragged. John was naturally paying maximum court and attention to her, so we didn't get into the real nitty gritty of German politics. But it's an old easy friendship and he has a great deal of wisdom and knowledge and I enjoyed talking to him very much. He dropped me at an S-Bahn and I got the train back up to Potsdam, a taxi home, to find the typical conference evening of beer being spilled in the bar, which I joined in for a moment and then went to bed.

SATURDAY 24 MARCH 2001

Up for the final conference session. I was dozing at the back of the hall, reading the newspapers and gossiping to John Kerr when suddenly Nigel Broomfield called me and I had to make a general waffle about the future of Europe. I acquitted myself well but only because the impact of the Thursday speech lingers on. Silke, my assistant in the Commons who is a young Königswinter participant, said that her group wanted me to repeat the speech to them. I gently explained that a good speech was about chemistry and striking the right sparks in response to what other people said and events of that day and the general atmosphere. It couldn't be repeated cold.

I went for a walk on the lakeside. So close to Berlin, there are these beautiful giant lakes. On the coach into the airport, we passed the Wannsee. There was a museum to the famous house where the Final Solution conference took place. Will all this be history to my children, I wonder? Of course, there is an immense lobby to keep the memory of the Holocaust alive. Rightly so, though it gets mixed up with Israeli state interests in the Middle East. But somehow I think history will move on.

MONDAY 26 MARCH 2001

Into the Commons for Blair's statement on the Stockholm Council. The statement is filled up with questions about foot and mouth and very little on Europe, save the usual whinge about European defence. Beside him, Gordon Brown sits. Glowering and nibbling at his badly bitten nails. Blair refers to him as 'my brilliant friend' over the issue of Third World debt, but Gordon barely breaks into a smile of acknowledgement. He just doesn't come over as a normal human being. I wonder, were he to be Prime Minister, if he would have Blair's grace under pressure or simply be brittle and crack.

TUESDAY 27 MARCH 2001

Into the Foreign Office for the last meeting to prepare for oral questions with Cook. I go into his room and he is standing, a rather slight and much older, less bouncy figure, looking out onto Horse Guards where the cavalry are playing a march.

'What's the music?' he asks into the air.

I tell him it is the 'Triumphal March' from *Aida*. That's the terrible thing about British parliamentary politics: there is no time for any culture.

Before going to see Robin, I had a phone call from a Swiss newspaper man who wanted to know how much MPs in Britain earned. I calculated that I did about a ninety-hour week and dividing that into my salary meant my pay was just £6.50 an hour.

We go through the questions, but there are no other ministers there. Robin is hardly interested. All he can think about is whether he has a future or not.

I go out and see Vaz and go over his questions with him. He has one on Kosovo. He looks up oddly and says in a plaintive tone, 'Can somebody draw me a map, please, so that I know exactly how Kosovo fits in with Macedonia and Albania.' He had asked the same question at his first meeting with officials when he became Europe Minister and Kosovo quickly rose to be a major issue. By now he might have learnt where Kosovo is. One of the female officials sketches out a map on a bit of paper. It's pathetic. In the corridor, I bump into John Kerr who is gossiping with Sherard. They have no pity left for Keith.

'Before the Foreign Affairs Select Committee hearing, he was briefed for just eight minutes and then just dismissed everyone. Of course he was eaten alive,' says Sherard.

Question time itself was fairly perfunctory. The only moment of excitement was when Andrew MacKinlay jumped up and started ranting at Vaz for not having visited the Balkans. Tory MPs stood up but Mick Martin simply moved on to the next question, which wasn't really the way you should do things. MacKinlay exploded out of his below-the-gangway frontbench seat and said, 'And we have to provide the opposition here as well' to Martin's obvious discomfort. He really is a very poor Speaker.

WEDNESDAY 28 MARCH 2001

Over to the Foreign Office – possibly my last outing? – where Robin was due to give a major speech on human rights to an invited audience of NGOs in the Locarno Room.

Cook's speech itself was an exposition of the hidden part of Foreign Office work that he has accomplished. Things that I didn't even know about. People have been seconded from NGOs to work in the Foreign Office and vice versa. Three hundred people have been on human rights training. He claimed he wanted to make a Foreign Office interest in and commitment to human rights 'irreversible'. I am sure it is sincere, but it reminded me of the efforts under the Callaghan government to get the Foreign Office interested in trade union issues. Mike Walsh, the TUC's international director, was seconded for two years and, of course, all that did was produce a great cry of outrage amongst the conspiracy theorists that the Foreign Office was taking over the TUC.

I sat at the back looking up at the beautiful, decorated ceiling of the Locarno Room. It has lovely, gilded decorations. I have enjoyed the aesthetics of the Foreign Office but it's time to move on. Afterwards in the reception, the Polish ambassador reminded me I was due to give a speech at the European Commission office for something called the Federal Trust, which is a pro-European organisation. I am to make it tomorrow morning and had completely forgotten about it. With three members of staff, I still don't seem to have a proper PA.

Geoff Martin, the European Commission boss in London, was there for the reception and he was complaining endlessly about Jack Straw. Apparently, Jack had given some annual lecture on British–French relations, which Geoff said was awful.

'It was the worst speech about France I have heard from any politician since Labour came in. I have known Jack since NUS days. He knows nothing about Europe. His speech was embarrassing. Fifteen years out of date.' Straw and Martin were both presidents of the National Union of Students and I expect the student rows from years ago still linger on.

This all sounds as if Geoff Martin is worried that Jack could be made Foreign Secretary, though of course, while I hope Robin will stay there, the use of Jack to Blair in that post would be to remove a euro-suspicious character in the Cabinet, send him to the Foreign Office and watch him go native.

Back over to the Commons to start thinking about my intervention in Prime Minister's Questions.

I had question number five and I think it's only the second time this parliament that I have had a question high enough to guarantee it being reached.

I squeezed into a place at the far end of the Chamber, just above the little side seats that people can sit in before you get to the bar of the House. Peter Mandelson was in one of them and told me proudly that he had spent Saturday and Sunday in Hartlepool distributing Labour Party leaflets.

'And you are going to do it next year as well,' I said with a grin. He grinned back. But somehow his fall from grace has made him more vulnerable and human and perhaps he is learning that arrogance isn't always the best policy.

We got to about 3.25 p.m. and then I was up. I started off very softly talking about the terrible plight of the farmers but then comparing it to the 6,000 steelworkers' families who would have their lives destroyed without a peep of sympathy from the party opposite or their string-pullers in the press. There was a huge roar behind me and I had that marvellous moment when the House is utterly focused and on my side utterly supportive and on the other side utterly silent as they have to listen. The main bulk of the question was to welcome the Corus–ISTC deal and to say that partnership was a way forward and that the government should support it in every way possible. And I then finished up raising my voice with a little shout at the Tories, who had butchered the steel industry in the 1980s. An immense roar of support again behind me and around me, and I sit down to everybody clapping me on the shoulder and turning round to give big thumbs-up signs. What I think I had done was given vent to the sense of frustration at the hypocrisy of the Conservative Party and the press who give two or three pages a day to the foot and mouth issue but have nothing at all to say about

any other of the terrible economic dislocations that our nation is
going through. At any rate, I felt pleased with myself. Even Tories
congratulated me, since doing well at Prime Minister's Question
Time is our equivalent of scoring a goal in an international.

'Bloody good, bloody good,' boomed Nicholas Soames. 'I even
thought for a minute you believed half of what you said,' he carried
on, chortling. Oh dear, it's shameful to admit these small pleasures.
Stuart Bell came up also to congratulate me and said, 'I'm still
pushing for you to be a minister, but you were so good in there
Tony will probably think he has to keep you in the Commons as a
backbencher as your talents can't be lost in the Chamber.' Thanks,
Stuart, but there's a little bit that's right in what he said.

On up to the LSE where Adair Turner is launching his book *Just
Capitalism*. All the usual gang are there; Ralf Dahrendorf, David
Simon, John Kay, David Goodhart – all the liberal New Labour
crowd who like capitalism just fine and believe it will deliver social
justice with just minor tweaks. I like Adair very much. He has such
a fine analytical mind and a generosity and largeness of spirit. Plus
he is pro-European. I buy a copy of his book which is being sold
by his two pretty daughters who have signed it for me in addition
to his own signature but on reading it later that evening find it is
just full of liberal Panglossianism. There is more a whiff of com-
placency. I think the rise in poverty and the ever-increasing differences between the wealthy – such as Adair and most of the people
in the room – and the rest of humanity will create at some stage
a counter-reaction and an explosion of anger that may produce a
new right-wing politics as workers will be told to blame their lost
job and poor wages on immigrants. 'Twas ever thus and dammit, I
don't accept that socialism is completely off the agenda.

SATURDAY 31 MARCH 2001

The Sun says the election will be on 7 June. Two weeks ago *The Sun* said it would be 3 May. In the end, I think Rory Bremner decides these things. It's a bore, but an extra month won't make much difference and perhaps it will mean that foot and mouth is a bit more under control. I go and hand out some leaflets in the town centre and people are pretty cheerful. All the hostile remarks are directed at William Hague. Poor man. Does he realise just how unpopular he is?

TUESDAY 3 APRIL 2001

This was a fun parliamentary day. There was the second reading of the bill on the International Criminal Court, and in a very thin House, I sat behind Cook as he ragged the Tories. Francis Maude, as customary, made a very poor speech. As usual, and fatally in a Commons speech, he quoted anonymous critics of the International Criminal Court procedure. Whenever I shouted out for him to name them, he was unable to do so. Alas, my chirping from the back benches got under his nose and he started snarling about the 'Foreign Secretary's PPS' and I said back across the Chamber, 'I'm not', whereupon Maude said that I was an even 'lowlier' person than he had imagined. It was absolute bliss to see the Tories getting so worked up over me when in fact I couldn't even make a contribution to the debate. Cheryl Gillan, winding up, referred to me as 'an immature nonentity' and my day was filled. It's shameless self-indulgence.

By chance I had had lunch with Bob Seely, who works as Maude's researcher and spin doctor. He is fed up with the constant sniping at Maude. But I told him that as long as Maude had to toe the anti-European and single-issue line, there would be no real hope for the Conservatives. I asked him why he wasn't trying to become a candidate and an MP himself and he said that he had been asked to stay on to help the front bench in opposition. I told him he was wrong. If he wanted a career, he had to get into the Commons early. 'Yes, I think I will be good at opposition. I enjoy opposition.' He's a nice, bright man and I hope he does well.

WEDNESDAY 4 APRIL 2001

At question time it was like a return to the old days. For some reason Mick Martin picked all the parliamentary stars – Dennis Skinner who asked a great question about the army taking over the Conservative Party, Ian Paisley who appealed for a national day of prayer to combat foot and mouth, Teresa Gorman who wants to bring back caning in schools – and so we had a wonderful end of term Prime Ministers' Questions instead of the usual pap and under pager control rubbish from crawlers on either side.

THURSDAY 5 APRIL 2001

In Portcullis House at midday I bump into Kamal Ahmed, the thin string-bean political editor of *The Observer*. The white commonwealth of lobby correspondents disdains him, but he's energetic and phones around a lot and I think puts together perfectly adequate narrative stories of political events. Now, of course, it is completely and utterly the accepted wisdom that 7 June was always the best idea, so that is where he is at. He talks about future promotions and as we run over the names, like Charles Clarke and Patricia Hewitt and Yvette Cooper, we suddenly realise how thin they are on the ground. David Lammy is often spoken of but he asked a question earlier this week and I thought he was very hesitant and poor on his feet, which is odd given that he is, I think, a barrister. But he has years ahead of him to catch up and he seems a very nice person. Siôn Simon has got Robin Corbett's seat in Erdington. He is a Labour loyal puppy who writes well and I wonder what future he will have in the Commons. Naturally, I insert my own name into the conversation. Why not? Steve Richards has given me a nice plug in *The Independent* and David Goodhart has said it's time for a minister who spoke foreign languages in *Prospect*. It won't make much difference, but if you don't sell yourself, no one else will sell you.

TUESDAY 17 APRIL 2001

I have been reading a very good book. They are lectures that Lucien Febvre gave at the Collège de France in the 1944–45 academic year. There in the devastation of Europe was an appeal to rebuild and reconstruct the Continent and do so on the basis of its geographic and historical roots. These are notes for an oral lecture and as such are rather rhetorical but flow with vitality and a simple abundant passion and commitment to constructing something different. But still, like all Frenchmen, he sees Europe as an extension of France. He wants a European republic, a European nation, just as today's French want a European state. It is finding a way of bridging these alternative visions of Europe that we have to achieve. There is also a friendly little book by Henri Weber, *La Gauche Expliquée à mes Filles*, which is an idiot's guide to why he is on the left. Again, almost entirely located in French context. Today's governing left are extraordinarily inward looking and based on the nation – not nationalistic but with very little European or wider international perspective.

French politics is in a bad way at the moment. Jospin lost his temper with a poor female journalist from AFP on a plane ride in Brazil the other week and screamed and shouted at her for reporting his remarks that the left had done badly in the municipal elections. All the other journalists on the plane protested and it has become one of those nasty stories of a bossy Prime Minister losing his rag with a humble female reporter. But Jospin is being put under huge pressure to make empty left declarations because of big job redundancies. He doesn't seem to have the stability to steer his way out of this, and for the first time I wonder if Chirac might win?

FRIDAY 20 APRIL 2001

In the evening a General Committee which was calm and peaceful. Even dear old Stan Crowther, my predecessor as MP for Rotherham 1976–92, was fairly cheerful. I had nothing much to say other than to express the hope that this famous second term would be more radical than the first. Once elected on our own merits, Labour could start to do real things. The problem, of course, will be Gordon Brown, who wants us simply to become a mini-America. I wonder what his real views even on something like capital punishment are.

SUNDAY 22 APRIL 2001

Robin Cook has helped to stir the pot by making a speech at the end of last week in which he said there was no such thing as a single

British race but we were all a mixture of races and that our national dish was a chicken tikka masala. The chicken tikka metaphor has, of course, captured all the headlines, as it was intended to. The *Daily Mirror* had two pages on it and served chicken tikka to Robin when he went to lunch there last Thursday. The *Daily Mail* and the *Daily Telegraph* have gone insane with anti-Cook rage, but both *The Guardian* and *The Sun* endorse the speech in editorials. One begins to remember that Cook can be a big player if he wants to be.

He phoned me up and asked how I thought the speech had gone down. I said it was very brave and like parachuting a neutron bomb into the Tory race row. He giggled from Edinburgh at the thought but sounded a bit nervous, unsure whether he had made some kind of gaffe or not. I expect the old women in Downing Street and the Brown–Mandelson gang at Millbank will be very iffy and brief that Robin should not have stepped into a Tory race row. Actually, the themes he picked up are almost word for word what I wrote in *The Observer* last year and we are now a much more complicated and mixed-up group of races and religions than ever before. Daniel Defoe put it well 300 years ago when he said we were a 'mongrel race', and he was right.

MONDAY 23 APRIL 2001

Walking over from my office I bumped into Bob Marshall-Andrews. He was pissed. He gave me a big hug and then grabbed my glasses and set them squarely and at right angles on my eyes. 'I'm on Freedom Road,' he growled. 'It's all over for me with the asylum seekers. But at least I can make sure your glasses are straight, dear boy,' he said. I guess if anyone is to pay a price it will be the Kent

MPs. Damn. I shall miss him enormously and even more so Derek Wyatt. Why do the best always lose their seats?

A call from Robin Cook's office. He is in Kosovo but he wants someone to take soundings in the tea room on his chicken tikka speech about British identity and the existence of the British race. By chance there is a division shortly after the call, so I go through the lobby approaching individuals or groups saying very simply, 'Cookie's chicken tikka speech, yes or no?' Almost without exception everybody says straight away 'no', or there is a kind of pause and a half shaking of the head and so I say, 'Don't worry, everybody else is saying the same thing.' The one exception was Clive Soley standing beside the Chief Whip, Ann Taylor, who was quite brutal about it. Tony Clarke, the Harwich MP, said that it had been raised when he was canvassing in working-class council estates in a very negative way. The general view was that the Tories were imploding on race, so why had Cook stepped in to draw attention away from Conservative disarray? Actually, I disagree with all of this. I think it was a brave speech and important that a senior politician stood up and said these things even at a sensitive time.

I called back to Cook's office and spoke to his private secretary, Sherard Cowper-Coles, who said that No. 10 were unhappy now about the speech and the reaction to it. I bet they are, I thought to myself, they are such craven cowards and don't know the meaning of the word leadership. I was patched through to Robin in Kosovo and asked him what the weather was like. Well, what else do you say on these ridiculous conversations? He said that Kosovo moved from a bitter winter to a boiling summer with no intervening spring and it was now a hot summer. I told him that MPs were not criticising his speech but when asked cold-bloodedly whether it had been helpful or not weren't that keen on the grounds that it drew attention away from the Conservative infighting on race. He sounded a bit glum, so I tried to cheer him up by saying that anybody who had actually read it in full thought it was very good and that compared to Gordon Brown's and Michael Wills's utterances on Britishness, which were really a discussion about why the Scots should keep running Britain, Robin's speech, which was located fully in a European context, was very positive. Anyway, I didn't disguise the results of my MPs' survey but didn't try to make him feel bad about it either. The speech had a positive mention in editorials in both *The Guardian* and *The Sun*, which is some going for a Labour Cabinet minister and I think secures Robin's purpose of still being a Cabinet minister with a clear left line. Being monstered by people like Simon Heffer and all the other right-wing extremist crowd will do him no harm now or in the long run.

TUESDAY 24 APRIL 2001

In the evening I have a glass of wine in the Portcullis House cafeteria with Jean Corston and Helen Jackson. Both go back a long way in the Labour Party and are great women. Jean told a story about the 1987 campaign when she was a Labour Party staffer:

I was sat in the meeting where people were going through a list of names of party spokesmen who could be put up on television to promote the party and the name of Robin Cook came up. Straight away Peter Mandelson said, 'Oh, I don't think so, Robin's got a new constituency to look after and he'll want to spend time digging himself in there.' Well, it was just obvious to everyone that Robin had a very safe new constituency, but, of course, Peter wasn't going to have him as a party spokesman at any price.

It's true. There's a Millbank or No. 10 selection committee that puts up the people it likes and knocks down those it doesn't and that's the end of it. Helen is on the NEC and I forgot to nominate her again for the MPs' section of it. But who really cares about the NEC at the moment? It's a non-body and unless somebody seriously organises on it, it will remain so.

WEDNESDAY 25 APRIL 2001

To lunch at *Private Eye* where I sit beside Jane Bonham-Carter who lives with one of the bosses of the Liberal Party and is their spin-doctor-in-chief. I complain about the Liberals using my speech on tactical voting in a stupid way and she says she will pass the message on. But the damage has been done. I want to gossip but it's too dangerous with all the journalists there, so I arrange to meet Francis Wheen for dinner tomorrow night where we can exchange a little low-grade intelligence.

MONDAY 30 APRIL 2001

Lunch with Tim Garton Ash. He had phoned up out of the blue to see if I was free. Of course I am, because he is one of the most intelligent people to talk to on Europe. I take him into the Strangers' Dining Room and he says, 'You are my candidate for Minister for

Europe.' I demur. I still don't think Blair will appoint me. Tim thinks that the Schröder–SPD initiative is very big. He disagrees with my view that Schröder's main interest is securing a relationship with Russia and control over the landmass to the east of Germany. 'Oh, there's nothing in that. That's always been Germany policy. They will remain Atlantic and interested in the whole of Europe. There won't be any Rapalloism.'

Tim said to me he thought there was no question of Britain going into the euro in the next parliament.

'It will be a Conservative Prime Minister who will lead us into the euro,' he said.

TUESDAY 1 MAY 2001

The first May Day of the new century. How many Firsts of May have I spent in marches or demonstrations with my beloved working class? In the rest of Europe, it's a day off. Here, it's a day when a few thousand demonstrators against the pollution of the planet by multinationals, new technology, repressive governments and the rape of the environment will gather around Oxford Circus and then suddenly be penned in by the police as if they were interned in a special holding area – unable to move, unable to eat, unable to piss – it's a shabby sight and shows how unconfident the state is.

But I will have none of this, since I have to do Foreign Office questions today. It's straight to the Foreign Office for the last one. Robin walks around in his white shirt which is always too big for what is really rather a small body.

'I wonder why Francis Maude never uses the PNQ [private notice question] technique. It's a good way of raising an issue. Of course, he never comes into Parliament before lunchtime with all the work he does in the City.'

I suggest that he should be gently mocking on Maude as it is Maude's last outing also at the despatch box as shadow Foreign Secretary. He will be replaced after the election, I think, whatever happens.

'Oh, don't start going soft on Maude, please, Denis,' says Robin.

He is in a bad-tempered truculent mood and the meeting finishes after only twenty minutes. Afterwards, I suggest to Sherard that Robin should invite all his ministers and political team and advisers and so on into his office for drinks after question time, but both Sherard and I know it won't happen.

WEDNESDAY 2 MAY 2001

I bump into Peter Mandelson in the lobby who says, 'We are going backwards on Europe.'

I said that we were losing our presence in Europe. Flattering his ego a bit, I told him that we had lost the plot since he had stopped networking around Europe when he was in the Cabinet Office. 'There is no one else doing it,' I told him. Peter, whose hair has got very lank and floppy around his face, as if he is trying to pose as a thoughtful intellectual, nodded in agreement at my wisdom in seeing his centrality on the question.

'Yes, we have rather lost the plot. There is no one who takes any interest in it.'

I keep fearing that Blair in the second term will not be the brave radical leader that, say, Hugo Young of *The Guardian* wants. Instead, it will be safety-first, let's win the third term, let's take no risks, let's be inward-looking and let's not ask the people of Britain to take brave decisions. This is all simply my instinct, but if you look at the people who surround Blair and the people he appoints to the Cabinet, they are all of the same mould. In the end, Gordon's only hopes of becoming Prime Minister will be to inherit it a bit like Anthony Eden after years and years of loyal service. I also think the world economy and other political and economic tensions will make everyone be very safety-first and that excludes style and leadership on Europe.

Gerry Sutcliffe, the Bradford MP, told me an interesting story. Blair went to the rugby league cup final last Saturday to present the cup. I guess he must have been bored rigid since rugby league must be to him what eating sushi and going to a Stockhausen concert would be to a Sunderland bus driver, but Gerry said that when Blair went onto the pitch to meet the teams before the kick off and the loud speaker announced his name, there was a round of booing in the crowd:

> It wasn't a big noise, just a low boo that went round and round picked up from each part of the crowd to the next. It was very clear if you were present at the stadium, though perhaps not big enough to have been caught by the television. And after the game, when the loudspeaker said that Tony was going to present the cup, the same booing started again. These were 66,000 white working-class males. I don't like it.

For what it's worth, they all come from our part of the country where we have our northern heartland seats, I didn't need to add.

It won't lead to losing seats this time. But bit by bit, the modern left is speaking to and for itself – graduates, at ease in Europe, liberal on race and gay rights but no longer listening to those left

behind, the workers who lost money and status as a result of glo-
balised deindustrialisation, who resent foreigners whether from
Pakistan or Poland who are everywhere while their children can't
find decent work or work of any sort. If this coalesces into real politics, Labour will be out.

THURSDAY 3 MAY 2001

A wonderful new discovery this morning. I had signed up for the
Commons tennis club, which plays for an hour and a half on Tuesday and Thursday mornings at the tennis courts of Westminster
School in Vincent Square. So after dropping Sarah off, I put on a
tracksuit, dug out a racquet and some balls, got on my bike and
pedalled round there. But there was no one there. It is all one-line
business today and the only person playing there was Edward Gar-
nier's wife, Anna. Luckily, we knew each other from a skiing week in
Davos and she is a magnificent sportswoman and very good fun and
easy to know and like. So we played a set and she was quite gentle
with me, since I saw a number of shots that would have knocked me
into 6-0 and 40-love every time if she had used them regularly. She
said she had run the London marathon and an article I had written
about it appeared in the official programme. It was a lovely sunny
morning and I went home to have a good shower and to just feel
better.

MONDAY 7 MAY 2001

I drive to Stansted Airport to get a Buzz flight to Berlin. An embassy
car picks me up and takes me out to the residence in the Grunewald.
It's an uninteresting large functional house from the 1930s.

Although I arrive late, there is a grand old dame who used to be a British ambassador in Denmark staying here with her companion. They had come back from a Mahler concert and so we got a nice if over-heavy dinner. When on earth will people realise you don't serve big meat dishes after 10 p.m.? I sit beside her companion who describes herself as a 'true blue' from Suffolk. She says she can't stand William Hague. 'Where did he get that ridiculous skinhead haircut? Who let him wear that ridiculous baseball cap? He's terrible. I shan't vote. I can't vote Labour. I shall simply stay at home and not vote at all.'

She delivers this with all the authority of an educated countryside bourgeoise. And having announced it, I expect she may actually carry it out. Everybody around the table including the ambassador's delightful blonde wife, one of the spooks in charge of intelligence and Paul Lever, the ambassador himself, when he turned up, said the same thing. There is just nothing going for Hague at all in the English establishment. What an opportunity, if only we knew how to recast things, but still in my guts I don't think the conservative establishment are happy at the idea of Labour in power and will only tolerate us providing we do exactly what they want.

And they don't want Europe.

TUESDAY 8 MAY 2001

Downstairs to say hello to Robin Cook who is going off early to the hotel where the Party of European Socialists congress is taking place. He seems cheerful. He had a speech written out. I had told him to busk it and just say nice things about other speakers, but he said, 'I need fifteen minutes on paper, Denis.' I said, 'Yes, even if one is a good speaker, it's handy to have a little Zimmer frame,' and he laughed.

François Hollande, the general secretary of the French Socialist Party, made a strong speech calling for a federal Europe of nations, grouped around an *avant-garde* based on a constitution and with a strong defence profile. As always, with any French speech, it had to have three points in it. It sounded federalistic but not in the German sense of a weak centre, a strong parliament and power transferred from governments to the commission. The French idea is for a federation of nations with strong governments cooperating and really a rather weak commission, and since the French don't understand what parliaments exist for, they have no interest in parliamentary control or accountability.

I talked to Hollande afterwards and asked if his speech would form the basis of the long-awaited speech on Europe by Jospin. He giggled in that chubby friendly way of his and shrugged his shoulders. He kept asking me when I would be publishing more articles and I said my French wife was so fed up with being in England she had gone on strike and refused to help me with translation.

I had good talks with Henri Weber and others of the Socialist Party gang. I also had a nice chat with Franz Müntefering, the general secretary of the SPD. He said that the SPD paper on Europe was published as a draft six months ahead of their congress to allow a proper debate. He regretted it had not been published a bit later after the British election but didn't actually seem to be that worked up about it. I'll pass these messages back on to Downing Street.

I drove back to the embassy with Hugo Powell. He is Jonathan's nephew and the son of Charles. He's absolutely charming, full of fun, interesting and clearly destined to be the third Powell to work at a high level in Downing Street under some Conservative Prime Minister in ten or fifteen years' time. He said he wanted to organise a sixtieth birthday party for his dad, which would be based on climbing Mont Blanc. I told him I would come along, since if I don't do it soon, it will never happen.

David Clark, Robin's adviser, says he will quit after the election. He is right. There's only so much time you can spend working as a special adviser. He doesn't want to be an MP. He claimed that he didn't know who had put Keith Vaz up to be Minister for Europe eighteen months ago. 'He certainly wasn't Robin's choice. And Robin was told he had to accept him.' David was very contemptuous of Gordon Brown. 'He is endlessly briefing against Robin. It is really quite bad at times. There will never be any stability in the government while Brown is there. He just can't help his endless poisonous activities.'

David was also critical about Peter Hain:

> Robin was really very upset when Peter gave one of his interviews
> to the *New Statesman* and said Robin had been wrong to talk about
> an ethical foreign policy. Peter thinks I organised the leak of the
> memo he sent Robin opposing national missile defence. As soon as
> it appeared, he was dead as far as Downing Street was concerned.

I listened to all of this old history and, as always, you just get one side as we drove back along the North Circular Road on a sunny May early evening. And it really was history. Who cares, who cares, who cares?

WEDNESDAY 9 MAY 2001

Nearly the last, last, last day. Hooray. I like elections on the whole. It sounds corny but it's no bad thing to meet voters.

Into Prime Minister's Questions for the last time of this parliament. Hague is deeply boring. He goes on and on about Europe. But it doesn't resonate. In the end, his famous advantage of mastery of the despatch box seems to be hollow. Tony Benn asks his last question with his usual snide, 'I have been absolutely right on everything and you, Blair, are absolutely wrong on everything' sort of tone. Blair thanks him for his parliamentary career and it's over. Tony, of course, is Westminster through and through. A prime example of the establishment who then became a small irritation, a pebble in the shoe that everybody knew was there but couldn't quite get out. He wasn't radical enough in the 1950s and '60s and then lost all touch with the working class in the 1970s and '80s. His upper-class courtesy and mannerisms mask a deep vanity and arrogance. Anti-European, anti-American, anti-the-aspirations-of-people-to-better-themselves. Naturally, John Bercow calls him the greatest living parliamentarian.

But the best moment is when Edward Heath gets up to make a personal statement. It is dripping with venom against Hague and his last final plea for engagement in Europe. This was a man who in the 1930s campaigned against Neville Chamberlain and who understands in a way that hardly anyone else in the Conservative Party has understood where history was taking his country. But he expressed it so badly. A prophet without honour in his own party never really makes a national breakthrough. When he sat down, we all burst out in applause. That's to say Labour and Lib Dem MPs clapped, Tony Blair slapped the side of his thigh, since I suppose the Prime Minister mustn't clap in front of the despatch box, but the entire Parliamentary Conservative Party sat in hate-filled silence. No, it wasn't hate. It was embarrassment. Because they knew that Heath was right. And they haven't been able to make their peace with that rectitude ever since they got rid of Thatcher. God, at times you need a Shakespeare to put into words what can happen at the high level of politics. It was an extraordinary moment of parliamentary history.

A brief chat with Harriet Harman who was nice about my *Today* interview on the German document on Europe. She thought we would have a big problem with all the MPs who would keep their seats, let alone the new ones:

All those who came in in '97 are bright, clever people. They've been able to tell themselves, their constituency parties and their families that all the work they've done on the back benches has simply been preparation time for when they will get some promotion. But it won't happen. Because there aren't enough jobs. And then things could turn quite sour.

I agree with her. Personnel management of what is going to be quite a fractious PLP will be a big problem.

Simon Walters of the *Mail on Sunday* said that David Blunkett, Geoff Hoon and Stephen Byers had all gone to see Blair saying that they would form a block against Gordon Brown in the next government. I mentioned this to Robin Cook when he had a farewell drink in his office at 6 p.m. today. He pooh-poohed the idea. 'Blair doesn't see people in groups,' he said. I reckon in any case that

Gordon wouldn't even notice he was eating Byers and Hoon and while Blunkett has quite a populist touch and can repeat formulae, he doesn't really have a wide policy grasp. It suits Blair to build him up so that Brown isn't the master of all he surveys. Blair wants to be *primus inter pares* and so every year or so someone has to have his profile raised to stop the almighty Brown.

John Kerr said he hoped to see me next time in the Foreign Office as a minister but added that he still thought my reputation as a maverick, or as he gently put it, 'someone who likes ideas too much', would stop me getting anything. Finally, and I'm conscious that this ludicrous ambition question has figured too much in my diary notes recently, I am completely at ease. Of course I want promotion, but if I don't get it, I shall simply go on a long holiday and rethink life and times in a big way.

I went down to say goodbye to Keith and he pointed at his chair saying, 'That's where you'll be sitting next month', while James, his nice private secretary, looked on giggling. I got a nice note from Colin Budd, who is head of the European Union desk, saying how much they enjoyed my interview on the SPD and how everyone was pushing for me to be a minister. Keith said that John Battle had cleared his desk and moved everything back to his office in the Commons. And yet Battle has steered the International Criminal Court Bill quite successfully through the Commons and I think does a perfectly adequate job. David Mathieson said Robin was fully supportive of me now and he has been quite friendly in the past two or three weeks. Oh well. We'll see. It's been a wonderful four years as a baby bag-carrier at the Foreign Office and I must say I have enjoyed every second of my time. If that is the total height which I will achieve in public life, I couldn't have wished for a better department to work in. The sheer aesthetics and style of it all make it more enjoyable to work in than any other government department.

THURSDAY 10 MAY 2001

I am hassled by the BBC *Today* programme wanting me to go for an interview tomorrow about tactical voting. Apparently, twenty Lib Dem and Labour councillors in Lewes have signed an appeal for tactical voting to keep the Lib Dem MP there and not allow a Tory to return. Although he is a prize chump and a completely idiosyncratic and vain MP, it is better to have Norman Baker, the Lib Dem, than some wretched Conservative. But, alas, the Labour candidate in Lewes is Paul Richards, who has more energy and drive and common sense than twenty Labour MPs put together. So I certainly don't want to dump on him. I phone Millbank and leave messages for Lance Price to find out whether I should accept the offer or not as I receive importuning calls from the *Today*'s political chap, Tim Franks.

In for the last vote of the session and unbelievably the Conservatives have voted against the International Criminal Court on the third reading. It is an outrageous piece of Tory cynicism. It is probably Robin Cook's finest achievement as Foreign Secretary. I tell John Battle to try to get some publicity denouncing the Conservatives for this hostility to international regulation even on an issue like crimes against humanity, but he shrugs his shoulders. 'Peter Hain would have done it,' I tease him and he bursts out laughing. Instead, I go and phone round PA and a bit of the lobby to see if I can get a splutter in.

Back home to see all the children as Nathalie is away and then I bike round to the fiftieth birthday party for Liz Symons and Phil Bassett. All the old gang is there: the ex-Labour correspondents like John Lloyd, Don Macintyre, Robert Taylor, Charlie Falconer and Howard Davies, their old friend and head of the Financial Services Authority who tells me there isn't really a north-south divide. What kind of world does this London elite live in?

Then off to the Thai restaurant off Vauxhall Bridge Road with Alan Howarth, Larry Whitty, Anji Hunter, Don Macintyre and Sarah Spanky, a nice pissy evening interrupted by a call from Lance Price to tell me that he had been told by Alastair Campbell that I should do this tactical voting interview. Damn. It will make me unpopular with a good chunk of the party and irritate some of the bigwigs who will say, 'What the hell is MacShane doing on the *Today* programme when I am a world-famous Cabinet minister?'

FRIDAY 11 MAY 2001

Into the Millbank studio to do the interview. I just keep calling the Conservative Party extremist and say that a mature electorate can make up its own mind on how to vote and that one shouldn't patronise voters by telling Labour voters to vote Lib Dem and vice versa. I got in the point that I was going to campaign for a maximum Labour vote in every constituency and dodged the question on whether some Labour councillor in Lewes should be expelled, before calling for a tactical vote. Ian Bruce, the boring Dorset Tory MP who has a majority of seventy-seven and who stands for absolutely nothing that I can identify, whinged and whined saying that a tactical vote was to vote Conservative, but I just rose above that and made my point fairly calmly.

I walked over to the Commons to have breakfast, but on this last Friday of this parliament, there were no kippers available, so I had a disgusting toasted sausage sandwich instead. Ian Pearson had heard the interview and said it was OK, but otherwise there were just a lot of very fat whips all lounging in armchairs cackling together. What does one call a grouping of whips? They were all like fat pashas, sitting over their coffee and tea in their armchairs, relaxed now that they didn't have a single vote to deliver. I suppose I shouldn't complain. They have, on the whole, been nice enough to me, but there is something sleek and self-important about them all that I find faintly distasteful.

SATURDAY 12 MAY 2001

Town centre activity this morning under wonderful sunshine.

Then we all have to go down to the Phoenix Sports Pavilion at Brinsworth. This is because Tony Blair is *going* to drop in there to look at the second half of the FA Cup final – Liverpool v. Arsenal – and watch it with party faithful and Tony Webb, the very right high Tory president of Rotherham United. Kevin Barron had said something to me and John Healey in the lobby on Thursday about keeping Saturday afternoon free but hadn't explained that it was a surprise visit by Blair. I am hugely pissed off because, of course, the sports ground and the pavilion are actually in my constituency. Kevin had told John and me in the morning that the three of us would greet Blair, walk him up to watch the television and then he would go down to a wedding reception to kiss the bride and be off fairly quickly. But as we all arrived, and of course his battle bus was late, it turns out Kevin is to do the meeting and greeting and I have a real row with Nan Sloane, the regional director of the party, and some hackette from Millbank who has to organise all of these things.

I got a call yesterday from Rachel Cowburn at Millbank asking me about Rotherham details as the idiots down there woke up to the fact that Tony would actually be coming to my constituency. It's a silly protocol thing, but Kevin has been very unpleasant to me if ever I have done anything to his constituency and it's just one of those little parliamentary rules that allow life to rub along between MPs. But that's Kevin. He has been eclipsed by the arrival of John Healey and myself as much more promotable MPs in Rotherham. I am sure he would just like to make me disappear.

It doesn't really matter as Tony and Cherie come up and I get kisses from her and from Fiona Millar, Alastair's partner who walks around with a little rucksack on her back, and a permanently stressed-out Anji Hunter, who just keeps snapping at everybody and looks very unhappy. Blair walks around saying hello to everybody, watches a bit of the FA Cup final and then in a pure South Yorkshire way Cherie is dumped in a little landing behind the main TV room where she sits with Carol Barron and Tony Webb's wife in front of a table full of biscuits and sandwiches, which she looks at with faint horror. I take the children over and Sarah and she have a discussion about the respective merits of Sacred Heart v. Lady Margaret. But she is completely imprisoned between these two Rotherham ladies and can't get out to smile at children and talk to ordinary people. Blair himself moves around from table to table and has his picture taken with everyone. I introduce veterans like Danny Willoughby and Joyce Oldham and, of course, Blair has a picture taken with Anna Chester, who just about faints with pleasure. He does a little speech for the faithful on the importance of the second term and carrying on with the mixture of economic progress and social justice. It all goes down very, very well and he does have a light popular touch with the party faithful.

Downstairs to kiss the bride at a wedding reception, which was the shock of her life, and then outside where Wath cricket team are playing a Phoenix cricket team. The players stop the game to come running over and offer their bats to Blair to be autographed. It's an extremely sunny, cheerful mood under an almost perfect English day of a bright green cricket pitch looking out over Canklow Woods and you really wouldn't know you were in the heart of industrial South Yorkshire.

Looking at all the players, I suddenly realised that four or five of them are actually Asian. They clearly fail the Norman Tebbit test, but for these South Yorkshire teams, it doesn't matter if the colour of your skin is not the same colour as your flannels – if you are a good batsman or bowler, then you're in. Then it's all over and away Blair goes. The Sky TV reporter asks him to answer questions on tax, but he just smiles and says, 'nice try' and goes on. One of the press people says to the reporter, if you want to interview someone on tax talk to Denis as he knows all the answers, but the Sky man says, 'I'd love to but under the Representation of the People Act, I can't talk to Denis without talking to all the other candidates in the constituency.' Not really true but it didn't matter.

MONDAY 14 MAY 2001

In Rotherham, to the first of many old people's homes. Nice people who are very pleased with the £200 they have got from Labour in the form of the winter fuel allowance. This, of course, is a pure little bribe and just crude fiscal electioneering to make up for the incredible negative impact of the 75p rise in the basic pension the year before. But it works and people are glad. Indeed, £200 wouldn't be noticed in the expense account of a London journalist, but in Rotherham it can make the difference between heating and eating. The opinion polls still give us a complete and utter victory. I wish I could be just so radiantly confident. All the young people are completely turned off politics. I write a letter for first-time voters and try to make it as *Sun*-like as possible in its appeal. I doubt if it will make any difference.

Actually, I don't do much work. There are no meetings. No adoption meetings. Nowhere that is a hustings. No door-to-door canvassing – it's all done on the telephone now. I am glad to be out of Westminster, but I don't feel I am taking part in an election.

WEDNESDAY 16 MAY 2001

I talk to Jonathan Powell about putting out a statement on the Silvio Berlusconi victory in Italy. He has won well, but the horrible Northern League Party has lost seats. 'Be cautious, Denis,' he says, 'we will have to work with him and Aznar after the election.' So there we have it – a little right-wing axis of London, Madrid and Rome against the northern social democrats and socialists. Christ. It sounds like the 1930s all over again. Do I really want a job as the Samuel Hoare or Rab Butler of an appeasement government?

More low-grade door-knocking and then it is into a tailcoat and white tie – yes, white tie and tails! Can I believe it?! In the middle of an election campaign to be a Labour MP, I have to dress up to go to the Cutlers' Feast – a kind of giant nosh for steelmakers in Sheffield. I phone Richard Caborn, the veteran Sheffield MP and steel industry union fixer, to ask whether I really should go and he was quite clear. 'Of course you should, Denis. You should go and talk to the Corus bosses and make peace with them. Steve Byers and all the DTI team are going to the CBI dinner in London next week.'

I rush round Rotherham in the morning to try to find a proper white waistcoat but none exists without a few days' notice being given. Well, if I hold my hands over my belly, nobody will notice I am not wearing one. But how ridiculous it feels to leave the poverty of Rotherham and go in a chauffeur-driven council limousine along with the nice mayor, Iain St John, to this event. As it is, it is full of steel industry friends as well as Clive Betts and Richard Allan, so I am not completely alone and idiotic as an MP.

The event is deeply tedious. I am on the top table between two past master cutlers, which just means they inherited steel companies from their papas and everybody in turn gets their year at the job. The main speech is by Digby Jones, the CBI director-general. It is one of the worst speeches I have ever heard. Rambling and zigzagging without any theme, or strong points, or clear message, let alone a rallying call. He is a nice self-satisfied Brummie corporate accountant and he does say something very strong on the need for a tolerant Britain and the need to accept immigrants and to be opposed to xenophobia. I see all these right-wing Tory reactionaries flinching at the thought of having to be nice to Pakistanis and to West Indians. But bravo for Digby. I go up afterwards and congratulate him and he gives me a little smile. He was immensely fat and his hair has become very thin. I don't think it can be that much fun being boss of a CBI with firms run by some of the most stupid businessmen in the world.

As we drive home, the driver, Fred, is bubbling with excitement. Apparently, John Prescott has hit a demonstrator who threw an egg straight into his face. It is all over television. An unseemly brawl. But I expect that people will love Prescott all the more for it. I certainly do. He is one of the few human beings in that wallpaper technocratic government.

SATURDAY 19 MAY 2001

Last Saturday it was Tony Blair. This Saturday it is John Prescott. Anna got a call late last night to say his battle bus would turn up at Percy Street to visit the party activists stuffing envelopes and working the phone at canvassing tables. And there he was. A couple of police protection officers, one of whom is bent over asking me where the toilet was. Prescott goes around shaking hands with everybody. He doesn't do much of a speech. The burly aggressive figure we know on television is just a rather overweight late-middle-aged man. His personality doesn't dominate. I ask him to go for a walk in the market. Joan Hammell, his PA and an old friend, blanches. 'Don't worry, Joan, it will be all right. I know Rotherham and John is very popular here.'

So we set off, we walk down the hill into the market and I take him round a few stalls and work up cheers and applause. Most people, as soon as they realise who they have in their midst, are full of friendly waves and appreciation and support for his punch against the man who tried to attack him. We walk past an egg stall. Two or three yards of nothing but eggs and he accelerates, walking briskly by. He mutters something about a photographer from the *Sunday Times* who is following him around and there is someone snapping away but the primeval politician's fear of being linked to what clearly was, on balance, a very embarrassing incident takes control and he wants nothing of it. But the risk paid off; he was well received. People were ready to talk to him. The handshakes were warm. He climbs back on his bus and away he goes.

I go back to London to be received with huge hugs. It's my fifty-third birthday in two days. Laura has written a magnificent poem. Called 'Fifty-Three'. This is how it goes:

> Fifty-three. What an age!
> Crumbly, wrinkled. Old wizard.
> Sad, grey.
> The list goes on. And on.
> And on. But you! Never!
> The body of fifty-three, the mind, younger than me.

I can't believe an eleven-year-old has written this. How I love her and all my family.

WEDNESDAY 23 MAY 2001

I talked to Jonathan Powell in Millbank. 'This place is terrible,' he says. 'I can't wait for this election to be over.' And so say all of us.

Back out doing routine door-knocking work or meeting people outside the school gates. It's all again very friendly. The papers are full of the European Commission's flatly denied stupid Conservative claim that a document on tax policy represented the march towards harmonisation. Oddly enough, both *The Times* and the *Daily Telegraph* last week reported the document as opposing tax harmonisation and so at their press conference in the morning, the Conservatives were heckled by most of the journalists. They look like a weird little sect.

In the evening, however, I watched Robin Cook on *Newsnight* and he is awful. Jeremy Paxman asks him if there are any political advantages about entering the euro. Robin simply loses the plot and starts snapping at him and doesn't answer the question. He looks extremely nervous and tense. Poor man. He, like all the other Cabinet ministers, hold these high offices of state but they're all terrified of getting the thumbs down from Alastair Campbell or in any way being considered dispensable by Blair. God, it is pitiless at the top. The powers that be are without mercy and since their entire lives hang and fall on the office they hold, they have little independent room for manoeuvre and this lack of confidence just oozes out of the television screen. The Tories, by contrast, know they are losing but have a cocky arrogance and a 'get-stuffed' approach to interviewers. I hope they lose seats big, big, however.

THURSDAY 24 MAY 2001

Another beautifully warm day. This is the sunshine election. I spent part of the time outside East Dene Primary School, serving one of the poorest communities in Rotherham today, and nobody wanted to discuss Europe. *Quelle surprise*! The headteacher, an energetic man good at networking called Howard White, came up beaming to say his budget had increased from £500,000 to £800,000 a year, so he was doing very well under Labour. I wonder if we can sustain these increases in public spending in the next parliament. If we don't, there may be a day of reckoning. But people aren't ready to take a new leap off the good ship, the welfare state, into the choppy waters of privatised pay-as-you-go provision.

Robin Cook's disastrous performance on *Newsnight* is still being talked about. Nick Sigler, Labour's international officer at Millbank, said it was toe-curling and embarrassing. I phone around a few people in Europe – Ian Black of *The Guardian* in Brussels, John Lichfield of *The Independent* in Paris and John Hooper of *The Guardian* in Berlin – to push forward the importance of Jospin's speech which will go head to head with the SPD–Schröder vision of Europe. It will muddy the waters considerably and bury the idea of an EU superstate being fashioned in Paris and Berlin.

The Tories can't be bothered to campaign in Rotherham and are away in the Hallam constituency in Sheffield trying to remove Richard Allan, the nice Liberal Democrat MP. That gives us a clear run, but I wish there were some young people joining the party.

SATURDAY 26 MAY 2001

Thomas Kielinger appears from Birmingham. He is the correspondent of *Die Welt* and we do town centre campaigning, where he starts noting down all the EU hostile remarks. I talk to a Pakistani who comes up to me complaining about asylum seekers. I ask him how long he has been in Britain and he says seven years. He says he works in a restaurant from 6 p.m. to 2 a.m. and for this eight-hour shift he is paid £20. 'Now one of the Kosovan asylum seekers who is much younger and stronger than me and can work much faster has come along and is willing to do it for £10. Something must be done about them, Mr MacShane.' He won't give me the name of the Rotherham curry restaurant and, of course, this is the eternal law of economic migration – the poor pushing the poor out of jobs by offering to do them for low pay. I tell him to talk to his other Pakistani friends and I will raise the issue by perhaps getting the minimum wage inspectors round to that restaurant. Rotherham is faced with opening up too many hostels for asylum seekers and I can sense a real explosion brewing up after the election.

TUESDAY 29 MAY 2001

A routine day of going round old people's homes for the postal votes and standing in the town centre to do it. There really is a good surge of support to enrol for postal votes and I think it could make a significant difference to the turnout and to the future of democratic participation in the UK. Though, as I keep telling Anna, we should enrol them to vote in this election but certainly not in any euro referendum. A constant refrain is that they hate the council, they like the government and they don't want to go into Europe. But on the forms that we are asking them all to fill in, the box to tick is to receive postal ballot papers for all future elections. Well, if they sign up for that then we won't be able to determine who actually votes in the next euro election or indeed the next European Parliament election. Good. All the more reason to have a very big campaign in favour of Europe as soon as the election is over. I am ready.

Laura and Emilie make a delicious vegetable soup which I gobble up after coming home from canvassing. All the children are in fine form. Emilie is now reading like an express train. Sarah and Laura went off to Meadowhall to watch a movie and in Sarah's case to buy a dress which she was proudly wearing when we got home. How awesomely pretty she looks with all the beauty of Ireland, Poland, France and Vietnam in her face. Oh Christ, when do the boys start?

WEDNESDAY 30 MAY 2001

I go down to Percy Street to talk to the Sheffield University politics professor, Pat Seyd, who is writing a book on the election campaign. I make three main points to him. Firstly, that this isn't a Millbank-run campaign. We are all doing our own thing. I haven't looked at a single briefing paper or line from Millbank since the election started. Partly I am confident enough in my own knowledge of what the government has been doing to defend its record but also there just simply aren't the events or engagements where you need the detailed information at your fingertips.

Second point is the focus on postal votes. This is an important extension of democracy and part of the constitutional change that has taken place under the new Labour government. So I am campaigning to get people to sign up for the postal vote register and that also offers a chance to talk to people about their own issues, but after I have, as it were, offered them a distinct new democratic right thanks to a Labour government.

But the third aspect of this campaign, which really is the most odd, is the complete absence of the trade unions. Not a single trade union official has turned up to campaign regularly. Nice Bernard Rooney from the ISTC pops in maybe once a week for a short bit of help, but that's it. The old days when full-time officials and full-time shop stewards from all the trade unions would detach themselves from work to carry out electoral tasks have disappeared. I know they are signing big cheques in London, but here in Rotherham, and I expect in other constituencies, they have simply absented themselves entirely from the political process. Do they sense in their inner hearts that Labour does much better when there is no association with trade unions? Have they finally learnt the lesson of the twentieth century that for Labour to be a trade-union-only party is actually extremely damaging to its electoral chances? Has there been some strategic thinking on this? I wish somebody would investigate it and find out.

The point is reinforced immediately after my talk with Seyd when four people from the Rotherham Technical College (RCAT) come in to complain about the financial state of the college and its general administration. Two are from the college lecturers' union NATFHE, one from the GMB union and one from Unison. All good people, but I say to them, where are you in terms of helping me in the election? And I put it to them bluntly, telling them, 'If you don't come and help me now [and I point at Tom Donaldson, the local NATFHE leader, who had actually signed the nomination papers for the Socialist Alliance candidate], why should I help you when you come and demand my support after the election?' They look a bit sheepish and admit it's true, but they have no answer. RCAT has grossly overspent in the expectation that EU money in the form of Objective One money would come flooding in to pay its bills. But Objective One is nearly two years late in its implementation and so there is a financial crisis.

Charles Kennedy is looking very chipper on the television, though there is absolutely no Lib Dem presence in Rotherham that I can see. Kennedy looks good on television with his 'plague on both your houses' style. However, he is being over-priggish with his claim that only his party stands for honesty. I know the political class at national and local level is a microcosm, but no one who has seen the Lib Dems in action would claim that this is an honest party at all. They lie and cheat at every possible opportunity. And their promises, of course, don't get any real scrutiny at all. Obviously, I want them to do well because the big enemy is the Conservative Party and if we can reduce the number of Tory MPs so much the better, but there is something deeply distasteful by Kennedy's pretence that his dirty and dishonest little party somehow operates at a purer level of political engagement than parties that are much closer to power and government.

Out to the only public meeting of the campaign. It was organised by the World Development Movement at Eastwood Mission. All the candidates were there, save the Lib Dems who didn't show up. My declared opponents are pretty weak. The Conservative Richard Powell was a very nervous speaker. Obviously, he doesn't know the audience or the local situation. It went off well enough. Perhaps I was over-rhetorical at times for what was a fairly churchy audience, but for God's sake, this is my only public meeting of the entire campaign, the only chance to engage with the public in any way at all. What a weird business politics is today. Face-to-face meetings only and no chance to develop ideas. I certainly let them have both barrels on Europe and offered no concessions on my pro-European stance.

FRIDAY 1 JUNE 2001

The *International Herald Tribune* publishes a front-page story date-lined 'Rotherham: England' by John Vinocur based on a visit here a week ago. It is pretty fair, but he is very cynical about Blair's refusal to discuss the euro in the context of the election. But why should he? It isn't yet a reality for the British people. It is an idea, an abstract notion and we cannot handle abstractions.

We need Europe to be seen and to be perceived as performing well economically, particularly in creating jobs. I also tell him and *IHT* readers that I cannot imagine Paris or Berlin or Brussels being happy with Britain being convulsed by a referendum campaign for months and months leading either to a possible defeat or to a very narrow and contested victory in the run-up to the launch of the currency itself. So *festina lente* is my permanent watchword. Not very courageous, but it's how I see things at the moment. Blair and especially Brown have failed utterly in the past four years to make any strong case for Europe, and until people are educated, they cannot be expected to understand what in effect is a new language.

SATURDAY 2 JUNE 2001

A goodish turnout in the town centre. I buy everybody red basketball hats which I got for £2.50 a piece in the market. We walk all over the place, handing out leaflets and again people are still pretty friendly. I talk to the UKIP candidate, a retired doctor except no one ever remembers him doing any doctoring in Rotherham. He is a perfectly nice old buffer seized by an anti-European hate. But, in general, the small party candidates are not to be seen. The Liberal

Democrat candidate has not circulated an election address and has literally never been seen in the town at all. There are no Lib Dem posters up anywhere and so the sleeping giant of Lib Dem voters in Thorpe Hesley may not be really woken up. In any case, the Lib Dem vote here is basically a petty bourgeois protest vote, so I don't have to worry about it too much… yet.

Afterwards, I drive down to London listening to *Yes Minister* tapes which Martin gave me as a birthday present. They are quite hilarious. Only after having sat at meetings with permanent secretaries does one realise just to what extent *Yes Minister* far from being a comedy is almost a perfect fly-on-the-wall documentary of both the mandarin style and the relationship between top civil servants and their ministers. They are so funny and accurate that I almost wish the three-hour journey could last longer so I could listen to more of them. Well done Martin for a brilliant present.

THURSDAY 7 JUNE 2001

A blustery, cold morning for the election. At least I am up early. At 7 a.m. walking down Wellgate, distributing leaflets, asking people to go out to vote.

At 8 a.m. outside the bus station the Trots from the Socialist Alliance are there handing out their own leaflets and snarling 'Wipe the smile off Denis MacShane's face. He wants to privatise your hospitals! Wipe the smile off Denis's face!' At least they are calling me Denis, and Anna gently tugs me away rather than risk any confrontation.

Over to East Herringthorpe with Andrew Fellows, who is a soul of good cheer as always. It is the most wretched and depressing place. A forgotten bit of poverty and lack of aspiration and no hope. It stretches down to Dalton, a hill of social despair. We loudspeaker and knock on doors and push leaflets through letterboxes, but not much is going to happen. Sheila Walker is with us. She has been away on holiday for much of the election campaign but turns up for the last two days. The other two councillors are nowhere to be seen.

Anna asks me to call her on the mobile and when we arrive at the count she has got all of our Rotherham constituency team gathered at the door and gives me a huge cheer as I come in. She is such a pet.

The count is over fairly quickly. The turnout is down by 12 per cent to just over 50 per cent. All the campaigning efforts and all the hard work to get postal votes have paid off in keeping us honourably above 50 per cent, but that's all. The turnouts in Wentworth and Rother Valley are similar. My majority drops to 13,077. I got 18,759 votes, which was 64 per cent of the total vote cast, over the Conservative score of 5,682. A ridiculous Trotskyist woman only got 352 and the UKIP man got 730 over the Green candidate's 577. So I am back as an MP. I make my little speech, saying very little, and just want to get away home. Anna drags me up to Ann Russell's house where she had organised a post-election party, but somehow we're just not in the mood. I have a glass of water and then that's it.

All day long, I had been trailed by a French radio journalist, who was quite fun, and as usual I will be a bigger figure in France than in my own country.

As the results come in, it is clear that absolutely nothing has changed. No one seems to have lost their seat. The Tories are the big losers with a loss of about ten seats compared to 1997. Hague has been crushed and will have to go. There is a deep satisfaction in that. But now the newspapers will become the opposition. They will pick up all his themes – hatred of Europe, semi-racist intolerance of foreigners, non-stop assaults on public service – and make them their own. I feel no sense of triumph at all, just a great battle won and endless campaigning and unreachable horizons ahead of us. No matter. I am going to have fun whatever. Back home to bed.

MONDAY 11 JUNE 2001

I go into the office in the Commons and put the printer back on the desk and dump all the papers from Rotherham which need sorting out. I wish I had an efficient PA. Yesterday, we bought a new mobile phone for me which won't keep going wonky like the old one. But neither it nor the pager goes off. I refuse to put on the radio or television. Downstairs getting some coffee, a tall redheaded woman who looks a bit like Patricia Hollis – a smiling face in a no-nonsense kind of way – comes up and introduces herself. She is Vera Baird. She is the new MP for Redcar replacing Mo Mowlam. A QC. I don't know who she is, but she recognises me and we have a friendly chat. I give her lots of tips on being an MP, all the problems of allowances and mileage and hiring staff and so forth.

How awful it must be to be one of the half-dozen or so seats we have lost. One of them is Chesterfield, which Tony Benn has managed to change into a Liberal Democrat seat. More pressure on us in South Yorkshire. Thanks, Tony, your final parting gift to the Labour Party, to which you did such historic damage, turning it away for twenty years from the possibility of social democratic reformism, was to deny your successor the chance of serving in Parliament.

Lunch with Gareth Thomas, whom I'm delighted to see back. All the people I'm really fond of like Derek Wyatt and Huw Edwards or Gareth himself or Ruth Kelly, who would have been swept away if there'd been a half-decent normal swing to the Tories, are back. There are also some wastrels and scoundrels but it's absolutely weird that absolutely nothing has changed. This is going to be the long non-Parliament. One of those decades in British history when the executive is all and Parliament is nothing.

Still no call and I take the bus home and get some clothes to take to the cleaners. Just going into the dry cleaners and my nice new mobile phone goes off.

'Hello Denis, it's Katie Kay here…' My heart leaps, my gut tenses. My sweet little Katie is, of course, Blair's PA, and the friendliness in her voice can only mean one thing.

'Tony would like to have a word with you, Denis, hang on and I'll put you through.'

'Hello Denis, how are you?' comes a voice that isn't that of Rory Bremner.

I babble. 'Tony, Prime Minister, congratulations, I hope you're well, sir. I hope Jonathan has shown you my article in yesterday's *Pittsburgh Post-Gazette* in which I say you can act as a bridge between America and Europe,' I waffle on.

He gets to the point. 'I'd like you to join my government in the Foreign Office, Denis. You'll be in charge of consular affairs and bits of Europe, but they'll tell you what it's all about,' he says dismissively.

Suddenly that ridiculous and stupid ambition turns into a sense of relief . 'Thank you, Tony, I'll do my best for you, you know that.'

'Yes, now you can show us what you can do. Good luck. The Foreign Office will be in touch on the details,' he says.

'Well, thank you very much, Tony. I'm looking forward to serving you. You'd better get off, you've got lots of other calls to make,' I say, breaking the connection.

Wow. Is that it? Fifty-three and one of Her Majesty's ministers. How long will it last? What will I do with it?

I phone Nathalie's number on the mobile. She left for Zurich at 6 a.m. but I get straight through. She whoops with joy and pleasure when I tell her, '*Je suis un ministre de sa Majesté*!' She is proud for me and pleased for me. The calls start coming in and Don Macintyre comes round and we drink two bottles of Sancerre and eat lots of smoked salmon and toast. He wishes me joy. It's a friendship going back more than thirty years now and it's just good to have friends around like that. Go to bed happy, drunk and wondering what the future holds.

INDEX

INDEX